Relevant No More?

RELIGION, POLITICS, AND SOCIETY IN THE NEW MILLENNIUM

Series Editors: Michael Novak, American Enterprise Institute, and Brian C. Anderson, Manhattan Institute

For nearly five centuries, it was widely believed that moral questions could be resolved through reason. The Enlightenment once gave us answers to these perennial questions, but the answers no longer seem adequate. It has become apparent that reason alone is not enough to answer the questions that define and shape our existence. Many now believe that we have come to the edge of the Enlightenment and are stepping forth into a new era, one that may be the most religious we have experienced in 500 years. This series of books explores this new historical condition, publishing important works of scholarship in various disciplines that help us to understand the trends in thought and belief we have come from and to define the ones toward which we are heading.

Beyond Self-Interest: A Personalist Approach to Human Action, by Gregory R. Beabout, et al.

Human Nature and the Discipline of Economics: Personalist Anthropology and Economic Methodology, by Patricia Donohue-White, et al.

The Free Person and the Free Economy: A Personalist View of Market Economics, by Anthony J. Santelli Jr., et al.

Meaninglessness: The Solutions of Nietzsche, Freud, and Rorty, by M. A. Casey

Boston's Cardinal: Bernard Law, the Man and His Witness, edited by Romanus Cessario, O.P.

Don't Play Away Your Cards, Uncle Sam: The American Difference, by Olof Murelius, edited by Jana Novak

Society as a Department Store: Critical Reflections on the Liberal State, by Ryszard Legutko

In God We Trust? Faith-Based Organizations and the Quest to Solve America's Social Ills, by Lewis D. Solomon

Deconstructing Diversity: Justice, Multiculturalism, and Affirmative Action in Jesuit Higher Education, by Peter Minowitz

Relevant No More? The Catholic/Protestant Divide in American Electoral Politics, by Mark D. Brewer

On Ordered Liberty: A Treatise on the Free Society, by Samuel Gregg

Relevant No More?

The Catholic/Protestant Divide in American Electoral Politics

Mark D. Brewer

LEXINGTON BOOKS
Lanham • Boulder • New York • Oxford

LEXINGTON BOOKS

Published in the United States of America
by Lexington Books
A Member of the Rowman & Littlefield Publishing Group
4501 Forbes Boulevard, Suite 200, Lanham, Maryland 20706

PO Box 317
Oxford
OX2 9RU, UK

Copyright © 2003 by Lexington Books

All rights reserved. No part of this publication may be reproduced, stored in a retrieval system, or transmitted in any form or by any means, electronic, mechanical, photocopying, recording, or otherwise, without the prior permission of the publisher.

British Library Cataloguing in Publication Information Available

Library of Congress Cataloging-in-Publication Data

Brewer, Mark D.
  Relevant no more? : the Catholic-Protestant divide in American electoral politics / Mark D. Brewer.
       p. cm. — (Religion, politics, and society in the new millennium)
  Includes index.
  ISBN 0-7391-0513-2 (cloth : alk. paper)
  1. Elections—United States. 2. Catholics—United States—Political activity. 3. Protestants—United States—Political activity. 4. Voting—Religious aspects. I. Title. II. Series.

JK1967.R35 2003
324.973'092'088204—dc21

2003044681

Printed in the United States of America

∞™ The paper used in this publication meets the minimum requirements of American National Standard for Information Sciences—Permanence of Paper for Printed Library Materials, ANSI/NISO Z39.48–1992.

For my loving wife, Tammy

Contents

List of Tables		ix
Preface		xv
1	The Issue Defined	1
2	The Conventional Wisdom: The Supposed Decline of the Catholic/Protestant Divide	11
3	The Conventional Wisdom Revisited	33
4	The Search for Sources of Catholic/Protestant Division	51
5	The Search Continued	67
6	Catholic/Protestant Division: A Religious Worldview Explanation	87
7	A Final Test: Multivariate Analyses	121
Conclusion		135
Bibliography		139
Index		157
About the Author		161

Tables

Table 3.1: Democratic Presidential Vote, House Vote, and Party ID, Catholics and Protestants, All Respondents, 1952-2000   34

Table 3.2: Democratic Presidential Vote, House Vote, and Party ID, Catholics and Protestants, All Respondents, by Decade, 1950s-1990s   35

Table 3.3: Democratic Presidential Vote, House Vote, and Party ID, Catholics and Protestants, Whites Only, 1952-2000   38

Table 3.4: Democratic Presidential Vote, House Vote, and Party ID, Catholics and Protestants, Whites Only, by Decade, 1950s-1990s   38

Table 3.5: Should Government Support Health Care? Catholics and Protestants, Whites Only, by Decade, 1950s-1990s   39

Table 3.6: Should Government Guarantee Jobs and a Good Standard of Living? Catholics and Protestants, Whites Only, by Decade, 1950s-1990s   40

Table 3.7: Government Aid to Blacks and Minorities, Catholics and Protestants, Whites Only, by Decade, 1970s-1990s   40

Table 3.8: Government Services and Spending, Catholics and Protestants, Whites Only, by Decade, 1980s-1990s   40

Table 3.9: Defense Spending, Catholics and Protestants, Whites Only, by Decade, 1980s-1990s   41

Table 3.10: Positions on Legality of Abortion, Catholics and Protestants, Whites Only, by Decade, 1970s-1990s   41

Table 3.11: Family Income Thirds for Catholics and Protestants, Whites Only, by Decade, 1950s-1990s   42

Table 3.12: Education Levels for Catholics and Protestants, Whites Only, by Decade, 1950s-1990s 43

Table 3.13: Democratic Presidential Vote, by Income Thirds, Catholics and Protestants, Whites Only, 1952-2000 44

Table 3.14: Democratic Presidential Vote, House Vote, and Party ID, by Income Thirds, Catholics and Protestants, Whites Only, by Decade, 1950s-1990s 45

Table 4.1: Catholic Democratic Presidential Vote, House Vote, and Party ID, Women and Men, Whites Only, 1952-2000 53

Table 4.2: Catholic Democratic Presidential Vote, House Vote, and Party ID, Women and Men, Whites Only, by Decade, 1950s-1990s 53

Table 4.3: Democratic Presidential Vote, House Vote, and Party ID, Catholics and Protestants, by Gender, Whites Only, by Decade, 1950s-1990s 54

Table 4.4: Democratic Presidential Vote, House Vote, and Party ID, Catholics and Protestants, by Age Group, Whites Only, by decade, 1950s-1990s 56

Table 4.5: Democratic Presidential Vote, House Vote, and Party ID, Catholics and Protestants, by Age Cohort, Whites Only, by Decade, 1980s-1990s 57

Table 4.6: Percentage Hispanic and Non-Hispanic in NES Sample, Catholics and Protestants, Whites Only, 1980-1998 59

Table 4.7: Democratic Presidential Vote, House Vote, and Party ID, Hispanic and White Catholics and Protestants, by Decade, 1980s-1990s 60

Table 4.8: Democratic Presidential Vote, House Vote, and Party ID, Catholics and Protestants, White, Non-Hispanics Only, 1980-1998 61

Table 4.9: Democratic Presidential Vote, House Vote, and Party ID, Catholics and Protestants, White, Non-Hispanics Only, by Decade, 1980s-1990s 61

Table 5.1: Church Attendance for Catholics and Protestants, Whites Only, by Decade, 1950s-1990s 71

Table 5.2: Democratic Presidential Vote for Catholics and Protestants, by Level of Church Attendance, Whites Only, 1952-2000 72

Table 5.3: Democratic Presidential Vote for Catholics and Protestants, by Level of Church Attendance, Whites Only, by Decade, 1950s-1990s 72

Tables xi

Table 5.4: Democratic House Vote for Catholics and Protestants, by Level of Church Attendance, Whites Only, 1952-2000   73

Table 5.5: Democratic House Vote for Catholics and Protestants, by Level of Church Attendance, Whites Only, by Decade, 1950s-1990s   73

Table 5.6: Democratic Party ID for Catholics and Protestants, by Level of Church Attendance, Whites Only, 1952-2000   74

Table 5.7: Democratic Party ID for Catholics and Protestants, by Level of Church Attendance, Whites Only, by Decade, 1950s-1990s   74

Table 5.8: Amount of Guidance from Religion for Catholics and Protestants, Whites Only, by Decade, 1980s-1990s   75

Table 5.9: Level of Religious Salience for Catholics and Protestants, Whites Only, by Decade, 1980s-1990s   76

Table 5.10: Democratic Presidential Vote for Catholics and Protestants, by Level of Religious Salience, Whites Only, 1980-2000   76

Table 5.11: Democratic Presidential Vote for Catholics and Protestants, by Level of Religious Salience, Whites Only, by Decade, 1980s-1990s   76

Table 5.12: Democratic House Vote for Catholics and Protestants, by Level of Religious Salience, Whites Only, 1980-2000   77

Table 5.13: Democratic House Vote for Catholics and Protestants, by Level of Religious Salience, Whites Only, by Decade, 1980s-1990s   77

Table 5.14: Democratic Party ID for Catholics and Protestants, by Level of Religious Salience, Whites Only, 1980-2000   77

Table 5.15: Democratic Party ID for Catholics and Protestants, by Level of Religious Salience, Whites Only, by Decade, 1980s-1990s   78

Table 5.16: Democratic Presidential Vote, House Vote, and Party ID, Catholics, Mainline Protestants, and Evangelical Protestants, Whites Only, 1960-1996   81

Table 5.17: Democratic Presidential Vote, House Vote, and Party ID, Catholics, Mainline Protestants, and Evangelical Protestants, Whites Only, by Decade, 1960s-1990s   81

Table 5.18: Differences in Democratic Presidential Vote, House Vote, and Party ID, Catholics, Mainline Protestants, and Evangelical Protestants, Whites Only, by Decade, 1960s-1990s   82

Table 6.1: Positions on Whether Government Should Guarantee Individuals Jobs and a Good Standard of Living, Catholics and Protestants, Whites Only, by Decade, 1950s-1990s   105

Table 6.2: Positions on Whether Government Should be Involved in Providing Health Care to Individuals, Catholics and Protestants, Whites Only, by Decade, 1950s-1990s   106

Table 6.3: Positions on Amount of Government Services and Spending, Catholics and Protestants, Whites Only, by Decade, 1980s-1990s   107

Table 6.4: Positions on Amount of Government Spending on Defense, Catholics and Protestants, Whites Only, by Decade, 1980s-1990s   107

Table 6.5: Positions on Whether Government Should Do More to Solve the Country's Problems, Catholics and Protestants, Whites Only, by Decade, 1980s-1990s   108

Table 6.6: Positions on Amount Government Spends on Assistance to the Poor, Catholics and Protestants, Whites Only, by Decade, 1980s-1990s   109

Table 6.7: Positions on Whether Government Should Do Something to Reduce Income Differences Between Rich and Poor, Catholics and Protestants, Whites Only, by Decade, 1980s-1990s   109

Table 6.8: Positions on Whether Government Should Do Something to Improve the Standard of Living of the Poor, Catholics and Protestants, Whites Only, by Decade, 1980s-1990s   110

Table 6.9: Democratic Presidential Vote by Position on Whether Government Should Guarantee Individuals Jobs and a Good Standard of Living, Catholics and Protestants, Whites Only, by Decade, 1950s-1990s   111

Table 7.1: Logit Estimates and Odds Increases for Catholic Affiliation, Age, Family Income, Gender, Church Attendance, Union Household, and Southern Residence on Presidential Vote, Whites Only, 1952-2000   123

Table 7.2: Logit Estimates and Odds Increases for Catholic Affiliation, Age, Family Income, Gender, Church Attendance, Union Household, and Southern Residence on House Vote, Whites Only, 1952-2000   124

Tables xiii

Table 7.3: Logit Estimates and Odds Increases for Catholic Affiliation, Age, Family Income, Gender, Church Attendance, Union Household, and Southern Residence on Party ID, Whites Only, 1952-2000   125

Table 7.4: Logit Estimates and Odds Increases for Catholic Affiliation, Age, Family Income, Gender, Hispanic Ethnicity, Religious Salience, Union Household, and Southern Residence on Presidential Vote, Whites Only, 1980-2000
127

Table 7.5: Logit Estimates and Odds Increases for Catholic Affiliation, Age, Family Income, Gender, Hispanic Ethnicity, Religious Salience, Union Household, and Southern Residence on House Vote, Whites Only, 1980-2000   128

Table 7.6: Logit Estimates and Odds Increases for Catholic Affiliation, Age, Family Income, Gender, Hispanic Ethnicity, Religious Salience, Union Household, and Southern Residence on Party ID, Whites Only, 1980-2000   129

Preface

This book grew out of the desire to answer a simple question: Does religion still matter in American politics? Specifically, I wanted to know if religious affiliation affects the electoral behavior of American citizens; if it plays a role in the candidates they vote for and in the party they identify with.

Throughout the vast majority of American history, knowledgeable political observers would have considered such questions silly. Of course religion mattered. It has long been recognized that nineteenth-century electoral politics, especially after the Civil War, was in many ways driven by ethnoreligious tensions and conflicts. Tensions and conflicts between Catholics and Protestants in particular were important in defining the electoral landscape that existed in the post-bellum period. These divisions retained their prominent place in electoral politics as the United States moved into the twentieth century, with the electoral differences between Catholics and Protestants serving as a significant factor in both the New Deal coalition created by Franklin Delano Roosevelt and maintained by Harry Truman, and also in the election of John F. Kennedy in 1960. Those who followed American electoral politics accepted as a matter of course that religion affected individuals' voting behavior and partisan identification.

This view began to change very quickly in the late 1960s. The New Deal coalition was breaking down, and religion was seen as one of the primary causes as Catholics began to leave the Democratic Party and behave (electorally at least) increasingly like Protestants. Throughout the 1970s the view that religion was increasingly irrelevant to American electoral politics gained acceptance. The Catholic/Protestant divide was thought to have become especially meaningless, and for many the behavior of these two religious groups in the 1980 presidential election marked the end of distinctive patterns of electoral behavior between Protestants and Catholics.

While Ronald Reagan's election signaled to many the demise of an electoral cleavage between Catholics and Protestants in the United States, it also served notice of a new type of religious divide at play. For the first time since at least the early years of the twentieth century, and perhaps farther back than that, evangelical Protestants were perceived as having played an important role in the presidential election. Evangelical groups, in particular Jerry Falwell's Moral Majority, had been very active in support of Reagan before the election, and early analyses in the wake of Reagan's victory attributed at least some of the credit for his win to evangelicals. This was the beginning of the rise to prominence of evangelicals in American electoral politics, and although their fortunes have ebbed somewhat in the past few years, evangelical Protestants are still widely regarded as an important force in the American electoral arena.

This rather sudden gaining of political influence by evangelicals served to jumpstart the study of religion and politics. For the most part ignored by political scientists (at least those who studied the United States) in the 1960s and 1970s, scholars in the field began devoting considerable attention to intersections between the political sphere and the religious sphere. Many researchers focused in particular on the effects of religion on individuals' electoral behavior and, to the surprise of many, often found that religion did indeed influence the manner in which people cast their ballots and selected a party to identify with.

Findings showing that religion affects electoral behavior should not, however, surprise anyone. We as social scientists know that many of the social and demographic characteristics possessed by individuals contribute heavily to their self-identities, to the way in which they define themselves. In other words, to how an individual sees himself or herself as a human being. Given the importance of these characteristics, it only makes sense that some attributes such as gender, income level, race, ethnicity, marital status, etc., have been shown to produce powerful effects on individuals' electoral behavior. Why should religion be any different? Religion, in the form of denominational affiliation, also serves as an important source of self-identity for many Americans. Religion by its very nature focuses on questions of ultimate meaning. In the attempt to provide answers to these questions, religion can equip its adherents with a particular worldview, or perspective through which to view the world around them. For some then, religion provides a lens that shapes their views of and helps them to interpret the society they live in. We should not be surprised that religion affects individual electoral behavior. We should, rather, be surprised if it does not do so.

Even as more and more research was conducted showing that religion affected electoral behavior, most of this work focused on the impact religion had among evangelical Protestants. Little attention was given to the more traditional Catholic/Protestant divide, and when this cleavage was addressed it was generally held that the differences between Catholics and Protestants were indeed a thing of the past. The electoral behavior of these two religious groups had become indistinguishable.

This is the claim that sparked the research that resulted in this book. If religion does have an impact on political behavior, then how could a religious-based electoral cleavage that had existed throughout most of American history suddenly become irrelevant in the space of less than twenty years? Had the Catholic/Protestant divide in American electoral politics really disappeared, and if it had why did it do so?

As I will show throughout this book, the differences in electoral behavior between Catholics and Protestants in the United States did not disappear. The two religious groups continue to differ dramatically in their patterns of voting and party identification, with Catholics being much more likely to support the Democratic Party than are Protestants. This finding obviously renders the second of the two questions that closed the above paragraph moot. It does, however, raise an even more interesting one: Why do Catholics and Protestants differ in their electoral behavior? I argue that the divergent electoral behavior exhibited by these two religious groups can be explained by differences in the worldviews articulated by the two religious traditions and inculcated into their respective adherents. Specifically, I argue that the Catholic worldview emphasizes values that are more communal in nature and focus more on equality than does the Protestant worldview, which tends to place greater emphasis on the values of individualism and freedom. These differences in worldviews explain, at least in part, why Catholics support the Democratic Party at higher levels than do Protestants, and vice versa. The reader's reaction to this argument once as he finishes this book will be the test of how well I have made my case.

As is the case with the undertaking and successful completion of any intellectual endeavor I have accumulated many debts along the way, none of which can ever be fully repaid but at the very least can be acknowledged here. Marie Provine provided sound advice and consistent encouragement during my first year of graduate school, reassuring me that I had what it takes to be a successful scholar at a time when I myself was not so sure. This book is a revision of my doctoral dissertation, and all the members of my committee deserve thanks for the assistance they have provided in helping me produce this finished work. Suzanne Mettler read the early versions of these chapters many times, and her keen insights always resulted in improvements. In addition, her belief in the value of this project in its beginning stages was much appreciated. The idea for this project developed out of a seminar directed by Rogan Kersh. Many subsequent conversations with him helped to refine the focus, and his vast knowledge of the literature in disparate fields yielded more than a few sources that I would not have otherwise encountered. Kristi Andersen also read the early versions of the chapters many times, and our discussions about the clarity of both my ideas and my writing have made this a stronger work. Joe Cammarano read the dissertation near its completion, but his comments led to some important improvements in the final version, especially in chapter 6.

Eric Petersen was a great colleague and friend in graduate school, and remains both today. Our many academic discussions improved the quality of this book, and our nonacademic discussions and activities improved the quality of life overall. Sandy Maisel has been very helpful during my time at Colby, providing me with a classroom schedule that enabled me to make the revisions to this work and also overall sound professional advice. Chris La Putt provided much needed and appreciated help with editing and formatting the final manuscript. My parents, Dave and Sharon Brewer, of course, deserve no small amount of thanks. Without their efforts it is very unlikely that I would have ever written anything, and they encouraged me during my writing even though I am sure they could not imagine how anyone could be a college student for so long.

Finally I would like to thank the two people who were most important to me in the researching and writing of this book. Jeff Stonecash served as the chair of my dissertation committee, and without him I am not sure I could have written this book. Even though he was incredibly busy doing his own research and writing, he always had time to help me in this process. Whether it was discussing ideas in his office, assisting me with one of my seemingly endless methodological dilemmas, or reading multiple iterations and drafts, Jeff always gave his full attention to my questions and to my work. It is impossible for me to conceive of any student having a better advisor. I was lucky to have Jeff as my advisor, and I am proud to now have him as a colleague and a friend.

My wife, Tammy, came back into my life during the early stages of this project. She has provided constant encouragement and support at all stages, and for this I will always be grateful. She has been and continues to be there for me always, no matter what. I love her more than anything, and I cannot imagine my life without her. Fortunately I do not have to.

The individuals named above all played important roles in the completion of this book. However, it of course goes without saying that they bear no responsibility for any errors of fact or judgment that exist herein. Those are the sole responsibility of the author.

Chapter One

The Issue Defined

Introduction: The Question Defined

American electoral politics has always been a group-based politics.[1] Differences between groups provide the "social fault lines" around which conflict develops and political parties in the United States are organized.[2] American parties are coalitional parties, aggregates of the many diverse groups and constituencies present in American society. Because of this fact, the study of electoral behavior in the United States has long been centered on the concept of party coalitions, with scholars attempting to determine the particular group components of party coalitions.[3] In addition to determining which groups support each of the two major political parties in the United States, scholars have also been extremely interested in explaining why these groups identify with their party of choice. Deciphering the social bases of American electoral behavior has proven to be a driving force in the study of American politics.

Religious affiliation is one of the many social characteristics that have shown an impact on individuals' electoral behavior. In their seminal studies of presidential elections in the 1940s, sociologists at Columbia University determined that religious group affiliation mattered a great deal in explaining the partisanship and voting behavior of Americans.[4] Using the survey results of the National Election Studies, political scientists at the University of Michigan found that religious group affiliation continued to be an important predictor of Americans' electoral behavior during the 1950s and 1960s.[5] Subsequent research has shown that religious affiliation has remained significant as a source of political cleavage and electoral behavior throughout the remainder of the twentieth century.[6]

These findings come as little surprise when one thinks about what religion is and what it represents. Religion is more than a set of beliefs regarding the divine.[7] It encompasses more than a contained thought process that deals only with matters relating to a supreme being or beings.[8] Religion is "an institutionalized system of symbols, beliefs, values, and practices focused on questions of ultimate meaning."[9] Seen in this light, religion is obviously more than a mere social classification.[10] Religion has the ability to provide individuals with a particular perspective, or lens, through which to view the world around them. This perspective offers believers a way to understand the temporal world they live in, as well as a framework for conducting themselves in their worldly affairs and activities.[11] As Andrew Greeley put it, religion provides human beings with "stories which are templates for interpreting and directing one's life."[12] Potentially, religious affiliation has greater importance for the believer than any other form of social identity because the messages and answers provided by religion are presented as pertaining to the ultimate meaning of life.[13] Given the nature of religion and religious beliefs, one can easily see how these factors could have a significant impact on individuals' electoral behavior.

This study will examine the electoral behavior of one religious group in the United States, Roman Catholics. Comprising about 25 percent of the population, Catholics are the largest religious denomination in the United States, but are a minority religious group when Protestantism is considered as a whole. This minority existence was not always a smooth or comfortable one for American Catholics. America's past history of anti-Catholicism is a well-documented fact. As Catholic journalist John Cogley observed, "Anti-Catholicism has been called America's oldest and most abiding prejudice."[14] Despite showing incredible disregard for the situation of African Americans in the United States, this claim aptly describes the environment facing Catholics for much of America's history. Anti-Catholic sentiment was widely evident in America's colonial period, exploded onto the national scene during the nineteenth century, and remained an important issue into the twentieth century.

Seventeenth-century England was a rabidly anti-Catholic society. The Reformation had swept through the country in the sixteenth century, resulting in the complete separation of the Church of England from the Roman Catholic Church. Catholicism was thoroughly discredited, portrayed as an authoritarian religion plagued by hierarchy, superstition, and an overreliance on ritual and dogma. These characteristics made the faith inherently dangerous to the emerging Enlightenment ideals of liberty and freedom. Catholicism was prohibited for a time in England, and numerous penal laws directed against Catholics and Catholicism were enacted.[15]

The anti-Catholic sentiment briefly described above was transported by the British to their American colonies, where it sank deep roots and grew stronger.[16] Many of the colonies passed laws aimed at punishing Catholics and in some cases banned Catholicism altogether.[17] By the time of American independence, anti-Catholicism had developed into a full-blown component of the American mindset. America's Protestant majority viewed Catholics as a distinct, somehow foreign element in its midst. Catholics were different. They were not fully American, and they were incapable of becoming so.

The existence of this belief on the part of American Protestants can be traced to three primary factors. The first is the nature of authority in the Catholic

Church. In religious matters, Catholics were required to be obedient to the Pope in Rome. Catholics had little, if any, voice in running their church. American Protestants believed the authority of the church over Catholics extended to temporal matters as well.[18] At its very core, Catholicism was perceived as inherently incompatible with the Enlightenment ideals of liberty, freedom, and individualism on which the United States was founded.[19] Because of the authoritarian and hierarchical nature of their faith, Catholics were believed to be incapable of performing the duties required of citizens in a democratic polity. More than being incapable of acting as good citizens, Catholics were also dangerous to the fledgling republic. Because of Catholics' fealty and obedience to the Pope, Protestants believed any conflict between American interests and the interests of the church would require American Catholics to place church interests ahead of those of the nation. The specter of a papal takeover loomed in the back of Protestants' minds when their thoughts turned to Catholics in America. This fear grew stronger as increasing numbers of Catholics began immigrating to the United States during the nineteenth century.[20] To the vast majority of Protestant Americans, Catholicism was equivalent to despotism and authoritarianism. The adherence to the Catholic faith made independence and liberty impossible.[21] The difference in the nature of authority between Catholicism and Protestantism is one of the major reasons why Catholics were marked as a distinct group in American society.

Differences between Catholic and Protestant notions of authority were not limited to the religious arena. The two groups differed dramatically in their theological worldviews, which led to opposing ideas on the proper nature of governmental authority as well. For Catholics, the responsibility and authority to deal with personal sin and morality rested solely with the church. Government had no authority over such matters. The possession of such a perspective by Catholics caused them to oppose efforts to extend the coercive power of the state into matters of personal morality. Many Protestants, on the other hand, viewed immorality as one of society's biggest problems, a condition that had to be eradicated by any means. Government intervention into the realm of personal morality was not only desirable, but also necessary in the battle to improve the moral character of society.[22] The conflict of the Catholic view of governmental authority with their own is another reason why American Protestants viewed Catholics as a distinct and separate group in American society.[23]

The final, and perhaps most obvious reason why American Protestants viewed Catholics as a distinct group was the ethnic stock of the majority of American Catholics. By 1850, American Catholicism was largely a church of immigrants.[24] As is often the case with immigrant groups, the newly arriving Catholics were poor. They immediately assumed a position at the very bottom of the socioeconomic scale. Protestants regarded this influx of poor Catholic immigrants as both a threat to the morals of society and a drain on the public coffers. In addition, the strange appearances, languages, cultures, and customs of these immigrants certainly served to mark them as distinct in the eyes of America's "native stock" Protestants. These same characteristics rendered the immigrants as impossible to assimilate into the American culture. Nativism, another hallmark of America's historical mindset, was often so closely intertwined with anti-Catholicism that it was difficult to separate the two. Both prejudices operated simultaneously.[25] The foreign background of the overwhelming majority of American Catholics combined with their religious faith to provide American Protestants two prominent reasons for viewing them as a distinct and separate group in American society.

It was not only Protestants that viewed American Catholics as different. Catholics too saw themselves as a distinct group in American society.[26] The open hostility displayed toward them by the Protestant majority fostered a sense of exclusion and separation among American Catholics.[27] Pre-Vatican II Catholicism held that Catholicism was the only "true" religious faith, and that the only way to salvation was through the Catholic Church.[28] Such a mindset, prominent among both clerical leaders and the laity, served to increase the tendency of Catholics to see themselves as different and apart from Protestants. By the 1850s, a majority of Catholic leaders openly advocated the separation of Catholics and Catholic culture from the American culture at large. This stance of separation from the Protestant majority taken by Catholics only served to increase the trepidation and hostility of American Protestants, resulting in additional tension and conflict between the two groups.

The picture painted above is necessarily simplistic, one that will be refined and fleshed out in later chapters. The key point is that American Catholics, both in their own eyes and in the eyes of America's Protestant majority, constituted a distinct group in American society. This distinctness resulted in differences in political beliefs and actions between the two groups, including significant differences in their respective electoral behavior. These differences remained large and meaningful throughout most of America's history.[29] We know Catholics once constituted a distinct group in American society, and that this distinction resulted in significant differences in electoral behavior between Catholics and Protestants in the United States. The important questions for this analysis focus on the present. Do Catholics remain a distinct group in American society? Does the electoral behavior of American Catholics still differ in significant and meaningful ways from that of American Protestants?

The short answer to the questions posed above, according to the conventional wisdom, is no. Catholics no longer constitute a distinct group in American society. The dominant view among academic and nonacademic observers alike is that since the end of World War II, Catholics have been thoroughly assimilated into mainstream American culture.[30] Since the end of large-scale white Catholic immigration in the 1920s, Catholics had been gradually moving up the socioeconomic ladder. This process had begun even earlier among the Catholic ethnic groups who had been first to immigrate to the United States, notably the Irish and the Germans.[31] The GI Bill that followed the end of the Second World War opened the doors of higher education to many American Catholics, allowing them to greatly increase their rate of ascent into the ranks of the middle class.[32] By the 1970s, Catholics had drawn almost even with or moved ahead of

America's Protestant denominations in terms of family income, education levels, and occupational status.[33] At least in terms of socioeconomic characteristics, American Catholics have become very much like the Protestant majority.

Catholics have become more like their Protestant counterparts in other ways as well. Catholic and Protestant attitudes regarding reproductive issues such as contraception, family planning, and fertility patterns have converged significantly in recent years.[34] The behavior of the two groups has also become increasingly similar on other issues such as divorce and church attendance. Some analysts have interpreted these findings as evidence for the argument that as Catholics moved up the socioeconomic ladder, they began to adopt values and attitudes more similar to America's Protestant middle class.[35] Growing out of the endorsements of religious toleration and increased ecumenism provided by the Second Vatican Council, interaction and cooperation between Catholics and Protestants have reached levels heretofore unseen.[36] Building on the argument first articulated by Herberg in his seminal work on religion in America,[37] some scholars see Catholics and Protestants in the United States as having reached a state of social and cultural similarity.[38] Much, if not all, of this newfound similarity is attributed to changes on the part of the Catholic Church and American Catholics. In the words of Catholic historian Philip Gleason: "As Catholics came up in the world so rapidly, they lost their sense of being outsiders. They saw the world in much the same light as other Americans. In short, they became thoroughly assimilated and Americanized."[39]

According to the conventional wisdom, the assimilation of American Catholics into mainstream American society combined with the increased similarity between Catholics and Protestants produced by this assimilation have resulted in the disappearance of significant differences in electoral behavior between the two groups. Catholics and Protestants now behave in essentially similar ways with regards to partisan affiliation and voting. The Catholic/Protestant divide, which dominated American electoral politics in the nineteenth century, and remained significant through the 1960s, is no longer in evidence.[40]

Is the conventional wisdom regarding Catholic and Protestant electoral behavior correct? Do differences in party identification and voting patterns between the two groups no longer exist? I argue that the conventional wisdom is not correct. Chapter 3 of this book will present data showing that American Catholics do continue to differ from American Protestants in their electoral behavior. Moreover, these differences remain relatively large and quite stable, despite the move of American Catholics into the socioeconomic and cultural mainstream. Anti-Catholicism is largely a thing of the past in American society, but divergence between Catholics and Protestants in their respective voting behavior most certainly is not. Something continues to exist which causes Catholics to act as a distinct group in American society when it comes to electoral behavior.

This analysis will examine the electoral behavior of American Catholics, with an eye toward documenting and explaining the trends and changes in this behavior. Particular emphasis will be given to answering the following question:

Why do American Catholics continue to support the Democratic Party at higher levels than do American Protestants?

Certainly it is possible that the differences in electoral behavior that exist between Catholics and Protestants could be caused by something other than religious affiliation. Catholics and Protestants could differ with respect to demographic characteristics such as family income level, education level, age distribution, gender distribution, or ethnic composition. Given what is known about the impact of these variables on electoral behavior, it is possible that differences between Catholics and Protestants on these social categories could result in differences in electoral behavior between the two religious groups. It is also possible that religious variables could cause differences in Catholic and Protestant electoral behavior. Growing divergence between mainline and evangelical Protestants is one possibility that comes to mind. Another relates to levels of religious salience, and the possible effects that differences in salience could have. All of these possibilities will be explored in this analysis.

However, it could also be that Catholicism and Protestantism continue to instill different values in their respective adherents, producing different worldviews. These different worldviews could produce differences in electoral behavior between Catholics and Protestants, much as they did in the nineteenth century. It could be that the Catholic Church emphasizes values that are more communal in nature and focus more on equality, while the central values of Protestantism tend to be more individualistic in nature and focus more on the idea of freedom. This is not a new claim. Tocqueville commented on the tendency of Catholicism to promote equality while Protestantism tended to promote individualism and independence.[41] Wuthnow noted that Catholicism tends to actively cultivate communal ties among its members to a much higher degree than does Protestantism.[42] Greeley states "for Protestantism the tendency has always been to emphasize the relationship of the individual with God while for Catholicism the tendency has always been to emphasize the individual relating to God as a member of a community."[43] People who espouse an individual religiosity focus on their own problems and needs, while those who adhere to a more communal religiosity tend to focus on the problems and needs shared by all people, and involve their interrelationships.[44] It could be that Catholics are more communal in nature than are Protestants, and that this tendency makes Catholics more likely to support the Democratic Party than are Protestants.

Using the contrast between communal and individualistic religious values in an attempt to explain political behavior is not new. Benson and Williams fruitfully utilized such an approach in their attempt to explain differences in voting among members of Congress.[45] Welch and Leege used the communal vs. individualistic approach in attempts to explain differences in political attitudes among Catholics.[46] Guth et al. used such an approach to explain differences in political attitudes among Protestant clergy.[47] However, an examination of differences in communal and individualistic values has never been utilized in an attempt to explain differences in electoral behavior between Catholics and Protestants. Such an approach will be utilized in this analysis.

In this book I will examine each of the above possibilities. However, before delving into these matters it is first necessary to briefly look into the past in order to more fully lay the groundwork for the analysis that will follow. How did Catholics and Protestants in the United States come to differ so dramatically in their respective electoral behavior? Why did these differences supposedly disappear? Chapter 2 will address these questions.

Notes

1. Norman H. Nie, Sidney Verba, and John R. Petrocik, *The Changing American Voter* (Cambridge, Mass.: Harvard University Press, 1976), 210-11.

2. John R. Petrocik, "New Party Coalitions and the Nationalization of the South," *Journal of Politics* 49, no. 2 (May 1987): 352.

3. See, for example, Robert Axelrod, "Where the Votes Come From: An Analysis of Electoral Coalitions, 1952-1968," *American Political Science Review* 66, no. 1 (March 1972): 11-20; William S. Maddox, "Changing Electoral Coalitions from 1952 to 1976," *Social Science Quarterly* 60, no. 2 (Sept. 1979): 309-13; Seymour Martin Lipset, ed., *Party Coalitions in the 1980s* (San Francisco: Institute for Contemporary Studies, 1981); John R. Petrocik, *Party Coalitions: Realignments and the Decline of the New Deal Party System* (Chicago: University of Chicago Press, 1981); Harold W. Stanley, William T. Bianco, and Richard G. Niemi, "Partisanship and Group Support over Time: A Multivariate Analysis," *American Political Science Review* 80, no. 3 (Sept. 1986): 969-76; Robert S. Erikson, Thomas D. Lancaster, and David W. Romero, "Group Components of the Presidential Vote, 1952-1984," *Journal of Politics* 51, no. 2 (May 1989): 337-46; Harold W. Stanley and Richard G. Niemi, "Partisanship and Group Support, 1952-1988," *American Politics Quarterly* 19, no. 2 (April 1991): 189-210; John R. Petrocik, "Reformulating the Party Coalitions: The 'Christian Democratic' Republicans" (paper presented at the 1998 annual meeting of the American Political Science Association, Boston, Mass., Sept. 1998).

4. Paul F. Lazarsfeld, Bernard Berelson, and Hazel Gaudet, *The People's Choice: How the Voter Makes Up His Mind in a Presidential Campaign*, 2d ed. (New York: Columbia University Press, 1948), 22-24; Bernard R. Berelson, Paul F. Lazarsfeld, and William N. McPhee, *Voting: A Study of Opinion Formation in a Presidential Campaign* (Chicago: University of Chicago Press, 1954), 62-71.

5. Angus Campbell, Philip E. Converse, Warren E. Miller, and Donald E. Stokes, *The American Voter* (New York: John Wiley & Sons, 1960).

6. Jeff Manza and Clem Brooks, "The Religious Factor in U.S. Presidential Elections, 1960-1992," *American Journal of Sociology* 103, no. 1 (July 1997): 39.

7. Mary T. Hanna, *Catholics and American Politics* (Cambridge, Mass.: Harvard University Press, 1979), 2.

8. Ronald R. Stockton, "The Evangelical Phenomenon: A Falwell-Graham Typology," in *Contemporary Evangelical Political Involvement: An Analysis and Assessment*, ed. Corwin E. Smidt (Lanham, Md.: University Press of America, 1989), 45.

9. Charles Y. Glock and Rodney Stark, *Religion and Society in Tension* (Chicago: Rand McNally & Company, 1965), 4. In formulating their definition of religion, Glock and Stark built on the famous definitions offered by Durkheim and Parsons. Emile Durkheim, *The Elementary Forms of Religious Life*, translated by Karen E. Fields (New York:

The Free Press, 1995), 44; Talcott Parsons, *The Social System* (New York: The Free Press, 1951), 367-68.

10. Clarke E. Cochran, Jerry D. Perkins, and Murray Clark Havens, "Public Policy & the Emergence of Religious Politics," *Polity* 19, no. 4 (Summer 1987): 598.

11. David C. Leege, "Religion and Politics in Theoretical Perspective," in *Rediscovering the Religious Factor in American Politics*, ed. David C. Leege and Lyman A. Kellstedt (Armonk, N.Y.: M. E. Sharpe, 1993), 3; Cochran, Perkins, and Havens, "Public Policy," 598; Paul Kleppner, *The Cross of Culture: A Social Analysis of Midwestern Politics, 1850-1900* (New York: The Free Press, 1970), 72-73; Glock and Stark, *Religion and Society*, 5.

12. Andrew M. Greeley, *Religious Change in America* (Cambridge, Mass.: Harvard University Press, 1989), 1.

13. Leege, "Religion and Politics," 10.

14. John Cogley, *Catholic America* (New York: The Dial Press, 1973), 2.

15. Jay P. Dolan, *The American Catholic Experience* (Notre Dame, Ind.: University of Notre Dame Press, 1992), chapter 3.

16. Dolan, *The American Catholic Experience*; James Hennesey, *American Catholics* (New York: Oxford University Press, 1981), chapters 4 and 5; John Tracy Ellis, *American Catholicism*, 2d ed., rev. (Chicago: University of Chicago Press, 1969), chapter 1.

17. Dolan, *The American Catholic Experience*, 84-86; Hennesey, *American Catholics*, 20; Ellis, *American Catholicism*, 19-21.

18. Robert Wuthnow, *The Restructuring of American Religion: Society and Faith since World War II* (Princeton, N.J.: Princeton University Press, 1988), 75.

19. Philip Gleason, *Keeping the Faith: American Catholicism Past and Present* (Notre Dame, Ind.: University of Notre Dame Press, 1987), 40.

20. Dolan, *The American Catholic Experience*, 295-96.

21. Lawrence H. Fuchs, *John F. Kennedy and American Catholicism* (New York: Meredith Press, 1967), 30.

22. Kleppner, *The Cross of Culture*, 70-76; Richard Jensen, *The Winning of the Midwest* (Chicago: University of Chicago Press, 1971), 64-68; Paul Kleppner, *The Third Electoral System, 1853-1892* (Chapel Hill, N.C.: University of North Carolina Press, 1979), 185-97.

23. This issue is discussed in much greater detail in chapter 2.

24. Dolan, *The American Catholic Experience*, 160-61; Thomas T. McAvoy, *A History of the Catholic Church in the United States* (Notre Dame, Ind.: University of Notre Dame Press, 1969), 148; Ellis, *American Catholicism*, 50-51.

25. For a discussion of how nativism and anti-Catholicism often went hand in hand, see Hennesey, *American Catholics*, chapter 10; Ray Allen Billington, *The Protestant Crusade, 1800-1860: A Study of the Origins of American Nativism* (New York: The Macmillan Company, 1938).

26. Dolan, *The American Catholic Experience*, 300.

27. Ellis, *American Catholicism*, 82.

28. Richard P. McBrien, *Catholicism*, Rev. ed. (San Francisco: HarperCollins Publishers, 1994), 7-8 and 385-88.

29. This point will be discussed thoroughly in chapters 2 and 3.

30. For one concise statement of this viewpoint, see Dean R. Hoge, "Interpreting Change in American Catholicism: The River and the Floodgate," *Review of Religious Research* 27, no. 4 (June 1986): 289-99.

31. Dolan, *The American Catholic Experience*, 356-58.

32. Charles R. Morris, *American Catholic* (New York: Random House, 1997), 256-57; Jay P. Dolan, R. Scott Appleby, Patricia Byrne, and Debra Campbell, *Transforming Parish Ministry* (New York: The Crossroad Publishing Company, 1989), 52-53; David C. Leege, "Catholics and the Civic Order: Parish Participation, Politics, and Civic Participation," *The Review of Politics* 50, no. 4 (Fall 1988): 707-9; Hennesey, *American Catholics*, 283.

33. Dolan, *The American Catholic Experience*, 426; William D'Antonio, James Davidson, Dean Hoge, and Ruth Wallace, *American Catholic Laity in a Changing Church* (Kansas City, Mo.: Sheed & Ward, 1989), 33; Andrew M. Greeley, *The American Catholic: A Social Portrait* (New York: Basic Books, 1977), 57-58; Andrew M. Greeley, "How Conservative Are American Catholics?" *Political Science Quarterly* 92, no. 2 (Summer 1977): 199-218.

34. D'Antonio, Davidson, Hoge, and Wallace, *American Catholic Laity*, 17-18; Wuthnow, *The Restructuring of American Religion*, 94.

35. D'Antonio, Davidson, Hoge, and Wallace, *American Catholic Laity*, 16-18.

36. Dolan, Appleby, Byrne, and Campbell, *Transforming Parish Ministry*, 297; Wuthnow, *The Restructuring of American Religion*, 93-94; Eugene C. Bianchi, *John XXIII and American Protestants* (Washington, D.C.: Corpus Books, 1968).

37. Will Herberg, *Protestant-Catholic-Jew*, Rev. ed. (Garden City, N.Y.: Anchor Books, 1960).

38. For one prominent example, see Wuthnow, *The Restructuring of American Religion*. See also Samuel A. Mueller, "The New Triple Melting Pot: Herberg Revisited," *Review of Religious Research* 13, no. 1 (Fall 1971): 18-33.

39. Philip Gleason, "Catholicism and Cultural Change in the 1960s," *The Review of Politics* 34, no. 4 (Oct. 1972): 95.

40. The development of this view is discussed at length in chapter 2, and thus no documentation is offered here.

41. Alexis de Tocqueville, *Democracy in America*, ed. Phillips Bradley, 2 volumes (New York: Vintage Books, 1990), Volume 1, 300-301; See also Hennesey. *American Catholics*, 102; Fuchs, *John F. Kennedy and American Catholicism*, 42.

42. Wuthnow, *The Restructuring of American Religion*, 55.

43. Andrew M. Greeley, "Protestant and Catholic: Is the Analogical Imagination Extinct?" *American Sociological Review* 54, no. 4 (Aug. 1989): 485.

44. Michael R. Welch and David C. Leege, "Religious Predictors of Catholic Parishioners Sociopolitical Attitudes: Devotional Style, Closeness to God, Imagery, and Agentic/Communal Religious Identity," *Journal for the Scientific Study of Religion* 27, no. 4 (Dec. 1988): 542.

45. Peter L. Benson and Dorothy L. Williams, *Religion on Capitol Hill: Myths and Realities* (San Francisco: Harper & Row Publishers, 1982).

46. David C. Leege and Michael R. Welch, "Religious Roots of Political Orientations: Variations Among American Catholic Parishioners," *Journal of Politics* 51, no. 1 (Feb. 1989): 137-62; Welch and Leege, "Religious Predictors," 536-52.

47. James L. Guth, John C. Green, Corwin E. Smidt, Lyman A. Kellstedt, and Margaret M. Poloma, *The Bully Pulpit: The Politics of Protestant Clergy* (Lawrence, Kans.: University Press of Kansas, 1997).

Chapter Two

The Conventional Wisdom: The Supposed Decline of the Catholic/Protestant Divide

The electoral behavior of Catholics in the United States continues to differ significantly from the electoral behavior of American Protestants. In some important ways, Catholics remain a distinct group in the United States. In order to determine the ways in which Catholic behavior differs, and more important, why these differences exist, it is first necessary to examine the history of Catholics and Catholicism in America. Such an examination enables us to determine the origins of Catholic distinctiveness in the United States, and to examine the purported disappearance of this distinctiveness. Delving into the past also allows for discussion of historical differences in electoral behavior between Catholics and Protestants, an exercise with the potential to shed some light on the present.

Nineteenth-Century America: Catholic/Protestant Conflict in Full Bloom

As discussed in chapter 1, anti-Catholic prejudice has a long history in America, and this bias played an important role in nineteenth-century American society. Tension between Protestants and Catholics was pervasive during this period. Issues such as lay trustee management of parishes, public education, and numerous others exacerbated this tension, and in many cases led to open conflict.[1] One phenomenon, however, provided the raw material for much of the tension that existed between Catholics and Protestants in the United States during the nineteenth century. That phenomenon was immigration.

America did not serve as a beacon for immigrant Catholics during its colonial and immediate post-Revolutionary eras. The Catholic population in the United States was small, with an estimated total of 26,000 people in 1765, and grew slowly during the early years of the nation, totaling only 195,000 by 1820.[2]

This situation changed dramatically and rapidly over the course of the nineteenth century. By 1850, the number of Catholics in the United States had increased to approximately 1.6 million, and Roman Catholicism had become the single largest denomination in the nation.[3] The American Catholic population continued to grow at a staggering rate, reaching 3.1 million by 1860,[4] 4.5 million in 1870,[5] 6.3 million in 1880,[6] 12 million in 1900,[7] and 16.4 million by 1910.[8]

Before the onset of widespread Catholic immigration in the 1840s, Catholics were "a quaint oddity in the United States. . . . In most towns and cities, Catholics were an invisible minority."[9] This paucity of Catholics made it easier for the anti-Catholic prejudice of America's Protestant majority to remain relatively latent, with most Protestants rarely seeing or interacting with Catholics on a large scale or on a regular basis. Those American Protestants who did regularly experience some interaction with Catholicism saw it as a mostly middle- and upper-class, Anglo-American, almost genteel religion, with many of its adherents possessing prominent family trees that stretched back to colonial times.[10] American Protestants perceived these types of Catholics as posing little threat to their culture and traditions.[11]

The exponential growth of Catholicism in the United States due to immigration completely altered this situation. As the number of Catholic immigrants increased, Protestants began to take notice. All immigrants to nineteenth-century America encountered a nation that was thoroughly Protestant in its culture, traditions, and norms.[12] This was especially problematic for Catholic newcomers, given the traditional anti-Catholic bias that had been ingrained in American Protestants. As Catholic immigrants settled in the Northeast and Midwest, they began instituting practices and making demands that clashed with the dominant worldview of Protestant Americans. The examples of lay trusteeship and public schools mentioned earlier are just two of the most prominent instances. As the Catholic population swelled, Protestants became increasingly concerned and troubled. Many Protestants worried about a possible papal takeover of the United States, and voiced this concern publicly.[13]

Immigration changed the complexion of the Catholic Church in America as well. As discussed above, the pre-immigration church was small and relatively homogeneous, made up mostly of middle- and upper-class Anglo-Americans. By 1850, the Catholic Church in America was a church of immigrants, with the remnants of Anglo-American Catholicism having been overwhelmed by the influx of foreign adherents.[14] As newcomers to a foreign, often hostile land, Catholic immigrants needed a means of identification, something that would allow them to retain their sense of self. Their religion became that means of identification, a marking Dolan went so far as to label a "badge."[15] Catholicism became the religion of America's poor and working class, the religion of the expanding cities and their developing ghettoes and slums.[16] The transformation of American Catholicism into a church of immigrants lowered the cultural position of Catholicism in the United States, both in terms of socioeconomic characteristics, and more important, in the eyes of America's Protestant majority.[17]

Faced with the ever-growing wave of poor, Catholic immigrants cascading onto their shores, American Protestants responded with concern, fear, and most of all prejudice. Writing in 1835, even before Catholic immigration to America began in earnest, Samuel F. B. Morse summed up the feelings of many of his fellow American Protestants regarding Catholic immigration. Alarmed at the increasing numbers of Catholics coming to the United States, Morse warned "that there is good reason for believing that the despots of Europe are attempting by the spread of Popery in this country, to subvert its free institutions."[18] Significant in the fact that he was one of the first prominent Protestants to sound the alarm against the evils of Catholic immigration, Morse's comments were perhaps even more significant in that they exemplified many of the charges leveled against Catholics by Protestants over the course of the nineteenth century in the United States.

Morse and those who would follow him were not expounding original ideas. As discussed earlier, anti-Catholicism already had a long tradition in nineteenth-century America, a tradition that provided both the intellectual material for anti-Catholic messages and an audience conditioned to be receptive to such messages. Although the United States is a nation founded at least in part on the principles of religious freedom and toleration, the extension of such freedom and toleration was long thought to be applicable to Protestants only. Writing in the 1700s, Yale minister Elisha Williams said, "By his very Principles he (a Roman Catholic) is an Enemy or Traytor to *a Protestant State:* and strictly speaking *Popery* is so far from deserving the name of *Religion*, that it is rather a conspiracy against it, against the Reason, Liberties, and Peace of Mankind."[19] Speaking in the early 1800s, future president John Quincy Adams called Catholicism a "portentous system of despotism and superstition."[20] Protestants viewed Catholicism as a foreign religion that placed unnecessary emphases on dogma, ritual, and most of all authority. In the eyes of Protestants, the Catholic Church demanded absolute loyalty and obedience from its members, forcing them to place their religion ahead of all other ties and alliances. Submission by Catholics to the dictates of their priests, bishops, and ultimately the Pope was accepted as fact. Perceptions such as these led many Protestants to question whether Catholics could be loyal American citizens. As stated by prominent Protestant clergyman Josiah Strong, "Roman Catholics are Catholics first and citizens afterward."[21] Given the fact that the majority of the early settlers (and, more important, their leaders) were schooled in the thought and traditions of the Reformation and Enlightenment, the presence and resiliency of anti-Catholic sentiment in the United States is not surprising.[22] In the words of historian Ray Allen Billington, "The average Protestant American of the 1850's had been trained from birth to hate Catholicism."[23] As immigrants dramatically increased the size of the Catholic Church in the United States, Protestants reacted as could be expected. Drawing on their collective history, American Protestants resurrected their traditional anti-Catholicism and propounded those views with new force and frequency.[24] Numerous anti-Catholic groups and organizations sprang up across the United States throughout the latter two-thirds of the 1800s. The

Know-Nothings and the American Protective Association, two of the most prominent anti-Catholic groups, became so powerful that they were able to have a substantial impact on elections at the local, state, and even national level.[25]

The anti-Catholicism exhibited by many nineteenth-century American Protestants was not entirely unjustified. Many Catholic lay and clerical leaders were openly suspicious of and sometimes even publicly hostile toward Protestants.[26] Catholics were advised by their clergy to avoid excessive fraternization with non-Catholics.[27] Separation from Protestant America was a key component of nineteenth-century American Catholicism. In the realm of public policy, Catholic clergy were aggressive in making their objectives and demands known to government officials, often asking these officials for government action favorable to Catholics.[28] To Protestants, these demands represented a very real threat to their value system and view of American society.[29] In addition, the hierarchical organization of the Catholic Church represented a dangerous contradiction to American democratic government. When examined in this context, the anti-Catholic prejudice exhibited by American Protestants becomes more understandable, although not any more acceptable.

Religious Conflict and the Development of Partisan Allegiances

Regardless of the reasons behind the animosity that existed between Catholics and Protestants, the fact is that this tension developed into one of the most prominent social cleavages in nineteenth-century America. Following a dynamic that has since become familiar in American politics, this social cleavage eventually became a political cleavage. The mechanism that enabled the transmission of this conflict into the political realm was the political party.

The latter two-thirds of the nineteenth century has been classified as the golden age of political parties in the United States. Parties "totally dominated" the American political landscape during this period, providing the primary means by which the nation's political affairs were organized and settled.[30] This system of party organization was marked by an underlying religious dimension, specifically the denominational divide between Catholics and Protestants.[31] At the most fundamental level, American politics outside of the South over the course of the latter two-thirds of the nineteenth century was a battle between Protestants and Catholics, a battle that was fought electorally through the vehicles of political parties.[32] Political parties and religious denominations enjoyed a "symbiotic relationship" in nineteenth-century America, with religious groups influencing the political agenda through parties and parties constructing their constituencies from the religious groups whose worldviews coincided with the party's philosophies and platforms.[33] The relationship between Protestants and Catholics, and the tension and conflict inherent in this relationship, provided one of the dominant political cleavages in nineteenth-century America.[34]

For American Catholics, the party of choice was the Democratic Party. Multiple reasons exist for this affiliation. First among them was the often-intense nativist hostility of much of the Whig, and later Republican Parties. These parties contained strong elements of the traditional American anti-Catholic and anti-immigrant biases discussed earlier.[35] Many of the individuals who affiliated with the various nativist anti-Catholic third parties prevalent in the first half of the nineteenth century eventually ended up as Whigs or Republicans after the demise of the third party in question.[36] For many nineteenth-century American Catholics, Republican affiliation simply was not an option.[37] In the North, the Republican Party was widely viewed as the anti-Catholic party, an image that Republican officeholders and activists worked hard to cultivate and maintain through their "acts, speeches, and postures." During the 1868 presidential campaign, the Republican Party made a huge effort to associate the Democrats with immigrants and "that abomination against common sense called the Catholic religion." Just a few days before the 1884 election, Protestant minister Samuel Burchard labeled the Democratic Party as the party of "Rum, Romanism, and Rebellion" at a public rally for Republican presidential candidate James Blaine.[38]

The Democratic Party had an equally strong image as the Catholic party.[39] At the high point of the American Protective Association's popularity, the Democratic Party officially condemned the organization while Republicans refused to do so.[40] As more and more Catholic immigrants flooded into northeastern cities, the Democratic Party machines that controlled many of these cities reached out to Catholics and forged a lasting alliance with them.[41]

Although by no means a central factor, social class also played a role in the partisan allegiance of nineteenth-century Catholics. As a denomination comprised mostly of recent immigrants, American Catholics were positioned toward the lower ends of the socioeconomic ladder. Even in the nineteenth century, the Democratic Party outside of the South was perceived as the party of the less fortunate, or at least of the common man in society.[42] Such a perception certainly served to reinforce the partisan affiliation Catholics were pushed toward by their religion.[43]

Last, and perhaps most important, was the theological outlook of the Catholic Church. Nineteenth-century Catholicism was a religion characterized by a "ritualistic" or "liturgical" perspective. Such a perspective stresses assent to historical doctrine and formalized ritual practices. Right belief is emphasized over (but not to the exclusion of) right behavior. The holder of a "ritualistic" or "liturgical" perspective views the world as an inherently sinful place, but sees that situation as one to be resolved by the private sector rather than changed through the action of the state. The church, not government, has the responsibility and authority to deal with matters of morality.[44] The possession of such a worldview by Catholics served to connect them to the Democratic Party, which at the time was the party opposed to extending the coercive power of the state into issues of morality.

A large portion of nineteenth-century American Protestantism, on the other hand, was characterized by what Kleppner and Jensen both term a "pietistic" worldview. The "pietistic" perspective is one that eschews ritual and devotions, instead laying personal salvation at the hands of the individual through a personal conversion experience directly with God. The holder of a "pietistic" perspective also sees the world as a sinful place, but one that is to be changed and molded into a society more representative of God's wishes. Sin must be eradicated by any means available, and government intervention is not only desirable, but also necessary in the battle against sin in society. Such a worldview pushed many nineteenth-century American Protestants toward the Republican Party, the party of "positive government action" and "great moral ideas."[45] Combined with the anti-Catholic image and tradition of the Republican Party described above, it is easy to see why many Protestants felt at home with the Grand Old Party.

As would be expected, the partisan split between Catholics and Protestants manifested itself at the ballot box. American Catholics had been strong supporters of the Democratic Party since the time of Andrew Jackson, and that support became stronger as the nineteenth century progressed.[46] The popularity of the Know-Nothings served to strengthen Catholic support for the Democrats,[47] as did the increasingly anti-Catholic nature of the Republican Party later in the century.[48] Prompted in part by increasing social status, American Protestants began their move into the Whig Party before the Civil War.[49] The religiously charged political atmosphere spurred even greater electoral support by Protestants for the Republicans after the Civil War. In their respective analyses of electoral behavior in the second half of the nineteenth century, both Kleppner and Jensen found that Catholics voted overwhelmingly Democratic while most Protestants voted largely Republican. The difference in vote choice between Catholics and Protestants remained significant even when controlling for other demographic characteristics such as region of residence, socioeconomic status, and ethnicity.[50] Tension and conflict between Protestants and Catholics had become so pervasive as to dictate the structure of politics during the second half of the nineteenth century. By the 1892 presidential election, Catholics were firmly established as the electoral base of the Democratic Party (in the non-South), while Protestants (again, non-southern) made up the core of the GOP.

The economic disturbances of the 1890s changed the American political landscape somewhat. Concerns over tariffs, the Depression of 1893, and the monetary standard replaced the Catholic/Protestant divide as the principal cleavage in American politics.[51] Not only was the denominational split removed from the center stage of American politics, but its partisan manifestations were shaken as well. The election campaigns produced by the political climate of the 1890s temporarily weakened the moorings of Catholics to the Democratic Party. The two factors primarily responsible for this phenomenon were the principal candidates in the 1896 presidential election, William McKinley and William Jennings Bryan.

While the primary issue of the 1896 campaign was whether to use gold or silver to back U.S. currency, both McKinley and Bryan made appeals designed to cause changes in the traditional partisan loyalties of Catholics and Protestants. McKinley's appeals to Catholics appear to have been successful while Bryan's overtures to Protestants clearly were not, and may have served only to alienate

Catholics from his candidacy and his party. In fact, Reichley claimed that the most direct effect of Bryan's appeals to "pietistic" Protestants was to free up "large numbers of Catholics to vote Republican" for the first time.[52] The end result of the 1896 campaign was a massive, although temporary, shift of Catholic voters to the Republican Party.[53]

The politics of the 1890s blurred the sharp line that had previously existed between Protestants and Catholics with regard to partisan affiliation and voting behavior. Catholic support for the Democratic Party was no longer guaranteed, and Catholic support for the Republican Party did increase from previous levels. However, empirical evidence indicates that Catholics gradually returned to the Democratic Party after the election of 1896, or at the very least were more Democratic than Republican in their partisan support.[54] During the early decades of the twentieth century, the party system slowly returned to its previous religious alignment, with Catholics supporting the Democrats and northern "pietistic" Protestants firmly entrenched in the Republican Party.[55] The return of Catholics to the Democratic fold was helped along by two factors: the formal development of a Catholic ethic of social justice and the actions of the Democratic Party itself beginning in the late 1920s. The former will be examined first.

Development of a Catholic Ethic of Social Justice

The Catholic Church has a long history of social action in the United States, beginning with the urban charity efforts of the early nineteenth century. As discussed earlier, many of the Catholic immigrants who began flooding into the nation during the 1830s and 1840s settled in the large cities of the Northeast. Many of these newcomers arrived poor and in immediate need of assistance, while those who were able to find work upon arrival were extremely vulnerable to the many economic downturns of the period. Faced with the reality of a large number of its members in dire financial straits, the church, through both lay and clerical organizations, responded with acts of charity. The clergy encouraged almsgiving and acts of mercy toward the poor, while lay organizations went about collecting money, food, and clothing to alleviate the hardship of poor Catholic families in the northeastern cities.[56] Catholic charity efforts continued to mount during the 1840s and 1850s, and after the Civil War Catholic efforts to help the poor took on the nature of a crusade.[57] The Society of St. Vincent de Paul is indicative of Catholic charity efforts of this period. Founded in France, the society was devoted to the exercise of charity, specifically to poor families. The first chapter of the society was organized in the United States in 1845, and local chapters quickly sprang up in most eastern cities. By the 1880s, the Society of St. Vincent de Paul was the most important charitable organization in the church, assisting needy families and providing care for young orphan boys throughout America's cities.[58]

Catholic social action was extensive prior to 1880. It was also very conservative in nature. The principal aim of Catholic social action was the salvation of souls by improving the lot of the individual through charity, almsgiving, and acts of mercy. Catholic social action before 1880 did not call for the changing of society through reform. Indeed, societal reform instituted by the state went against the basic nature of Catholic thought during this period, as discussed earlier in this chapter. The church would do all in its power to alleviate the social ills of the time, but government action to reform society was not an option the Catholic Church could support.[59] Catholic social action of the time was characterized by efforts of the church and church-based groups to help individuals with their problems. Calls for large-scale societal reforms involving the government were noticeably absent.

In the 1880s, the nature of Catholic social thought began to change. A few Catholic liberals began to argue that the plight of the poor in society required more than charity and mercy. The economic changes brought on by the industrial revolution demanded a new approach to Catholic social action, one that focused on achieving actual social justice for the less fortunate members of society.[60] This new strand of Catholic social thought had its roots in the thought and writings of the liberal European clergy and theologians known as the Liege School.[61] Although doubtlessly influenced by the Liege School on some level, the shift of American Catholic social thought to concerns of social justice can be traced primarily to the emerging labor movement in the United States.[62]

As the industrial revolution progressed, tensions began to mount between employers and workers. Throughout the 1860s and 1870s workers began to organize in the hope of achieving shorter hours, higher wages, and better working conditions. As a predominantly working-class group, American Catholics supported the goals of the labor movement, and many became involved in its efforts.[63] Labor organizations were originally viewed as highly suspect by members of the Catholic clergy and hierarchy, mostly because they usually required their members to take oaths of secrecy, a practice frowned upon by many clerical leaders of the church.[64] Labor unions continued to gain in popularity among the laity, however, and by the 1880s their cause was also being championed by the Catholic press.[65] In 1884, the Vatican issued a ruling forbidding Canadian Catholics from belonging to the Knights of Labor, the largest labor organization of the 1880s. Realizing that many American Catholics were members of the Knights, prominent members of the American hierarchy led by Cardinal James Gibbons lobbied the Pope not to condemn the Knights of Labor in the United States. Gibbons and his colleagues argued that workers had the right to organize in order to protect their self-interest in light of the "social evils, public injustices . . . heartless avarice" that afflicted the United States. Failure to allow Catholic workers to act in such a manner would result in massive losses for the church among the working classes. Eventually, the Vatican agreed and lifted the ban on the Knights.[66]

The removal of the ban on the Knights of Labor by the Vatican represented a watershed event in the relationship of American Catholicism and the labor movement. For the first time, the American hierarchy had stood behind the laity in their support of labor activity. More important, the press widely reported the efforts of Gibbons in securing approval of the Knights, a move that firmly established Catholic hierarchy as supportive of labor in the minds of the American public.[67] From this point forward, the Catholic Church would be clearly and officially on the side of organized labor, a point reinforced by the papal encyclical *Rerum Novarum* in 1891. By the first decade of the twentieth century, Catholic social reformers had expanded their calls for social justice beyond labor to include such issues as poverty and housing.

By the end of World War I, American Catholicism possessed a clear and well-established social justice tradition.[68] Symbolic of this development was the *Bishops' Program of Social Reconstruction*, issued in 1919. Written largely by Monsignor John A. Ryan but issued by the American bishops as a whole, the program called for radical reorganization of the American economic system. Laissez-faire capitalism was condemned as a severely deficient philosophy for dealing with the modern economic system. The bishops called upon the national government to institute sweeping reforms, including the institution of minimum wage laws, the establishment of unemployment, old-age, and health insurance programs for workers, and legal protection of labor's right to organize.[69] The *Bishops' Program* drew accolades for its progressive nature from many of the liberal reform groups of the period, both Catholic and non-Catholic.[70] The social thought of American Catholicism had been transformed from conservative and individual-focused to liberal and community-focused. Catholic social teaching now very clearly endorsed an active role for the state in the achievement of a variety of egalitarian goals. This emphasis on social justice would eventually correlate well with the policy positions advocated by the rapidly changing Democratic Party, serving to further increase Catholics' affinity for the party.[71]

Strengthening of an Old Alliance: Catholics and the Democratic Party, 1928-1964

At the 1924 Democratic convention, New York Governor Alfred E. Smith was among those vying for the party's presidential nomination. Smith was a Catholic, having risen through the ranks of New York City's Tammany Hall political machine. Many within the Democratic Party expressed concerns over nominating a Catholic for the nation's highest office. These concerns were amplified by the Ku Klux Klan, the most prominent nativist and anti-Catholic organization of the time. The Klan of the 1920s, four to five million strong at its peak, targeted blacks, immigrants, and Jews, but saved its most venomous attacks for Catholics.[72] The Klan became heavily involved at the 1924 Democratic convention, working diligently to deny Smith the nomination. The convention degenerated into a raucous affair, deeply dividing the party and requiring over 100 ballots to choose the party's nominee. Smith did not receive the nomination.[73] American Catholics were put on notice that deep anti-Catholic sentiment still existed in the nation, indeed even within their own party, and that such feelings could become potent when aroused.

The events surrounding Smith and the 1924 convention served as a prelude for the presidential campaign of 1928. Smith received the Democratic nomination in 1928, as the northern, urban wing of the party was able to secure Smith's selection over the objections of the southern and rural elements of the party.[74] This decision by the Democrats ignited the most intense episode of anti-Catholicism in the twentieth century.[75] Smith's nomination provided an opportunity for those with anti-Catholic inclinations to express them publicly. Although the Klan was not as strong as it had been in 1924, anti-Catholic demonstrations followed Smith along the campaign trail throughout the South and the Midwest. Old fears of a papal takeover were revived with the possibility of a Catholic in the White House. Smith's Catholicism was the dominant issue of the 1928 campaign, monopolizing public discussion and debate. Even though they had long experienced anti-Catholic sentiment in the United States, Catholics were still somewhat surprised at the extent and intensity of the prejudice against them brought out by the 1928 campaign. Once again they were portrayed as un-American, a group to be feared because of their religious affiliation.[76]

The 1928 presidential campaign did more than put American Catholics on the defensive. It further cemented their allegiance to the Democratic Party.[77] Feeling compelled to defend their fellow Catholic against the many false charges being leveled against him because of his religion, many previously unattached or apathetic Catholics became supportive of the Democratic Party.[78] By extending their presidential nomination to a Catholic, the Democratic Party provided Catholics with the ultimate sense of "recognition, acceptance, and legitimacy."[79] This alliance between Catholics and the Democratic Party would be further strengthened by Franklin Delano Roosevelt and the New Deal.

The onset of the Great Depression in 1929 produced desperate times in American politics. Americans, many in the most dire of straits, wanted financial assistance and solutions to the economic disaster that had befallen them. In the presidential election of 1932, Franklin Delano Roosevelt attempted to provide such assistance, offering Americans a new style of national government, a more activist and involved federal government that stood in direct contrast to the laissez-faire philosophy traditionally espoused by the government in Washington. As witnessed by his victory in 1932, many Americans were supportive of Roosevelt's plans, but perhaps none more so than American Catholics.

By the 1920s many American Catholics had begun to question the rectitude of laissez-faire capitalism. In light of the church's newly developed emphasis on government responsibility for social justice, placing the good of the nation at the whims of unfettered markets filled many Catholics with a growing sense of unease. The onset of the Depression intensified these feelings, and the hands off approach of the Hoover administration in dealing with the nation's economic disaster made Catholics in general very unhappy.[80] Realizing that many Catholics, especially among Catholic leadership, were already favorably predisposed to his ideas, Roosevelt acted to increase and solidify his support among Catholics. Roosevelt carefully cultivated American Catholics, making frequent appearances before Catholic audiences.[81] During these appearances, Roosevelt praised the papal encyclicals *Rerum Novarum* and *Quadragesimo Anno*,[82] the latter of which had been especially well received by American Catholics.[83] Roosevelt often quoted from these encyclicals, and went to great lengths to note the similarity of the ideas contained in these papal documents with his own ideas about government.[84] After quoting at length from *Quadragesimo Anno* during a 1932 campaign speech in Detroit, FDR called the document "just as radical as I am" and "one of the greatest documents of modern times."[85]

American Catholics responded favorably to Roosevelt and his message, supporting him overwhelmingly at the polls in 1932.[86] The correspondence between Catholic ideas of social justice and Roosevelt's plans for governing increased Catholic support of FDR, building upon their historical support for messages of social egalitarianism (such as Roosevelt's) and of the Democratic Party.[87] Once Roosevelt was in office, Catholics responded very positively to the New Deal.[88] From the hierarchy and from the Catholic press, Catholics were deluged with messages about how closely the programs of the New Deal matched the social teachings of the church.[89] *Sign* magazine, an important Catholic publication, proclaimed to its readers that Roosevelt stood "among the leaders of the world as one of the foremost advocates of the principles of Pope Leo XIII."[90] Members of the Catholic hierarchy lavished praise on Roosevelt and his programs, a practice repeated in the Catholic press, by Catholic organizations, and ultimately among the laity.[91] Once in office, Roosevelt reciprocated in kind, continuing to reach out to American Catholics and their leaders much as he had on the campaign trail.[92] Roosevelt was publicly friendly with many Catholic ecclesiastics, inviting them to prominent national events and publicly seeking their counsel on national matters. After his election in 1932, FDR named two Catholics, James Farley and Thomas Walsh, to his cabinet, an unprecedented move.[93] Roosevelt also appointed more Catholics to public office than any president had before.[94] Through his actions, Roosevelt demonstrated to American Catholics that their support was important to him, that their ideas were relevant to the American experience, and that their loyalty would be rewarded. The New Deal served to securely bind Catholics to the Democratic Party.[95] Despite tensions between Catholics and Roosevelt over the recognition of communist Russia, U.S. policy toward Mexico, and the anti-Roosevelt tone that popular radio personality Father Charles E. Coughlin had adopted by 1936, Catholic support of the Democratic Party remained strong throughout the Roosevelt years.[96]

The friendly treatment Catholics received from the Roosevelt administration helped to ease the sting of the 1920s anti-Catholicism that had marked Smith's presidential efforts. Taken as a whole, the New Deal experience had served to further legitimize the place of Catholics in American society. The pace of Catholics' entrance into the American mainstream would quicken considerably in the years following World War II. Legislation severely restricting immigration to the United States had been passed in the 1920s, reducing the number of new arrivals to a trickle. America's Catholic population no longer increased every year due to the arrival of mostly lower-class immigrants, allowing Catholics as a group to improve their socioeconomic status.[97] The GI Bill opened the door to higher education for many working-class servicemen, a development that Catholics took full advantage of. Already moving up the socioeconomic ladder, Catholics used the GI Bill to climb exponentially.[98] By the 1950s, many members of the Catholic laity were socially and economically confident enough to offer their visions and ideas to the greater population, knowing they would be listened to as citizens, not as members of a suspect minority group.[99] During this period, Catholics began, for the first time, to approach mainline Protestants in regards to education and income levels.[100] The mobility of Catholics during the war and their subsequent travels in search of higher education, combined with their rising socioeconomic status, led to the breakdown of "ghetto Catholicism," as Catholics left urban centers and moved to the rapidly developing suburbs.[101] As Catholics spread out geographically, became more educated, and increased their income and status levels throughout the 1950s, they had increasing success in the electoral realm. In 1958 and 1959, Catholic governors were elected in the predominantly non-Catholic states of Pennsylvania, Ohio, California, and Hawaii. The Senate class of 1958 included Catholics from Connecticut, Massachusetts, Michigan, Minnesota, Maine, Montana, and Alaska.[102] As a result of the Democratic landslide of 1958, the percentage of Catholics in Congress corresponded to the percentage of Catholics in the American population for the first time.[103] American Catholics of the 1950s were finally confident enough of their acceptance into society to reach out beyond their ward or city for a place in American politics. The 1960 presidential election would provide American Catholics with confirmation of their acceptance into the mainstream of American politics and society. In hindsight, some political observers also saw in this election the beginning of the end of Catholic distinctiveness in terms of their electoral behavior.

In 1960 John F. Kennedy became the second Roman Catholic to run for the office of president of the United States on the line of a major political party. As in the 1928 campaign of Al Smith, some groups worked against the election of Kennedy simply because he was Catholic. This time, however, such anti-Catholic sentiment was neither as widespread nor as acceptable.[104] The position of Catholics in American society had improved much from 1928 to 1960, a fact that Kennedy's campaign and subsequent victory helped to confirm. From the very beginning, Kennedy unequivocally stated that his oath and duty to the nation would take precedence over his religion. He told voters that religion was a personal matter, and that "the separation of church and state must be absolute."[105] Kennedy's victory put an end to the unwritten rule that a Catholic could not be president of the United States. For Catholics, Kennedy's election confirmed their acceptance into the mainstream of American society.[106] Historian Lawrence Fuchs has said that the importance of Kennedy in opening minds and easing doubts about Catholics cannot be overestimated: "For many non-Catholics, Kennedy proved that Catholicism was not incompatible with freedom."[107]

Like Al Smith, John F. Kennedy was a Democrat. And like Smith, Kennedy enjoyed the overwhelming electoral support of his fellow Catholics. Reliable estimates show that over 80 percent of American Catholics voted for Kennedy in 1960, a figure that is truly staggering when one considers that Catholics made up around 25 percent of the national voting age population at that time.[108] While the level of Catholic support for the Democrat Kennedy was extraordinarily high, the fact that Catholics supported the Democratic candidate was true to form. As stated earlier, Catholics emerged from the Roosevelt era as staunch supporters of the Democratic Party, continuing a trend that stretched back to the earliest days of universal male suffrage. Catholic allegiance to the Democrats remained strong even after the death of FDR, with 66 percent of Catholics voting for Harry Truman in 1948.[109] Even as large numbers of Catholics defected from the Democratic ranks to vote for Eisenhower in 1952 and 1956, Catholics as a group still voted for the Democratic candidate at much higher levels than did their Protestant counterparts.[110] As noted above, the Democrats' nomination of Kennedy in 1960 produced a record level of Catholic support for the party in that election, a level that was nearly matched in the 1964 presidential election.[111] In the mid-1960s, Catholics remained stalwart supporters of the Democratic Party, providing one of the strongest components of the party's electoral coalition.[112]

A Crumbling Alliance? Catholics and the Democratic Party, 1968-Present

In the 1968 presidential election, the level of Catholic support for the Democratic Party nominee dropped significantly compared to the levels of Catholic support in the previous two presidential elections. In 1972, George McGovern actually lost among Catholic voters, only the second time a Democratic presidential nominee had met such a fate since reliable national estimates for voting percentages among social groups had been available.[113] The New Deal coalition was perceived as breaking down, with the decline in Democratic support among Catholics named as a major cause.[114]

Almost as soon as the decline in Democratic support among Catholics was noted, political observers attempted to explain the phenomenon. Early, non-academic analysts attributed the decline to the Democratic Party's liberal stand on the "social question," which included such issues as crime, student/youth rebellion, welfare, and pornography. The Democrats, by their liberal positions on these (among other) issues, had alienated many members of the Catholic community, thus driving them away from the party.[115] Some academics soon joined in offering a similar explanation, claiming that the Democratic Party had simply become too liberal for the taste of American Catholics.[116] This explanation still holds considerable legitimacy today.[117]

Other analysts chose more specific portions of the social question as the basis for their explanation of declining Catholic support for the Democratic Party. Race became a prominent explanation for why Catholics left the Democratic Party, although the connection of the race issue specifically to Catholics was sometimes implied. The argument generally offered here is that as the Democratic Party pushed through civil rights legislation, more and more blacks began to compete with blue-collar whites for high-paying union jobs. This alienated these whites from the Democratic Party.[118] This explanation relates to Catholics because of the fact that many of these blue-collar whites happened to be Catholic ethnics.[119] Jensen made such a claim openly: "The Southern and Catholic backlash against civil rights programs demonstrated that ethnocentric traditionalism was not dead in America. Democratic presidential candidates found it increasingly difficult to keep together the Roosevelt coalition of Catholics, blacks, and white Southerners."[120]

Abortion became the basis of another popular explanation for the decline of Democratic support among Catholics. The opposition of the Catholic Church to abortion in any form and for any reason is well known. Those who focus on abortion as the reason for their explanation of the decline in Catholic support for the Democratic Party argue that the party's liberal position regarding abortion in the post-*Roe v. Wade* era has forced many Catholics to leave the party.[121] In many examples, those who offer explanations centering on the social question use the Democratic Party position on a combination of issues to build the case in favor of their explanation. These variations focusing on the social question represent one of the two most common explanations offered for the decline in Catholic support for the Democratic Party.

The other prevalent explanation offered for the decline centers on the rise in socioeconomic status that American Catholics have enjoyed since the 1950s. After World War II, the income and education levels of American Catholics rose steadily, becoming almost equal to the levels attained by America's mainline Protestant population by the 1970s.[122] As early as 1948, Wesley and Beverly Allinsmith advanced the claim that socioeconomic status, not religious affiliation, was the determining factor in Catholic support for the Democratic Party. The Democrats were the party of the poor and the working class, and at that time in American history many Catholics qualified for inclusion in these groups. Class, not religious affiliation, was what caused Catholics to be Democrats.[123]

The logical extension of the Allinsmiths' argument is that as the socioeconomic status of American Catholics changed, so too would their party affiliation. As Catholics increased their socioeconomic status and moved into the suburbs, their interests would naturally fall out of line with the Democratic Party. They would gradually leave the Democrats in favor of the Republicans. In a seminal article, sociologist Scott Greer claimed this was happening in St. Louis during the late 1950s,[124] and political scientist Michael Parenti predicted in 1967 that it would eventually happen elsewhere.[125] Ladd et al. fully articulated this argument, claiming that by the late 1960s, the socioeconomic position of Catholics in American life had changed. "Many had moved up the socioeconomic ladder, were now *haves* rather than *have-nots*. They were less and less a beneficiary group, and more and more a contributing group in Democratic welfare policies."[126]

This explanation slowly gained advocates in the academic community. In 1976, Nie et al. presented evidence showing that while lower-status Catholics were remaining Democrats, upper-status Catholics were increasingly likely to vote Republican.[127] Ladd and Hadley expanded on the argument they had originally made in 1971.[128] By 1997, the socioeconomic status explanation for the decline in Democratic support among Catholics had become so commonplace[129] that Manza and Brooks called it "the main explanation for this hypothesized shift among Catholics."[130]

It appears that the academic community has reached a consensus regarding the electoral behavior of American Catholics. Catholics are no longer more Democratic than Republican. Perhaps more important, Catholics no longer differ from Protestants in their voting behavior and party identification. There are, however, numerous reasons to question the conventional wisdom regarding Catholic electoral behavior outlined above. Chapter 3 will discuss these reasons, presenting evidence that will show why the electoral behavior of American Catholics is in need of reexamination.

Notes

1. For extended discussions of the battles over lay trusteeship and public schools see: Ray Allen Billington, *The Protestant Crusade 1800-1860: A Study of the Origins of American Nativisim* (New York: Macmillan, 1938), chapter VI; Jay P. Dolan, *The American Catholic Experience* (Notre Dame, Ind.: University of Notre Dame Press, 1992), chapters 4, 6, and 10; John Tracy Ellis, *American Catholicism*, 2d ed., revised (Chicago: University of Chicago Press, 1969), 41-69; Vincent P. Lannie, "Alienation in America: The Immigrant Catholic and Public Education in Pre-Civil War America," *Review of Politics* 32, no. 4 (Oct. 1970): 503-21; Charles R. Morris, *American Catholic* (New York: Random House, 1997), 72-75.
2. Dolan, *The American Catholic Experience*, 201, 87, 160.
3. Patrick W. Carey, *The Roman Catholics* (Westport, Conn.: Greenwood Press, 1993), 31; John A. Coleman, "American Catholicism," in *World Catholicism in Transition*, ed. Thomas M. Gannon (New York: Macmillan Publishing Company, 1988), 234; Dolan, *The American Catholic Experience*, 160-61; Ellis, *American Catholicism*, 88.
4. Dolan, *The American Catholic Experience*, 161.
5. Carey, *The Roman Catholics*, 31.
6. James Hennesey, *American Catholics* (New York: Oxford University Press, 1981), 173.
7. Ellis, *American Catholicism*, 88.
8. Hennesey, *American Catholics*, 173.
9. Dolan, *The American Catholic Experience*, 158.
10. Dolan, *The American Catholic Experience*, chapter IV; Thomas T. McAvoy, *A History of the Catholic Church in the United States* (Notre Dame, Ind.: University of Notre Dame Press, 1969), chapter 4.
11. Coleman, "American Catholicism," 232.
12. Dolan, *The American Catholic Experience*, 158; McAvoy, *A History*, 240.
13. Dolan, *The American Catholic Experience*, 295.

14. Dolan, *The American Catholic Experience*, 160-61; McAvoy, *A History*, 148; Ellis, *American Catholicism*, 50.
15. Dolan, *The American Catholic Experience*, 163.
16. Hennesey, *American Catholics*, 175.
17. McAvoy, *A History*, 148.
18. Lannie, "Alienation in America," 505; Berton Dulce and Edward J. Richter, *Religion and the Presidency: A Recurring American Problem* (New York: The Macmillan Company, 1962), 21.
19. Elisha Williams, "The Inalienable Rights of Conscience," in *Puritan Political Ideas, 1558-1794*, ed. Edmund S. Morgan (Indianapolis, Ind.: The Bobbs-Merril Co., 1965), 282.
20. Dulce and Richter, *Religion and the Presidency*, 14.
21. Josiah Strong, *The Twentieth Century City* (1898; reprint, New York: Arno Press, 1970), 95.
22. Billington, *The Protestant Crusade*, 4.
23. Billington, *The Protestant Crusade*, 345.
24. Dolan, *The American Catholic Experience*, 201-2.
25. Tyler Anbinder, *Nativism and Slavery: The Northern Know Nothings and the Politics of the 1850's* (New York: Oxford University Press, 1992); Donald L. Kinzer, *An Episode of Anti-Catholicism: The American Protective Association* (Seattle: University of Washington Press, 1964).
26. Billington, *The Protestant Crusade*, 290-93.
27. R. Laurence Moore, *Religious Outsiders and the Making of Americans* (New York: Oxford University Press, 1986), 48-71; Dolan, *The American Catholic Experience*, 313.
28. Paul Kleppner, *The Third Electoral System, 1853-1892* (Chapel Hill, N.C.: University of North Carolina Press, 1979), 231.
29. Paul Kleppner, *The Cross of Culture: A Social Analysis of Midwestern Politics, 1850-1900* (New York: The Free Press, 1970), 117.
30. Joel H. Silbey, "The Rise and Fall of American Political Parties, 1790-1993," in *The Parties Respond*, 2d ed., ed. L. Sandy Maisel (Boulder, Colo.: Westview Press, 1994), 3-18; William Gienapp, "Politics Seem to Enter into Everything: Political Culture in the North, 1840-1860," in *Essays on American Antebellum Politics, 1840-1860*, ed. Stephen E. Maizlish and John J. Kushma (College Station, Tex.: Texas A&M University Press, 1982), 15-69.
31. Everett Carll Ladd, Jr. with Charles D. Hadley, *Transformations of the American Party System* (New York: W. W. Norton & Company, 1975), 46.
32. It is important to note that this discussion of religious groups and political parties in the nineteenth century does not apply to the American South. It is well known that the South of this period was strictly a one-party system. An overwhelming majority of southerners belonged to the Democratic Party despite the fact that southerners were also almost entirely Protestant. As Ladd and Hadley note, failure to recognize this fact partially conceals the significance of the Protestant/Catholic divide in structuring nineteenth-century American politics. Ladd with Hadley, *Transformations*, 52. All discussion of religious denominations and political parties during the nineteenth century in this study will exclude the South, unless otherwise noted.
33. Robert P. Swierenga, "Ethnoreligious Political Behavior in the Mid-Nineteenth Century: Voting, Values, and Cultures," in *Religion and American Politics: From the*

Colonial Period to the 1980s, ed. Mark A. Noll (New York: Oxford University Press, 1990), 161.

34. Kleppner, *The Third Electoral System*; David Knoke, *Change and Continuity in American Politics* (Baltimore, Md.: Johns Hopkins University Press, 1976), 19.

35. Andrew M. Greeley, *The American Catholic: A Social Portrait* (New York: Basic Books, 1977), 92; Lee Bensen, *The Concept of Jacksonian Democracy: New York as a Test Case* (Princeton, N.J.: Princeton University Press, 1961), chapter 11.

36. Paul Lopatto, *Religion and the Presidential Election* (New York: Praeger, 1985), 5.

37. Knoke, *Change and Continuity*, 19.

38. Vincent P. De Santis, "Catholicism and Presidential Elections, 1865-1900," *Mid-America* 42, no. 2 (April 1960): 68-75.

39. Kleppner, *The Third Electoral System*, 231-32.

40. McAvoy, *A History*, 314-15.

41. Greeley, *The American Catholic*, 92; Knoke, *Change and Continuity*, 19.

42. Jensen, *The Winning of the Midwest*, 15-16.

43. The term "reinforce" needs to be stressed here. Both Kleppner and Jensen clearly show that class was of secondary importance to religious affiliation in determining the partisan affiliation of nineteenth-century Americans. The fact that the majority of nineteenth-century Catholics was situated in the lower economic tiers of society was not the primary reason for their overwhelmingly Democratic allegiance. Class standing did, however, provide an additional impetus for the Democratic allegiance toward which Catholics were already pushed by their religious denomination. The same holds true for Protestants as well. Ladd with Hadley, *Transformations*, 52: Jensen, *The Winning of the Midwest*, xii; Kleppner, *The Cross of Culture*, 35.

44. This discussion of "ritualistic" and "liturgical" religious worldviews is based on the work of Paul Kleppner and Richard Jensen. Although both men discuss essentially the same religious perspective, Kleppner uses the term "ritualistic" while Jensen uses "liturgical." See Kleppner, *The Third Electoral System*, 185-97; Kleppner, *The Cross of Culture*, 70-76; Jensen, *The Winning of the Midwest*, 64-68.

45. Bensen, *The Concept of Jacksonian Democracy*, chapter 11; Jensen, *The Winning of the Midwest*, 67-68; Kleppner, *The Cross of Culture*, 75-76.

46. A. James Reichley, *Religion in American Public Life* (Washington, D.C.: The Brookings Institution, 1985), 183; Ladd with Hadley, *Transformations*, 50-51.

47. Kleppner, *The Cross of Culture*, 76.

48. Greeley, *The American Catholic*, 92.

49. Lopatto, *Religion and the Presidential Election*, 3-5.

50. Kleppner, *The Third Electoral System*; Jensen, *The Winning of the Midwest*; Kleppner, *The Cross of Culture*.

51. James L. Sundquist, *Dynamics of the Party System*, Rev. ed. (Washington, D.C.: The Brookings Institution, 1983), chapter 7.

52. Reichley, *Religion in American Public Life*, 210-11.

53. Sundquist, *Dynamics of the Party System*, chapter 7; David Burner, *The Politics of Provincialism: The Democratic Party in Transition, 1918-1932* (New York: Alfred A. Knopf, 1968); Paul Kleppner, *Continuity and Change in Electoral Politics, 1893-1928* (Westport, Conn.: Greenwood Press, 1987); Walter Dean Burnham, "The Changing Shape of the American Political Universe," *American Political Science Review* 59, no. 1 (March 1965): 7-28.

54. John M. Allswang, *A House for All Peoples: Ethnic Politics in Chicago, 1890-1936* (Lexington, Ky.: University Press of Kentucky, 1971), chapters 2 and 3; Burner, *The Politics of Provincialism*; Kleppner, *Continuity and Change in Electoral Politics*, chapter 7; J. Joseph Huthmacher, *Massachusetts People and Politics, 1919-1933* (Cambridge, Mass.: Belknap Press, 1959).

55. Sundquist, *Dynamics of the Party System*, 168.

56. Dolan, *The American Catholic Experience*, 322-324; Aaron I. Abell, *American Catholicism and Social Action: A Search for Social Justice, 1865-1950* (Notre Dame, Ind.: University of Notre Dame Press, 1963), chapter 1.

57. Abell, *American Catholicism and Social Action*, 27.

58. Dolan, *The American Catholic Experience*, 323-24.

59. Dolan, *The American Catholic Experience*, 325-26; Abell, *American Catholicism and Social Action*, chapters 1 and 2.

60. Dolan, *The American Catholic Experience*, 329; Abell, *American Catholicism and Social Action*, 72-73.

61. Abell, *American Catholicism and Social Action*, 72-73.

62. Dolan, *The American Catholic Experience*, 329; Abell, *American Catholicism and Social Action*, chapter 3.

63. Dolan, *The American Catholic Experience*, 329-31; Abell, *American Catholicism and Social Action*, 54-55.

64. Dolan, *The American Catholic Experience*, 312-13, 330-31; McAvoy, *A History*, 307.

65. Dolan, *The American Catholic Experience*, 332.

66. Dolan, *The American Catholic Experience*, 332-33; Abell, *American Catholicism and Social Action*, 66-71.

67. Dolan, *The American Catholic Experience*, 333; McAvoy, *A History*, 279-81.

68. Dolan, *The American Catholic Experience*, 329-44.

69. Dolan, *The American Catholic Experience*, 329-44; George Q. Flynn, *American Catholics & the Roosevelt Presidency, 1932-1936* (Lexington, Ky.: University of Kentucky Press, 1968), 23; Abell, *American Catholicism and Social Action*, 199-202; John A. Ryan, "The Bishops' Program of Social Reconstruction," *American Catholic Sociological Review* 5 (Mar. 1944): 25-33.

70. Dolan, *The American Catholic Experience*, 344-45; Abell, *American Catholicism and Social Action*, 203-4.

71. This social justice tradition is of vast importance to twentieth-century American Catholicism, and will be discussed in much greater detail in chapter 6.

72. Hennesey, *American Catholics*, 246; Ladd with Hadley, *Transformations*, 49.

73. Hennesey, *American Catholics*, 246-47; Jerome M. Clubb, "Party Coalitions in the Early Twentieth Century," in *Party Coalitions in the 1980s*, ed. Seymour Martin Lipset (San Francisco: Institute for Contemporary Studies, 1981), 107-26.

74. Burner, *The Politics of Provincialism*, 190-92; Allswang, *A House for All Peoples*, 96-97.

75. Philip Gleason, "Pluralism, Democracy, and Catholicism in the Era of World War II," *Review of Politics* 49, no. 2 (Spring 1987): 208-30. For some examples of anti-Catholic rhetoric during the 1928 campaign, see Dulce and Richter, *Religion and the Presidency*, chapter 7.

76. This discussion of Al Smith and the 1928 presidential campaign draws on: Morris, *American Catholic*, 159-60; Dolan, *The American Catholic Experience*, 351; Hennesey, *American Catholics*, 246-47; McAvoy, *A History*, 399-400.

77. Lopatto, *Religion and the Presidential Election*, 8; E. J. Dionne, Jr., "Catholics and the Democrats: Estrangement but Not Desertion," in *Party Coalitions in the 1980s*, ed. Seymour Martin Lipset (San Francisco: Institute for Contemporary Studies, 1981), 307-25; Richard L. Rubin, *Party Dynamics: The Democratic Coalition and the Politics of Change* (New York: Oxford University Press, 1976), 30-31.

78. Allswang, *A House for All Peoples*, 135; McAvoy, *A History*, 400; Huthmacher, *Massachusetts People and Politics*, chapter 6.

79. Ladd with Hadley, *Transformations*, 268-69.

80. Flynn, *American Catholics & the Roosevelt Presidency*, 23-35.

81. David J. O'Brien, *American Catholics and Social Reform* (New York: Oxford University Press, 1968), 55.

82. *Quadragesimo Anno* was issued by Pope Pius XI in 1931. Intended as an update of *Rerum Novarum*, the encyclical called for, among other things, workers to share in profits through ownership and management, the obligation of employers to pay a "living wage" to their workers, and the responsibility of government to intervene in society to protect the common good. In general, Pius endorsed a "law of social justice." Dolan, *The American Catholic Experience*, 402; McAvoy, *A History*, 407. Much more will be said about both of these encyclicals in chapter 6.

83. Dolan, *The American Catholic Experience*, 402; O'Brien, *American Catholics and Social Reform*, 47.

84. O'Brien, *American Catholics and Social Reform*, 52.

85. Hennesey, *American Catholics*, 260; Flynn, *American Catholics & the Roosevelt Presidency*, 17.

86. Ladd with Hadley, *Transformations*, chapter 1; Flynn, *American Catholics & the Roosevelt Presidency*, 20.

87. Reichley, *Religion in American Public Life*, 219-20; Lawrence Fuchs, quoted in Albert J. Menendez, *Religion at the Polls* (Philadelphia: The Westminster Press, 1977), 111; Angus Campbell, Philip E. Converse, Warren E. Miller, and Donald E. Stokes, *The American Voter* (New York: John Wiley & Sons, 1960), 159.

88. Flynn, *American Catholics & the Roosevelt Presidency*, 36; O'Brien, *American Catholics and Social Reform*, 51.

89. Flynn, *American Catholics & the Roosevelt Presidency*, chapter 3.

90. Quoted in O'Brien, *American Catholics and Social Reform*, 52.

91. Hennesey, *American Catholics*, 259-60; Flynn, *American Catholics & the Roosevelt Presidency*, 78.

92. John M. Allswang, *The New Deal and American Politics: A Study in Political Change* (New York: John Wiley & Sons, 1978), 42-43.

93. O'Brien, *American Catholics and Social Reform*, 51; Flynn, *American Catholics & the Roosevelt Presidency*, 50-51.

94. Philip Gleason, "Pluralism, Democracy, and Catholicism," 208.

95. Ladd with Hadley, *Transformations*, 50-51.

96. Ladd with Hadley, *Transformations*, chapters 1 and 2.

97. Dolan, *The American Catholic Experience*, 356.

98. Hennesey, *American Catholics*, 283.

99. Patrick Allit, *Catholic Intellectuals and Conservative Politics in America, 1950-1985* (Ithaca, N.Y.: Cornell University Press, 1993), 5.

100. More will be said about this rise in socioeconomic status among Catholics later in this chapter. For a description of this ascent, see: Greeley, *The American Catholic*;

Andrew M. Greeley, *The Catholic Myth: The Behavior and Beliefs of American Catholics* (New York: Charles Scribner's Sons, 1990).

101. Morris, *American Catholic*, chapter 10; Dolan, *The American Catholic Experience*, 357-58.

102. While a Catholic senator from Connecticut, Massachusetts, and Michigan may not be surprising, the other states listed here were at the time predominantly non-Catholic. For more on these elections, see Lawrence H. Fuchs, *John F. Kennedy and American Catholicism* (New York: Meredith Press, 1967), 148-49.

103. Mary T. Hanna, *Catholics and American Politics* (Cambridge, Mass.: Harvard University Press, 1979), 48.

104. Morris, *American Catholic*, 281; Allit, *Catholic Intellectuals*, 85.

105. Dolan, *The American Catholic Experience*, 421; Fuchs, *John F. Kennedy and American Catholicism*, 164-79.

106. Morris, *American Catholic*, 280-81; Dolan, *The American Catholic Experience*, 421-22; Hennesey, *American Catholics*, 308-9; Ellis, *American Catholicism*, 188-89; McAvoy, *A History*, 458-59.

107. Fuchs, *John F. Kennedy and American Catholicism*, 236.

108. Data from the National Election Studies (NES) put the percentage of American Catholics voting for Kennedy in 1960 at 82, a percentage similar to the figure reported by Ladd and Hadley using Gallup data. Ladd with Hadley, *Transformations*, 118. Percentage of population figure taken from Morris, *American Catholic*, 256.

109. The 1948 NES Pilot Survey puts the level of Catholic support for Truman in 1948 at 66 percent. Once again, Ladd and Hadley report a similar figure using Gallup data. Ladd with Hadley, *Transformations*, 118.

110. Ladd with Hadley, *Transformations*, 116-21; Robert Axelrod, "Where the Votes Come From: An Analysis of Electoral Coalitions, 1952-1968," *American Political Science Review* 66, no. 1 (Mar. 1972): 11-20; Campbell, Converse, Miller, and Stokes, *The American Voter*, 301.

111. Based on NES data.

112. Harold W. Stanley and Richard G. Niemi, "Partisanship and Group Support, 1952-1988," *American Politics Quarterly* 19, no. 2 (Apr. 1991): 189-210; Robert S. Erikson, Thomas D. Lancaster, and David W. Romero, "Group Components of the Presidential Vote, 1952-1984," *Journal of Politics* 51, no. 2 (May 1989): 337-46; Harold W. Stanley, William T. Bianco, and Richard G. Niemi, "Partisanship and Group Support over Time: A Multivariate Analysis," *American Political Science Review* 80, no. 3 (Sept. 1986): 969-76; Andrew M. Greeley, "How Conservative Are American Catholics?" *Political Science Quarterly* 92, no. 2 (Summer 1977): 199-218; David Knoke, "Religion, Stratification and Politics: America in the 1960s," *American Journal of Political Science* 18, no. 2 (May 1974): 331-45; Axelrod, "Where the Votes Come From," 11-20.

113. The first time was the 1956 election.

114. Jeffrey Levine, Edward G. Carmines, and Robert Huckfeldt, "The Rise of Ideology in the Post-New Deal Party System, 1972-1992," *American Politics Quarterly* 25, no. 1 (Jan. 1997): 19-34; Paul R. Abramson, John H. Aldrich, and David W. Rohde, *Change and Continuity in the 1992 Elections* (Washington, D.C.: Congressional Quarterly Press, 1995), 158-61; Timothy A. Byrnes, "The Politics of the American Catholic Hierarchy," *Political Science Quarterly* 108, no. 3 (Fall 1993): 499.

115. For examples, see William A. Rusher, *The Making of a New Majority Party* (New York: Sheed and Ward, 1975); Patrick Buchanan, *The Conservative Choice* (New

York: Quadrangle, 1975); Kevin Phillips, *The Emerging Republican Majority* (New Rochelle, N.Y.: Arlington House, 1969).

116. A. James Reichley, "Religion and the Future of American Politics," *Political Science Quarterly* 101, no. 1 (1986): 33; James L. Sundquist, "Whither the American Party System?" *Political Science Quarterly* 88, no. 4 (Dec. 1973): 565, 578.

117. Levine, Carmines, and Huckfeldt, "The Rise of Ideology," 19-34.

118. Abramson, Aldrich, and Rohde, *Change and Continuity in the 1992 Elections*, 158; Carol Weitzel Kohfeld and Robert R. Huckfeldt, *Race and the Decline of Class in American Politics* (Urbana, Ill.: University of Illinois Press, 1989).

119. Samuel G. Freedman, *The Inheritance* (New York: Simon & Schuster, 1996), chapters 8-10; Greeley, "How Conservative Are American Catholics?" 199-201.

120. Richard Jensen, "Party Coalitions and the Search for Modern Values: 1820-1970," in *Party Coalitions in the 1980s*, ed. Seymour Martin Lipset (San Francisco: Institute for Contemporary Studies, 1981), 82-83.

121. Reichley (1986) makes this claim openly (33), while it is alluded to in Hanna, *Catholics and American Politics*, chapter 5.

122. Greeley, *The American Catholic*, chapter 3.

123. Wesley Allinsmith and Beverly Allinsmith, "Religious Affiliation and Politico-Economic Attitudes: A Study of Eight Major U.S. Religious Groups," *Public Opinion Quarterly* 12, no. 3 (Fall 1948): 377-89.

124. Scott Greer, "Catholic Voters and the Democratic Party," *Public Opinion Quarterly* 25, no. 4 (Winter 1961): 611-25.

125. Michael Parenti, "Political Values and Religious Cultures: Jews, Catholics, and Protestants," *Journal for the Scientific Study of Religion* 6, no. 2 (Fall 1967): 259-69.

126. Everett Ladd, Jr., Charles Hadley, and Lauriston King, "A New Political Realignment?" *The Public Interest*, no. 23 (Spring 1971): 56. Italics in original.

127. Norman H. Nie, Sidney Verba, and John R. Petrocik, *The Changing American Voter* (Cambridge, Mass.: Harvard University Press, 1976), 231-32.

128. Ladd with Hadley, *Transformations*, see especially chapter 5.

129. For some examples, see Reichley, "Religion and the Future of American Politics," 32; Lyman A. Kellstedt and Mark A. Noll, "Religion, Voting for President, and Party Identification, 1948-1984," in *Religion and American Politics: From the Colonial Period to the 1980s*, ed. Mark A. Noll (New York: Oxford University Press, 1990), 355-79; Abramson, Aldrich, and Rohde, *Change and Continuity in the 1992 Elections*, 158-60.

130. Jeff Manza and Clem Brooks, "The Religious Factor in U.S. Presidential Elections, 1960-1992," *American Journal of Sociology* 103, no. 1 (July 1997): 43-44.

Chapter Three

The Conventional Wisdom Revisited

Introduction: Evidence for the Conventional Wisdom

In the wake of Nixon's landslide defeat of George McGovern in 1972, a majority of interested political observers became convinced that Catholics were leaving the Democratic Party. Whether the reason for the decline in Catholic support for the Democrats was the liberal stance of the party on selected social issues, the rapid rise of Catholics in socioeconomic status, or a combination of both, Catholics were said to be coming loose from their traditional political moorings. Having been fully integrated into the American mainstream, Catholics were seen by many political analysts as no longer constituting a distinct bloc of voters. By the late 1970s, the desertion of the Democratic Party by Catholics had been established as the prevailing conventional wisdom, despite the lack of supporting empirical evidence. As Andrew Greeley stated, Catholic defection from the Democratic Party became a "myth" that did not need to be proven.[1]

Subsequent research has provided greater support for the claim of a Catholic exodus from the Democratic Party. Catholic support for the Democrats does appear to have eroded somewhat since 1968.[2] Catholics now make up a greater percentage of the Republican coalition than ever before, and they have become increasingly likely to vote Republican in presidential elections.[3] At least at the presidential level, American Catholics are now usually portrayed as swing voters, equally likely to vote for either the Democratic or Republican candidate.[4] Tables 3.1 and 3.2 lend support to these claims. The percentages of Catholics voting Democratic in presidential and House elections have declined somewhat since the 1960s, as has the percentage of Catholics identifying with the Democratic Party.[5] The differences between Catholics and Protestants in their support for the Democrats have also decreased. Those offering early proclamations of Catholic defection from the Democratic Party would seem to have been correct, their claims apparently upheld by later empirical analysis.

Table 3.1: Democratic Presidential Vote, House Vote, and Party ID, Catholics and Protestants, All Respondents, 1952-2000

	President			House			Party ID		
Year	Cath.	Prot.	Diff.	Cath.	Prot.	Diff.	Cath.	Prot.	Diff.
1952	52	36	16	55	45	10	68	52	16
1954	--	--	--	--	--	--	64	54	10
1956	46	36	10	61	48	13	59	46	13
1958	--	--	--	72	54	18	67	51	16
1960	82	36	46	79	45	34	73	46	27
1962	--	--	--	75	50	25	67	48	19
1964	79	62	17	72	62	10	70	58	12
1966	--	--	--	68	51	17	64	50	14
1968	56	34	22	61	47	14	65	52	13
1970	--	--	--	58	51	7	63	51	12
1972	39	31	8	66	51	15	63	46	17
1974	--	--	--	72	56	16	63	48	15
1976	57	46	11	63	53	10	63	46	17
1978	--	--	--	64	55	9	65	48	17
1980	41	39	2	59	52	7	55	50	5
1982	--	--	--	66	53	13	65	51	14
1984	46	37	9	61	50	11	52	45	7
1986	--	--	--	66	57	9	55	49	6
1988	52	42	10	67	55	12	51	46	5
1990	--	--	--	65	62	3	56	49	7
1992	50	44	6	62	56	6	55	46	9
1994	--	--	--	49	42	7	52	43	9
1996	55	49	6	49	45	4	55	49	6
1998	--	--	--	51	40	11	52	49	3
2000	50	48	2	53	45	8	50	48	2

Note: In this table, and in all subsequent tables showing party identification, those respondents leaning toward a party are considered as identifying with that party.[6] House vote was not asked in 1954. Source: All data for years 1952-1998 taken from the *American National Election Studies Cumulative Data File, 1948-1998* (hereafter NES Cumulative File) vcf0106, vcf0128, vcf0705, vcf0707, and vcf0303. Data for 2000 are drawn from the *American National Election Studies Cumulative Data File, 1948-2000*. This is true for all analyses conducted in this study unless noted otherwise. The reasoning behind this decision is laid out in chapter 4, endnote 32. Variable numbers are the same in both versions of the Cumulative File.

Table 3.2: Democratic Presidential Vote, House Vote, and Party ID, Catholics and Protestants, All Respondents, by Decade, 1950s-1990s

	President			House			Party ID		
Dec.	Cath.	Prot.	Diff.	Cath.	Prot.	Diff.	Cath.	Prot.	Diff.
1950s	49	36	13	62	48	14	65	50	15
1960s	72	45	27	71	52	19	68	51	17
1970s	47	38	9	65	53	12	64	48	16
1980s	47	39	8	64	53	11	55	48	7
1990s	52	46	6	56	50	6	54	47	7

Source: NES Cumulative File, vcf 0106, vcf0128, vcf0705, vcf0707, and vcf0303.

To many analysts, the decline in Catholic support for the Democrats meant that the distinctive nature of Catholic electoral behavior had come to an end.[7] Upward economic mobility, increased educational levels, and suburban migration had combined to produce a Catholic population whose values, beliefs, and attitudes were quite similar to those held by Protestants.[8] In the words of William Prendergast, "Catholics went through the melting pot and came out very much like other Americans."[9] As a result, many observers claimed Catholic electoral behavior had become indistinguishable from that of Protestants.

Catholic Electoral Behavior: An Alternate Perspective

Have American Catholics abandoned their traditional preference for the Democratic Party? Are they equally likely to support Democrats and Republicans? Has the electoral behavior of Catholics lost its distinctive nature, becoming essentially the same as that of Protestants? Perhaps judgment has been passed too quickly on these matters. Certainly, Catholic support for the Democratic Party has declined somewhat across all party support indicators since 1968, and Catholics have become more likely to vote for Republican presidential candidates, particularly Ronald Reagan during the 1980s. However, these phenomena do not mean that Catholics have come unattached from their traditional Democratic moorings. The key questions for this chapter are: Does the empirical evidence support the claim that Catholics are now no more likely to support the Democratic Party than the Republican Party? Is their electoral behavior now indistinguishable from that of Protestants? The remainder of this chapter will attempt to answer these questions.

Incomplete Analyses

There are numerous reasons to reexamine the conventional wisdom regarding Catholics and the Democratic Party. Despite the supporting evidence cited above, scholarly analysis of the decline in Democratic support among Catholics, and of Catholic electoral behavior in general, is still incomplete. In fact, the scholarly community has failed to produce a complete analysis of Catholic electoral behavior. The extant literature even lacks a complete analysis of the years from 1952 to 1998, the period in which Catholics supposedly abandoned the Democratic Party. Works by earlier authors, such as Ladd with Hadley and Nie et al., end their analyses in the 1970s.[10] Still others, such as Levine et al. and Layman, select the 1970s and 1980s respectively as the starting points for their studies.[11] Finally, other studies that have been cited as important examinations of Catholic electoral behavior utilize surveys covering small blocks of time or selected years.[12] A recent work by Prendergast would seem to rectify this situation, but it too fails to provide a complete examination.[13] Given these weaknesses, a more complete examination of Catholic electoral behavior is clearly in order.[14] This study will provide such an examination.

Methodological Shortcomings of Existing Analyses

The story of Catholic defection from the Democratic Party also has not been established as fully as its status as conventional wisdom would indicate, and there are several shortcomings that need to be addressed. Many studies of Catholic electoral behavior focus exclusively on presidential elections. This creates two problems. First, presidential elections tend to be the most volatile elections, with many factors at work simultaneously. Short-term forces unique to each presidential election can significantly influence the results, making interpretation difficult even after the fact.[15] Second, focusing only on presidential elections may cause some analysts to judge the decline of Catholic support for the Democrats from the inflated levels of the 1960 campaign, when Catholics overwhelmingly supported the party at least in part as a response to the Democrats' presidential nomination of a fellow Catholic. This causes the decline of Catholic support for the Democratic Party to appear much larger than it really is.[16] Indeed, the relatively few analysts who have examined Catholic voting behavior in congressional elections have found that their support for Democratic candidates remained strong and relatively unchanged.[17] Catholic support for Democratic House candidates has declined recently, but that decline started in 1994, not 1968. The almost exclusive focus on presidential elections and corresponding lack of attention paid to congressional elections is problematic in studies of Catholic electoral behavior.

Perhaps more important, an increase in Republican identification among Catholics to the degree predicted by the current thinking regarding Catholics abandoning the Democratic Party simply has not materialized.[18] Some scholars even argue that there has been no distinctive net trend in Catholic support for the Democratic Party in either direction since the 1950s.[19] Catholics still continue to support the Democratic Party at higher levels than do Protestants in both voting and party identification, a fact of American political life that Greeley has reiterated consistently since the 1970s.[20] The Republican Party has certainly registered gains among Catholics over the last thirty years. However, with the exception of Jews, the GOP has increased its membership among all predominantly white religious groups in the United States over this period. The Republican inroads among Catholics have been significantly smaller than the gains achieved among the other religious groups, and Catholics continue to exhibit a greater propensity toward Democratic allegiance.[21]

This fact becomes even more apparent when one examines the electoral behavior of Catholics and Protestants among whites only. African-American voters have undergone one of the most rapid and complete realignments in American electoral history, having become perhaps the social group most supportive of the Democratic Party since 1964.[22] The passage of the Voting Rights Act and grassroots mobilization efforts such as the Voter Education Project also significantly increased the number of blacks registered to vote in the United States, especially in the South where registration rose from 29 percent in 1960 to 62 percent in 1970.[23]

The electoral behavior of African Americans is relevant to this analysis for the following reason. African Americans are overwhelmingly Protestant in their religious affiliation. The almost complete movement of blacks to the Democratic Party since 1964, combined with their relatively substantial increase as a percentage of the electorate, results in significant increases in the percentage of Protestants supporting the Democratic Party. Removing African Americans from the analysis results in a different picture of the electoral behavior of Catholics and Protestants than was presented in tables 3.1 and 3.2. When whites only are examined, differences between Catholics and Protestants in support for the Democratic Party remain quite large, and relatively stable. Tables 3.3 and 3.4 present these results. Aside from elections held in the 1960s, the differences between white Protestants and white Catholics in their support for the Democrats appear very similar across time. White Catholics support the Democratic Party at higher levels than do white Protestants.[24] While there has been a decline in Catholic support for the Democratic Party, this decline has not been as dramatic as suggested by the literature, especially if one examines the electoral behavior of whites only.[25]

The data presented in tables 3.3 and 3.4 raise serious questions about the perception, widely held, that Catholic Americans have abandoned their historical preference for the Democratic Party. The levels of support exhibited by Catholics for the Democrats in the 1990s across all three indicators are quite similar to the levels that existed in the 1950s, the period from which decline supposedly took place. Some decline has occurred among Catholics in their support of the Democrats, but the magnitude of this decline only appears substantial if one begins measuring the drop from the inflated levels of the 1960s.[26] However, one would have a difficult time gleaning these facts from the current literature.[27] Through a careful reexamination of the data, this analysis will attempt to determine to what extent or under what conditions previous claims regarding Catholic electoral behavior seem valid.

Table 3.3: Democratic Presidential Vote, House Vote, and Party ID, Catholics and Protestants, Whites Only, 1952-2000

	President			House			Party ID		
Year	Cath.	Prot.	Diff.	Cath.	Prot.	Diff.	Cath.	Prot.	Diff.
1952	51	33	18	55	42	13	68	51	17
1954	--	--	--	--	--	--	64	53	11
1956	45	34	11	60	46	14	59	45	14
1958	--	--	--	72	52	20	66	51	15
1960	82	34	48	79	44	35	73	46	27
1962	--	--	--	75	47	28	68	46	22
1964	78	57	21	72	58	14	69	54	15
1966	--	--	--	67	47	20	63	47	16
1968	55	26	29	60	43	17	63	46	17
1970	--	--	--	56	48	8	63	46	17
1972	36	24	12	65	47	18	62	43	19
1974	--	--	--	72	52	20	62	43	19
1976	55	40	15	61	47	14	61	41	20
1978	--	--	--	63	51	12	65	43	22
1980	40	31	9	58	46	12	54	44	10
1982	--	--	--	65	48	17	65	45	20
1984	44	28	16	59	45	14	52	38	14
1986	--	--	--	66	50	16	55	40	15
1988	51	33	18	66	49	17	49	37	12
1990	--	--	--	63	56	7	58	41	17
1992	48	34	14	61	50	11	55	38	17
1994	--	--	--	49	36	13	53	34	19
1996	54	41	13	49	38	11	55	42	13
1998	--	--	--	49	35	14	51	40	11
2000	47	40	7	51	39	12	46	40	6

Source: NES Cumulative File vcf0106, vcf0128, vcf0705, vcf0707, and vcf0303.

Table 3.4: Democratic Presidential Vote, House Vote, and Party ID, Catholics and Protestants, Whites Only, by Decade, 1950s-1990s

	President			House			Party ID		
Dec.	Cath.	Prot.	Diff.	Cath.	Prot.	Diff.	Cath.	Prot.	Diff.
1950s	48	34	14	62	46	16	64	50	14
1960s	72	39	33	70	48	22	67	48	19
1970s	45	31	14	64	49	15	63	43	20
1980s	46	31	15	63	48	15	54	40	14
1990s	51	37	14	55	44	11	55	39	16

Source: NES Cumulative File vcf0106, vcf0128, vcf0705, vcf0707, and vcf0303.

Evaluation of the Explanations for Decline

Given the problematic nature of the accepted accounts of Catholic electoral behavior, it stands to reason that the conventional wisdom explanations of Catholic defection from the Democratic Party have weaknesses as well. Although data has already been presented showing the continued support by Catholics for the Democratic Party, explanations of phenomena often take on a life of their own, so to speak. Thus a critical evaluation of the explanations regarding Catholics' desertion of the Democratic Party may prove useful in its own right. As explained in the previous chapter, the move of Catholics away from the Democrats is usually explained by the increasing socioeconomic status of Catholics or their dissatisfaction with the liberal positions of the Democratic Party on selected social issues.[28] I will examine the merits of these explanations one at a time, beginning with the latter.

Ideology

It is possible that the explanation focusing on Catholics' unhappiness with the liberal stands of the Democratic Party is simply wrong. First, public opinion data regularly show that American Catholics as a group tend to be more liberal than the rest of the population as a whole across a range of issues, including most of the social question issues discussed earlier.[29] Although far from perfect for the task, the NES dataset allows for some demonstration of the tendency of Catholics to be more liberal than their Protestant counterparts. Tables 3.5 through 3.9 present the attitudes of Catholics and Protestants on five political issues by decade. Across all five issues, Catholics are more liberal than Protestants.

Table 3.5: Should Government Support Health Care?
Catholics and Protestants, Whites Only, by Decade, 1950s-1990s

	Yes			Neutral		No		
Decade	Cath.	Prot.	Diff.	Cath.	Prot.	Cath.	Prot.	Diff.
1950s	75	61	14	--	--	25	39	-14
1960s	73	61	12	--	--	27	39	-12
1970s	53	35	18	12	15	35	50	-15
1980s	43	35	8	20	20	37	45	-8
1990s	45	36	9	20	22	35	41	-6

Note: In the 1950s and 1960s, respondents were offered only the option of yes or no. Beginning in 1970, a 7-point scale was offered to respondents, with 1 representing a government insurance plan and 7 a private insurance plan. Responses 1-3 have been coded as supporting government health care, 4 as a neutral response, and 5-7 as being against government sponsored health care. Source: NES Cumulative File vcf0128, vcf0805 and vcf0806.

Table 3.6: Should Government Guarantee Jobs and a Good Standard of Living? Catholics and Protestants, Whites Only, by Decade, 1950s-1990s

	Yes			Neutral		No		
Dec.	Cath.	Prot.	Diff.	Cath.	Prot.	Cath.	Prot.	Diff.
1950s	73	62	11	--	--	27	38	-11
1960s	50	41	9	--	--	50	59	-9
1970s	28	21	7	24	24	49	55	-6
1980s	29	23	6	25	22	47	55	-8
1990s	30	24	6	24	23	46	53	-7

Note: In the 1950s and 1960s, respondents were offered only the option of yes or no. Beginning in 1970, a 7-point scale was offered to respondents, with 1 representing the view that government should see to a job and a good standard of living for all and 7 the view that government should let each person get ahead on his own. Responses 1-3 have been coded as supporting government guaranteeing jobs and a good standard of living, 4 as a neutral response, and 5-7 as being against government guaranteeing jobs and a good standard of living. Source: NES Cumulative File vcf0128, vcf0808 and vcf0809.

Table 3.7: Government Aid to Blacks and Minorities, Catholics and Protestants, Whites Only, by Decade, 1970s-1990s

	Support			Neutral		Oppose		
Dec.	Cath.	Prot.	Diff.	Cath.	Prot.	Cath.	Prot.	Diff.
1970s	28	23	5	25	26	47	51	-4
1980s	25	19	6	32	30	43	51	-8
1990s	22	16	6	27	26	51	58	-7

Note: Question asks respondents about their opinion on whether or not government should make the effort to improve the social and economic position of blacks and minorities. Again, a 7-point scale is used. Responses 1-3 have been coded as supportive of government efforts to aid blacks and minorities, 4 as a neutral response, and 5-7 as being against government aid to blacks and minorities. Source: NES Cumulative File vcf0128 and vcf0830.

Table 3.8: Government Services and Spending, Catholics and Protestants, Whites Only, by Decade, 1980s-1990s

	Increase			Same		Decrease		
Dec.	Cath.	Prot.	Diff.	Cath.	Prot.	Cath.	Prot.	Diff.
1980s	42	30	12	31	31	27	39	-12
1990s	37	30	7	32	31	32	40	-8

Note: A 7-point scale was presented to respondents. Responses 1-3 have been coded as favoring reduced spending and fewer services, 4 as favoring keeping spending and services the same, and 5-7 as favoring increased spending and more services. Source: NES Cumulative File vcf0128 and vcf0839.

Table 3.9: Defense Spending, Catholics and Protestants, Whites Only, by Decade, 1980s-1990s

	Increase			Same		Decrease		
Dec.	Cath.	Prot.	Diff.	Cath.	Prot.	Cath.	Prot.	Diff.
1980s	38	43	-5	31	31	31	25	6
1990s	22	28	-6	34	38	43	34	9

Note: Once again, a 7-point scale was presented to respondents. Responses 1-3 have been coded as favoring reduced spending, 4 as favoring keeping spending the same, and 5-7 as favoring increased spending. Source: NES Cumulative File vcf0128 and vcf0843.

Even attitudes on the issue of abortion, about which so much has been said relating to Catholics, fail to provide any evidence in support of a Catholic desertion of the Democrats on the basis of liberal stands on social issues. While they may have differed from Protestants in the 1970s, when *Roe v. Wade* first thrust the issue of abortion onto the national agenda, this situation has changed. Catholics have become more accepting and supportive of legal abortions over the past twenty years.[30] Catholic attitudes are now very similar to those of Protestants as a whole, despite the efforts of the church.[31] Table 3.10 presents these results.

Table 3.10: Positions on Legality of Abortion, Catholics and Protestants, Whites Only, by Decade, 1970s-1990s

	Pro-Life			Pro-Choice		
Decade	Cath.	Prot.	Diff.	Cath.	Prot.	Diff.
1970s	18	8	10	19	25	-6
1980s	15	11	4	33	34	-1
1990s	14	11	3	38	38	0

Note: The numbers in the table represent the percentages of respondents selecting the absolute pro-life and pro-choice positions, respectively. The percentages of respondents choosing situational positions (e.g., rape, incest, woman's life in danger, etc.) are also very similar for Catholics and Protestants, with the greatest difference being 4 percentage points. Source: NES Cumulative File vcf0128, vcf0837 and vcf0838.

As Carmines and Layman admit, it seems unlikely that Catholics have become less attached to the Democratic Party because of the party's stands on social issues.[32] The data presented above show that Catholics are more liberal than Protestants on a variety of issues, and possess attitudes quite similar to Protestants as a whole on the issue of abortion. As noted earlier in this chapter, research by other scholars has shown that Catholics remain highly liberal on economic issues, supportive of an activist national government, and more liberal than Protestants on the vast majority of social issues. In addition, Guth and Green present data showing that congressional districts with a high percentage of Catholics tend to produce members of Congress with liberal voting records.[33]

Findings such as these raise considerable doubt about the argument that Catholics have been alienated from the Democratic Party by its liberal positions on social issues.

Socioeconomic Status (SES)

The explanation centered on socioeconomic status has great intuitive appeal. Class has long been recognized as one of the most important social bases of electoral behavior,[34] and it is widely recognized that religious denominations often reflect social class divisions.[35] The claim that Catholics moved away from the Democratic Party as they moved up the socioeconomic ladder appeals to what we as social scientists know about the interaction of social class and electoral behavior. As discussed in chapter 2, the socioeconomic status of American Catholics rose rapidly in the years after World War II. The expanded educational opportunities provided by the GI Bill, a rapidly expanding national economy, and greater assimilation all contributed to an increase in the socioeconomic status of Catholics. Analysts determined that by the 1960s, Catholics had pulled even with Protestants in terms of family income and education levels.[36] Tables 3.11 and 3.12 attest to this development. As early as the 1950s, Catholics exhibited higher percentages in the middle- and upper-income thirds than did Protestants as a whole. By the 1960s, education levels for Catholics and Protestants were virtually the same. Whether one examines family income or education levels, it is clear that Catholics have risen to a condition of parity with Protestants, and have been in such a position since at least the 1960s.[37]

Table 3.11: Family Income Thirds for Catholics and Protestants, Whites Only, by Decade, 1950s-1990s

	Lower			Middle			Upper		
Dec.	Cath.	Prot.	Diff.	Cath.	Prot.	Diff.	Cath.	Prot.	Diff.
1950s	26	35	-9	32	28	4	42	36	6
1960s	22	33	-11	35	32	3	43	35	8
1970s	24	31	-7	35	35	0	41	34	7
1980s	27	31	-4	36	36	0	37	33	4
1990s	27	31	-4	35	35	0	38	34	4

Note: The NES Dataset divides respondents into 5 percentiles based on their family income. Those respondents in the lower 2 income percentiles (0-16 percent and 17-33 percent) have been recoded here as "lower," those in the third percentile (34-67 percent) have been recoded as "middle," and those in the upper 2 percentiles (68-95 percent and 96-100 percent) have been recoded as "upper." Source: NES Cumulative File vcf0114 and vcf0128.

Table 3.12: Education Levels for Catholics and Protestants Whites Only, by Decade, 1950s-1990s

	≤8		9-12		HS		HS +		SomeC		BA		> BA	
D	C	P	C	P	C	P	C	P	C	P	C	P	C	P
50s	35	32	20	21	22	18	11	9	9	11	4	9	--	--
60s	22	25	18	19	24	21	14	10	12	14	8	9	2	2
70s	17	18	15	16	25	21	15	14	17	16	9	11	3	4
80s	11	10	11	12	26	28	10	10	25	22	12	13	6	6
90s	6	6	11	10	32	35	--	--	25	25	18	16	8	8

Note: Bachelor's degrees and higher degrees were coded together during the 1950s. After 1984, respondents were no longer given the option of high school diploma plus non-academic training (HS +). Source: NES Cumulative File vcf0128 and vcf0140A.

Identifying this rise in SES as the causal mechanism for the decline of Democratic support among Catholics would seem to constitute a sound approach for explaining the phenomenon. The problem here lies in the lack of convincing empirical evidence offered to support this explanation.[38] Much of the evidence offered to support this claim is inconclusive at best, with some analysts claiming that socioeconomic status explains very little about Catholic electoral behavior.[39] With the exception of a few more careful observers, most claims of socioeconomic status pushing Catholics away from the Democratic Party consist of little more than noting the rise in SES among Catholics, the decline in their support of the Democrats, and citing the increase in SES as the reason for the decline in party support. No discussion of which Catholics were moving away from the Democrats is provided.[40] While the rise in socioeconomic status among American Catholics may indeed explain at least part of the decline in their support for the Democratic Party, stronger empirical evidence needs to be presented before this explanation can be accepted.

Tables 3.13 and 3.14 attempt to provide such evidence. Table 3.13 presents the Democratic presidential vote percentages for Catholics and Protestants in the lower-, middle-, and upper-income thirds along with the difference between Catholics and Protestants in each third since 1952. Table 3.14 presents the Democratic percentages for Catholics and Protestants, along with the difference between the two groups in each third, for all three party support indicators by decade since the 1950s. Beginning in the 1970s, a clear cleavage has developed between upper-income Catholics and those Catholics in the lower- and middle-income thirds. Those Catholics in the lower- and middle-income thirds are much more likely to support the Democratic Party than are those Catholics in the upper-income third.[41] These results parallel recent findings showing a resurgence of class cleavages in American politics generally.[42] The rise in socioeconomic status among Catholics does appear to have produced a shift of Catholics away from the Democratic Party, but not among all Catholics. Upper-income Catholics are the ones moving to the Republican Party, while those Catholics in the lower and middle thirds of the income distribution remain strong in their support of the Democrats.

Increasing SES among Catholics does appear to have moved those Catholics in the upper third of the income distribution away from the Democratic Party. It is not, however, all Catholics, or even a majority of Catholics who have been motivated to join the Republican ranks as a result of the group's ascent up the socioeconomic ladder. This development of a class cleavage within American Catholicism is an important phenomenon, one that is only recently beginning to garner attention from scholars. It will be discussed more fully in the conclusion.

The more important question at the moment is whether or not the electoral behavior of Catholics remains distinct from that of Protestants across class levels. Do Catholics in the lower-, middle-, and upper-income thirds support the Democratic Party at higher levels than do Protestants who occupy the same income categories? Tables 3.13 and 3.14 also provide the answer to this question.

The results presented in these two tables are quite clear. Regardless of their income level, Catholics support the Democratic Party at substantially higher levels than do Protestants. This is true for all support indicators. Catholics in the lower- and middle-income thirds consistently give the Democrats a clear majority in both voting and partisan identification. Catholics in the upper-income third do not support the Democrats at these same majority levels, but they are also not lining up solidly behind the Republican Party, as are their Protestant counterparts in the upper third of the income distribution. Simply put, Catholics are more likely than Protestants to support the Democratic Party. Catholic electoral behavior remains distinct from that of Protestants.

Table 3.13: Democratic Presidential Vote, by Income Thirds Catholics and Protestants, Whites Only, 1952-2000

	Lower			Middle			Upper		
Year	Cath.	Prot.	Diff.	Cath.	Prot.	Diff.	Cath.	Prot.	Diff.
1952	63	35	28	47	40	7	48	30	18
1956	40	39	1	49	36	13	46	29	17
1960	77	36	41	85	40	45	83	28	54
1964	85	65	20	81	66	15	73	46	27
1968	58	27	31	56	25	31	53	23	28
1972	35	29	6	40	26	14	33	20	13
1976	67	47	20	61	43	18	45	33	12
1980	42	41	1	43	28	15	33	26	7
1984	59	38	21	44	31	13	36	22	14
1988	61	40	21	56	35	21	39	26	13
1992	57	47	10	55	35	20	37	27	10
1996	66	55	11	59	42	17	47	32	15
2000	57	42	15	48	40	8	44	37	7

Source: NES Cumulative File vcf0114, vcf0128, and vcf0705.

Table 3.14: Democratic Presidential Vote, House Vote, and Party ID, by Income Thirds, Catholics and Protestants, Whites Only, by Decade, 1950s-1990s

	Presidential Vote			House Vote			Party ID		
	L	M	U	L	M	U	L	M	U
1950s									
Cath.	51	48	47	70	62	57	66	64	64
Prot.	37	37	30	49	52	41	52	53	45
Diff.	14	11	17	21	10	16	14	11	19
1960s									
Cath.	74	72	71	75	73	66	70	70	63
Prot.	44	43	33	53	50	43	51	50	43
Diff.	30	29	38	22	23	23	19	20	20
1970s									
Cath.	50	48	39	73	68	56	69	68	55
Prot.	37	33	26	56	51	44	48	44	37
Diff.	13	15	13	17	17	12	21	24	18
1980s									
Cath.	55	48	36	73	61	58	64	55	46
Prot.	40	32	25	56	48	43	48	41	35
Diff.	15	16	11	17	13	15	16	14	11
1990s									
Cath.	61	57	41	66	59	47	64	58	46
Prot.	50	38	29	58	46	33	48	40	30
Diff.	11	19	12	8	13	14	16	18	16

Source: NES Cumulative File vcf0114, vcf0128, vcf0705, vcf0707, and vcf0303.

Conclusion

The findings presented in this chapter point to a need for reexamination of conventional wisdom regarding the electoral behavior of American Catholics. Catholic support for the Democratic Party has declined, but not as dramatically as is commonly asserted. Portraying this movement as an exodus, a desertion, or an abandonment, is certainly an exaggeration. Claims that Catholics left the Democrats for ideological reasons are not supported by the evidence we currently possess. The increase in socioeconomic status among American Catholics does seem to at least partially explain the movement of Catholics away from the Democratic Party, but appears to be relevant mostly for those Catholics in the upper third of the income distribution. Last, and most important, white Catholics in the United States continue to support the Democratic Party at much higher levels than do white Protestants. This is true across income levels and support indicators. The electoral behavior of American Catholics remains distinct from that of American Protestants. Now that this distinction has been established, it needs to be explained. Chapter 4 will provide the beginnings of such an explanation.

Notes

1. Andrew M. Greeley, "Catholics and Coalition: Where Should They Go?" in *Emerging Coalitions in American Politics*, ed. Seymour Martin Lipset (San Francisco: Institute for Contemporary Studies, 1978), 273-74.

2. Paul R. Abramson, John H. Aldrich, and David W. Rohde, *Change and Continuity in the 1992 Elections* (Washington, D.C.: Congressional Quarterly Press, 1995), 156; Harold W. Stanley, William T. Bianco, and Richard G. Niemi, "Partisanship and Group Support over Time: A Multivariate Analysis," *American Political Science Review* 80, no. 3 (Sept. 1986): 972-75.

3. Geoffrey C. Layman, "Religion and Political Behavior in the United States: The Impact of Beliefs, Affiliations, and Commitment from 1980 to 1994," *Public Opinion Quarterly* 61, no. 2 (summer 1997): 288-316; Harold W. Stanley and Richard G. Niemi, "Partisanship and Group Support, 1952-1988," *American Politics Quarterly* 19, no. 2 (Apr. 1991): 205; James M. Penning, "Changing Partisanship and Issue Stands among American Catholics," *Sociological Analysis* 47, no. 1 (Spring 1986): 34.

4. William B. Prendergast, *The Catholic Voter in American Politics: The Passing of a Democratic Monolith* (Washington, D.C.: Georgetown University Press, 1999), 218; Barry A. Kosmin and Seymour P. Lachman, *One Nation under God: Religion in Contemporary American Society* (New York: Harmony Books, 1993), 191; Timothy A. Byrnes, "The Politics of the American Catholic Hierarchy," *Political Science Quarterly* 108, no. 3 (Fall 1993): 500; Timothy A. Byrnes, *Catholic Bishops in American Politics* (Princeton, N.J.: Princeton University Press, 1991), 4.

5. Unless otherwise noted, all data in this study are taken from the National Election Studies Cumulative Data File. All NES data for years from 1952-1998 are taken from: Warren E. Miller and the National Election Studies, *American National Election Studies Cumulative Data File, 1948-1998* [computer file], 10th ICPSR version. Ann Arbor, Mich.: University of Michigan, Center for Political Studies [producer], 1999, Ann Arbor, Mich.: Inter-University Consortium for Political and Social Research [distributor], 1999. NES data for the year 2000 only are taken from: Virginia Sapiro, Steven J. Rosenstone, and the National Election Studies, *American National Election Studies Cumulative Data File, 1948-2000* [computer file] Ann Arbor, Mich.: University of Michigan, Center for Political Studies [producer and distributor], 2001. Why the most recent version of the NES Cumulative File is not used for all years in this analysis is explained chapter 4, endnote 32.

6. Given the overwhelming evidence that "independent leaners" behave much the same as partisans of the party that they lean toward, I believe it is appropriate to classify leaners as party identifiers. For support of this practice, see Bruce E. Keith, David B. Magleby, Candice J. Nelson, Elizabeth Orr, Mark C. Westlye, and Raymond E. Wolfinger, *The Myth of the Independent Voter* (Berkeley, Calif.: University of California Press, 1992).

7. Prendergast, *The Catholic Voter*, 203; Kosmin and Lachman, *One Nation under God*, 10; and Arthur H. Miller and Martin P. Wattenberg, "Politics from the Pulpit: Re-

ligiosity and the 1980 Elections," *Public Opinion Quarterly* 48, no. 1, B, (Spring 1984): 301-2.

8. William D'Antonio, James Davidson, Dean Hoge, and Ruth Wallace, *American Catholic Laity in a Changing Church* (Kansas City, Mo.: Sheed and Ward, 1989), 16; Dean R. Hoge, "Interpreting Change in American Catholicism: The River and the Floodgate," *Review of Religious Research* 27, no. 4 (June 1986): 289-99.

9. Prendergast, *The Catholic Voter*, 32.

10. Everett Carll Ladd, Jr. with Charles D. Hadley, *Transformations of the American Party System* (New York: W.W. Norton & Company, 1975); Norman H. Nie, Sidney Verba, and John R. Petrocik, *The Changing American Voter* (Cambridge, Mass.: Harvard University Press, 1976).

11. Jeffrey Levine, Edward G. Carmines, and Robert Huckfeldt, "The Rise of Ideology in the Post-New Deal Party System, 1972-1992," *American Politics Quarterly* 25, no. 1 (Jan. 1997); Layman, "Religion and Political Behavior."

12. Lyman A. Kellstedt, John C. Green, James L. Guth, and Corwin E. Smidt, "Religious Voting Blocs in the 1992 Election: The Year of the Evangelical?" *Sociology of Religion* 55, no. 3 (Fall 1994): 307-26; Penning, "Changing Partisanship,"; Joan L. Fee, "Party Identification among American Catholics, 1972, 1973," *Ethnicity* 3, no. 1 (Mar. 1976): 53-69; David Knoke, "Religion, Stratification and Politics: America in the 1960s," *American Journal of Political Science* 18, no. 2 (May 1974): 331-45.

13. Prendergast, *The Catholic Voter*.

14. Bendyna and Jelen also call for a closer examination of Catholic electoral behavior. Mary E. Bendyna and Ted G. Jelen, "Catholic Political Behavior in the United States: An Overview and Agenda" (paper presented at annual meeting of the American Political Science Association, Boston, Mass., Sept. 1998), 1.

15. Clubb and Allen provide an excellent discussion of this possible problem. Jerome M. Clubb and Howard W. Allen, "The Cities and the Election of 1928: Partisan Realignment?" *The American Historical Review* 74, no. 4 (April 1969): 1209. Nie, Verba, and Petrocik raise similar concerns. Nie, Verba, and Petrocik, *The Changing American Voter*, 34.

16. Converse cautioned against making claims about the impact of religion on American electoral behavior based on the 1960 election, in large part because of the unique role religious affiliation played in that particular election. Philip E. Converse, "Religion and Politics: The 1960 Election," in *Elections and the Political Order*, ed. Angus Campbell, Philip E. Converse, Warren E. Miller, and Donald E. Stokes (New York: John Wiley & Sons, 1966), 122-23. Manza and Brooks echo these sentiments, attributing the high levels of Catholic support for Kennedy in 1960 to a form of "identity politics." Jeff Manza and Clem Brooks, "The Religious Factor in U.S. Presidential Elections, 1960-1992," *American Journal of Sociology* 103, no. 1 (July 1997): 53, 59, and 66-67.

17. Abramson, Aldrich, and Rohde, *Change and Continuity in the 1992 Elections*, 301-2; Andrew M. Greeley, "How Conservative Are American Catholics?" *Political Science Quarterly* 92, no. 2 (summer 1977): 202; Ladd with Hadley, *Transformations*, 269.

18. Bendyna and Jelen, "Catholic Political Behavior," 6; David C. Leege, "Catholics and the Civic Order: Parish Participation, Politics, and Civic Participation," *Review of Politics* 50, no. 4 (Fall 1988): 720-21.

19. Manza and Brooks, "The Religious Factor," 66-67.

20. Greeley, "How Conservative Are American Catholics," 199-218; Andrew M. Greeley, *The American Catholic: A Social Portrait* (New York: Basic Books, 1977), 92-

104; Greeley, "Catholics and Coalition," 271-95; Andrew M. Greeley, *Religious Change in America* (Cambridge, Mass.: Harvard University Press, 1989), 82-84.

21. George Gallup, Jr. and Jim Castelli, *The American Catholic People: Their Beliefs, Practices, and Values* (Garden City, N.Y.: Doubleday and Co., 1987), 137-38; George Gallup, Jr. and Jim Castelli, *The People's Religion: American Faith in the 90's* (New York: Macmillan, 1989), 219-22; Bendyna and Jelen, "Catholic Political Behavior," 6-7.

22. Paul Allen Beck, *Party Politics in America*, 8th ed., (New York: Longman, 1997), 144; Stanley, Bianco, and Niemi, "Partisanship and Group Support," 975; Edward G. Carmines and James A. Stimson, *Issue Evolution: Race and the Transformation of American Politics* (Princeton, N.J.: Princeton University Press, 1989).

23. U.S. Bureau of the Census, *Statistical Abstract of the United States, 1971*, 92nd ed. (Washington, D.C.: Government Printing Office, 1971), 365. See also Richard J. Timpone, "Mass Mobilization or Government Intervention? The Growth of Black Registration in the South," *Journal of Politics* 57, no. 2 (May 1995): 425-42; Harold W. Stanley, *Voter Mobilization and the Politics of Race: The South and Universal Suffrage* (New York: Praeger, 1987).

24. Kenski and Lockwood note this as well. Henry C. Kenski and William Lockwood, "The Catholic Vote from 1980 to 1986: Continuity or Change?" *Religion and Political Behavior in the United States*, ed. Ted G. Jelen (New York: Praeger, 1989), 136-37; Kenski and Lockwood, "Catholic Electoral Behavior in 1988: A Critical Swing Vote," in *The Bible and the Ballot Box: Religion and Politics in the 1988 Election*, ed. James L. Guth and John C. Green (Boulder, Colo.: Westview Press, 1991), 176-78.

25. Unless otherwise specified, all subsequent discussion and analyses in this study will pertain to whites only. It should be noted at this point that the category "whites only" utilized in this study does include some Hispanics, specifically those who were identified as "white." Until the latest version of the NES Cumulative File (2001), race and ethnicity were recorded in such a way as to allow respondents to be identified as both "white" (or "black") *and* Hispanic. Those Hispanics who were identified as "white" are included among whites in this study. The reasons behind this decision, this categorization scheme and its implications will be discussed at length in chapter 4. At this point suffice it to say that some Hispanics are included in the "whites only" category and that the effects of Hispanic ethnicity will be controlled for in subsequent analyses in this study.

26. As discussed earlier, Catholics voted overwhelmingly for Kennedy in 1960. As Lopatto relates, Kennedy became a hero of mythic proportions to many Americans, and especially to Catholics, after his assassination in 1963. This fact likely contributed to the substantial support Lyndon Johnson and the Democrats received from Catholics in the 1964 elections. Given these facts, judging levels of Catholic support for the Democratic Party by comparing them to the levels of the 1960s can lead to questionable conclusions. Paul Lopatto, *Religion and the Presidential Election* (New York: Praeger, 1985), 162.

27. As noted above, Greeley and Kenski and Lockwood stand out as analysts who have brought attention to the continuing differences in electoral behavior between white Catholics and white Protestants.

28. Lyman A. Kellstedt, "Evangelicals and Political Realignment," in *Contemporary Evangelical Political Involvement: An Analysis and Assessment*, ed. Corwin E. Smidt (Lanham, Md.: University Press of America, 1989), 99.

29. Benjamin I. Page and Robert Y. Shapiro, *The Rational Public* (Chicago: University of Chicago Press, 1992), 306; Kenski and Lockwood, "Catholic Voting Behavior in 1988," 184; Greeley, *Religious Change in America*, 93; Jerome L. Himmelstein and

James A. McRae, Jr., "Social Issues and Socioeconomic Status," *Public Opinion Quarterly* 52, no. 4 (Winter 1988), 505; Gallup and Castelli, *The American Catholic People*, chapter 9; Penning, "Changing Partisanship," 46; Lopatto, *Religion and the Presidential Election*, 80-111; Greeley, "Catholics and Coalition," 290; Greeley, "How Conservative Are American Catholics?," 203-209; Greeley, *The American Catholic*, 92-93.

30. Gallup and Castelli, *The People's Religion*, 175.

31. D. Paul Sullins, "Catholic/Protestant Trends on Abortion: Convergence and Polarity," *Journal for the Scientific Study of Religion* 38, no. 3 (Sept. 1999): 354-69; Page and Shapiro, *The Rational Public*, 307; Kenski and Lockwood, "Catholic Voting Behavior in 1988," 182-84; Greeley, *Religious Change in America*, 93; Gallup, Jr. and Castelli, *The People's Religion*, 167-79; Gallup and Castelli, *The American Catholic People*, chapter 8; E. J. Dionne, Jr., "Catholics and the Democrats: Estrangement but Not Desertion," in *Party Coalitions in the 1980s*, ed. Seymour Martin Lipset (San Francisco: Institute for Contemporary Studies, 1981), 319.

32. Edward G. Carmines and Geoffrey C. Layman, "Issue Evolution in Postwar American Politics: Old Certainties and Fresh Tensions," in *Present Discontents: American Politics in the Very Late Twentieth Century*, ed. Byron E. Shafer (Chatham, N.J.: Chatham House Publishers, Inc., 1997), 106-7.

33. John C. Green and James L. Guth, "Religion, Representatives, and Roll Calls," *Legislative Studies Quarterly* 16, no. 4 (Nov. 1991): 577.

34. Seymour Martin Lipset, *Political Man*, Anchor Books Edition (Garden City, N.Y.: Doubleday & Co., 1963).

35. H. Richard Niebuhr, *The Social Sources of Denominationalism* (Hamden, Conn.: The Shoe String Press, 1954).

36. Greeley, *The American Catholic*; Norval D. Glenn and Ruth Hyland, "Religious Preference and Worldly Success: Some Evidence from National Surveys," *American Sociological Review* 32, no. 1 (Feb. 1967): 73-85.

37. James D. Davidson and Andrea S. Williams, "Megatrends in 20th-century American Catholicism," *Social Compass* 44, no. 4 (Dec. 1997): 511; Kosmin and Lachman, *One Nation under God*, 256.

38. Greeley, "How Conservative Are American Catholics?" 199-203.

39. Manza and Brooks, "The Religious Factor."

40. For works that examine the electoral behavior of Catholics by class level, see Stephen D. Johnson, "What Relates to Vote for Three Religious Categories," *Sociology of Religion* 55, no. 3 (Fall 1994): 263-75; John R. Petrocik, *Party Coalitions: Realignments and the Decline of the New Deal Party System* (Chicago: University of Chicago Press, 1981), 64-90; Dionne, "Catholics and the Democrats," 311; Nie, Verba, and Petrocik, *The Changing American Voter*, 231-32.

41. Dionne notes this development as well. Dionne, "Catholics and the Democrats," 311.

42. Jeffrey M. Stonecash, *Class and Party in American Politics* (Boulder, Colo.: Westview Press, 2000); Mark D. Brewer and Jeffrey M. Stonecash, "Class, Race Issues and Declining White Support for the Democratic Party in the South," *Political Behavior* 23, no. 2 (June 2001): 131-55; Jeffrey M. Stonecash, Mark D. Brewer, Mary P. McGuire, R. Eric Petersen, and Lori Beth Way, "The Survival of the Democrats: Secular Realignment outside the South," *Political Research Quarterly* 53, no. 4 (Dec. 2000): 731-52.

Chapter Four

The Search for Sources of Catholic/Protestant Division

Introduction

The previous chapter provided an empirical examination of the electoral behavior of white Catholics and white Protestants in the United States. Claims that American Catholics have abandoned their traditional loyalty to the Democratic Party were rendered, at best, dubious. While there has been some decline in Catholic support for the Democrats over the last thirty to forty years, Catholics are still more Democratic than Republican. More important, the data showed quite convincingly that substantial differences in support for the Democrats continue to exist between Catholics and Protestants in terms of their presidential vote, House vote, and party identification. The data also showed that these differences remained sizeable when controlling for family income. Regardless of income level, Catholics give greater support to the Democrats than do Protestants.

Why are Catholics more Democratic than Protestants? Although family income was unable to account for this phenomenon, it is possible that some other variable or combination of variables other than religious affiliation is causing the differences in electoral behavior that exist between Catholics and Protestants. This chapter begins the search for an explanation of these differences by examining the effects of the demographic characteristics of age, gender, and Hispanic ethnicity on Catholic electoral behavior.

Gender

The difference between the electoral behavior of men and women has become a hot topic in the social sciences. The tendency of women to support the Democratic Party at higher levels than do men over the last twenty years, especially in presidential elections, has received significant attention from scholars across a range of disciplines. While there has been and continues to be considerable debate about the phenomenon known as the gender gap, it is now relatively widely accepted that it does exist. Since about 1980, women have shown a tendency to be more Democratic than men.[1]

While the difference between men and women in their electoral behavior is an important matter in its own right, it is specifically relevant to this study in two ways. The first is the role of the gender gap in the electoral behavior of Catholics. How does the voting behavior and partisan identification of Catholic women compare to that of Catholic men? Tables 4.1 and 4.2 present this information. Since 1960, Catholic women have consistently been more Democratic in their presidential vote than Catholic men. Beginning in 1968, female Catholics have also identified with the Democratic Party at higher levels than their male counterparts. Only on the House vote indicator is there no clear trend of difference between Catholic men and women, although a sizable gap does appear in the 2000 House elections. A gender gap is clearly in evidence among Catholics, at least in terms of presidential vote and partisan identification. As other analysts have reported, Catholic women are now more Democratic than Catholic men.[2]

More important for this analysis is the effect of gender when Catholic electoral behavior is compared with that of Protestants. What impact, if any, does the separation of respondents by gender have on the differences in electoral behavior exhibited by Catholics and Protestants that were discussed in chapter 3? This matter takes on particular importance when one considers the fact that almost two-thirds of Catholics who regularly attend Mass are women.[3] If there is something inherent in Catholicism that results in greater support for the Democratic Party, it makes sense that those who attend Mass more regularly will exhibit stronger effects.[4] Is the continued gap in support for the Democrats between Catholics and Protestants due to overwhelming Democratic proclivities on the part of Catholic women?

Table 4.3 provides the answer to this question. The table, which presents the Democratic percentages for presidential vote, House vote, and party identification for Catholic and Protestant men and women by decade since the 1950s, shows that Catholic women are not solely responsible for the difference in Democratic support between Catholics and Protestants. As was the case in tables 4.1 and 4.2, Catholic women have been consistently more Democratic than Catholic men since the 1970s. Catholic women have also been more Democratic than Protestant women, by relatively large margins. However, Catholic men also exhibit higher levels of support for the Democratic Party than Protestant men. The margins of greater Democratic support are quite similar for male and female Catholics. It is also important to note that, despite the development of the gender gap in American electoral politics, Catholic men support the Democrats at higher levels than do Protestant women, across all decades and support indicators. While the gender gap may be increasingly relevant to American Catholic electoral behavior, it is not the cause of observed differences between Catholics and Protestants.[5]

Table 4.1: Catholic Democratic Presidential Vote, House Vote, and Party ID, Women and Men, Whites Only, 1952-2000

	Presidential Vote			House Vote			Party ID		
Year	Wom.	Men	Diff.	Wom.	Men	Diff.	Wom.	Men	Diff.
1952	52	50	2	54	56	-2	64	72	-8
1954	--	--	--	--	--	--	59	70	-11
1956	40	50	-10	56	66	-10	57	63	-6
1958	--	--	--	79	65	14	68	65	3
1960	85	78	7	82	74	8	75	71	4
1962	--	--	--	74	76	-2	65	71	-6
1964	80	77	3	74	70	4	70	68	2
1966	--	--	--	64	70	-6	63	63	0
1968	57	52	5	60	61	-1	68	57	11
1970	--	--	--	58	52	6	64	62	2
1972	39	33	6	65	65	0	65	58	7
1974	--	--	--	73	70	3	63	60	3
1976	57	52	5	61	61	0	61	61	0
1978	--	--	--	64	63	1	70	59	11
1980	42	38	4	57	60	-3	58	48	10
1982	--	--	--	75	52	23	74	53	21
1984	48	39	9	59	60	-1	54	50	4
1986	--	--	--	69	62	7	60	49	11
1988	52	50	2	63	69	-6	52	47	5
1990	--	--	--	67	59	8	59	55	4
1992	54	43	11	62	60	2	60	51	9
1994	--	--	--	48	49	-1	57	49	8
1996	58	51	7	51	48	3	61	50	11
1998	--	--	--	51	47	4	55	48	7
2000	53	39	14	59	43	16	53	39	14

Note: House vote not asked in 1954. Source: NES Cumulative File vcf0104, vcf0128, vcf0705, vcf0707, and vcf0303.

Table 4.2: Catholic Democratic Presidential Vote, House Vote, and Party ID, Women and Men, Whites Only, by Decade, 1950s-1990s

	Presidential Vote			House Vote			Party ID		
Dec.	Wom.	Men	Diff.	Wom.	Men	Diff.	Wom.	Men	Diff.
1950s	46	50	-4	61	62	-1	62	67	-5
1960s	73	70	3	71	70	1	68	66	2
1970s	47	42	5	64	63	1	65	60	5
1980s	48	43	5	64	62	2	58	49	9
1990s	55	46	9	57	53	4	59	51	8

Source: NES Cumulative File vcf0104, vcf0128, vcf0705, vcf0707, and vcf0303.

Table 4.3: Democratic Presidential Vote, House Vote, and Party ID, Catholics and Protestants, by Gender, Whites Only, by Decade, 1950s-1990s

	Presidential Vote		House Vote		Party ID	
1950s	Men	Women	Men	Women	Men	Women
Cath.	50	46	62	61	67	62
Prot.	36	32	49	43	52	47
Diff.	14	14	13	18	15	15
1960s						
Cath.	70	73	70	71	66	68
Prot.	40	39	51	46	49	47
Diff.	30	34	19	25	17	21
1970s						
Cath.	42	47	63	64	60	65
Prot.	29	33	50	48	42	43
Diff.	13	14	13	16	18	22
1980s						
Cath.	43	48	62	64	49	58
Prot.	27	33	47	48	39	42
Diff.	16	15	15	16	10	16
1990s						
Cath.	46	55	53	57	51	59
Prot.	31	42	40	47	34	43
Diff.	15	13	13	10	17	16

Source: NES Cumulative File vcf0104, vcf0128, vcf0705, vcf0707, and vcf0303.

Age

Age is another demographic characteristic that may affect individuals' electoral behavior. The concepts of time and age have been shown to influence people's beliefs and attitudes in many different ways. First, changes in society or specific events at particular times may modify or alter the attitudes and beliefs of all individuals living through these events. This is known as a period effect. Second, the life changes human beings go through as they age may significantly alter attitudes or rearrange their priorities regarding what is important to them. This is known as a life-cycle effect. Finally, individuals may be forever marked by the characteristics of the time period in which they grew to adulthood. Peoples' worldviews may be permanently impacted by the social and cultural landscapes that existed during their formative years, producing effects on their attitudes and beliefs throughout their entire lives. This is known as a generational effect.[6] All of these age-related factors may be operating simultaneously to affect the beliefs and attitudes of individuals. Regardless of which of these mechanisms are at work, differences in age may result in substantial differences in the attitudes, beliefs, and most important, behaviors of individuals.

Once again, the importance of age to this project is how it relates to the two key issues analyzed here: the electoral behavior of Catholics and the difference in Catholic electoral behavior from that of Protestants. Some scholars have found that younger Catholics are less Democratic than older Catholics.[7] If Democratic support is indeed more pronounced among older Catholics than younger Catholics, then this phenomenon could have important implications for the differences in electoral behavior between Catholics and Protestants. As we know, partisan allegiance becomes stronger and more lasting as individuals get older.[8] Older Catholics, who came of age politically when Catholicism was highly correlated with Democratic identification, likely remain strong Democrats in the present. Overwhelming Democratic support among older Catholics may have the effect of skewing Catholic partisan support as a whole toward the Democratic Party.

Are younger Catholics less Democratic than older Catholics? As shown in table 4.4, the answer is yes. The data in this table, which presents the Democratic support percentages for all three indicators among Catholics and Protestants in three age groups by decade since the 1950s, clearly show that since the 1970s Democratic support among Catholics has decreased as age decreased. The differences between the oldest age group (55 and older) and the youngest age group (17-34) were quite large in the 1980s, and although they have declined in the 1990s, remain sizeable. However, table 4.4 also shows that younger Catholics were much more Democratic than their youthful Protestant counterparts, as were Catholics in the other two age groups. And Catholics in the youngest age group have always been more supportive of the Democrats than Protestants in any age group. Differences in Democratic support remain substantial between Catholics and Protestants in all three age groups. Age does prove to have an impact on the electoral behavior of Catholics. Older Catholics are clearly more Democratic than younger ones. However, this does not affect the differences between Catholics and Protestants. Regardless of age, Catholics are more Democratic than Protestants.

Table 4.4: Democratic Presidential Vote, House Vote, and Party ID, Catholics and Protestants, by Age Group, Whites Only, by Decade, 1950s-1990s

	Presidential Vote			House Vote			Party ID		
Dec.	17-34	35-54	55+	17-34	35-54	55+	17-34	35-54	55+
1950s									
Cath.	47	51	45	57	64	64	65	66	60
Prot.	37	34	30	49	48	42	53	51	45
Diff.	**10**	**17**	**15**	**8**	**16**	**22**	**12**	**15**	**15**
1960s									
Cath.	72	71	73	68	72	70	65	68	67
Prot.	40	41	38	47	49	47	48	50	46
Diff.	**32**	**30**	**35**	**21**	**23**	**23**	**17**	**18**	**21**
1970s									
Cath.	47	40	48	60	62	69	61	61	68
Prot.	35	30	30	52	48	48	40	44	44
Diff.	**12**	**10**	**18**	**8**	**14**	**21**	**21**	**17**	**24**
1980s									
Cath.	42	43	53	57	64	66	47	56	63
Prot.	29	29	33	50	45	48	37	40	44
Diff.	**13**	**14**	**20**	**7**	**19**	**18**	**10**	**16**	**19**
1990s									
Cath.	46	51	54	53	53	59	51	55	58
Prot.	32	35	43	42	40	48	35	37	45
Diff.	**14**	**16**	**11**	**11**	**13**	**11**	**16**	**18**	**13**

Source: NES Cumulative File vcf0102, vcf0128, vcf0705, vcf0707, and vcf0303.

An especially significant generational effect may play a role in the electoral behavior of Catholics as well. The Second Vatican Council was held from 1962-1965. As historian Philip Gleason observed, Vatican II "shook everything loose" in Roman Catholicism.[9] The decisions and documents that came out of the council produced profound changes in Catholicism in general, and in American Catholicism in particular.[10] The language of the Mass was changed to the vernacular from the traditional Latin. Laity involvement in Mass was greatly increased, and the rule prohibiting the eating of meat on Fridays was abolished.[11] Documents produced by the council, such as the "Decree on Ecumenism," the "Declaration on the Relationship of the Church to Non-Christian Religions," and especially the "Declaration on Religious Freedom" served to remove barriers and lessen suspicions that existed between Catholics and non-Catholics. As a result, increased ecumenical efforts on the part of the church soon followed.[12] Older Catholic emphases on authority and obedience on the part of the laity were gradually replaced by new emphases on freedom of conscience and personal responsibility.[13] Rather than a fortress against the evils of the modern world, the church now presented itself as integrated with contemporary society, positioned to act as a force for good and justice.[14] Vatican II was an experience unique to Catholics: no other religious group in American society has recently experienced such a profound and dramatic event. Catholics who came of age after Vatican II received a significantly different religious upbringing than did Catholics who were raised in the pre-Vatican II church.[15] In many ways, the two groups experienced very different churches during their formative years. Seen in this light, any analysis of Catholic electoral behavior that failed to investigate the possible effects of the Second Vatican Council would be seriously remiss.[16]

Davidson and his colleagues have examined the faith and beliefs of American Catholics by generation. In their division of Catholics into pre-Vatican II, Vatican II, and post-Vatican II generations, Davidson et al. have shown that significant differences in religious beliefs and attitudes regarding faith do exist among these three generations of Catholics.[17] The important question for this analysis is whether similar differences in electoral behavior exist among these three generations. Following Davidson et al.'s generational scheme, I have divided Catholics into three age cohorts and examined their electoral behavior along the three support indicators of presidential vote, House vote, and party identification. Because the number of Catholics per age cohort in individual years is in some cases quite small, table 4.5 presents the results by decade beginning with the 1980s (1980 is the first year a significant number of post-Vatican II Catholics would have been eligible to vote).[18] Results for Protestants are also included in table 4.5, as the other main focus of this analysis is the difference in electoral behavior between Catholics and Protestants.

Table 4.5: Democratic Presidential Vote, House Vote, and Party ID, Catholics and Protestants, by Age Cohort, Whites Only, by Decade, 1980s-1990s

	Pres. Vote			House Vote			Party ID		
Age Cohort	1	2	3	1	2	3	1	2	3
1980s									
Cath.	41	43	49	53	62	66	44	51	61
Prot.	31	29	32	51	49	47	35	38	44
Diff.	**10**	**14**	**17**	**2**	**13**	**19**	**9**	**13**	**17**
1990s									
Cath.	46	53	52	51	54	58	50	55	59
Prot.	32	34	42	40	42	47	34	37	44
Diff.	**14**	**19**	**10**	**11**	**12**	**11**	**16**	**18**	**15**

Note: Codes for Age Cohorts: 1 = born 1959-present, 2 = born 1943-1958, 3 = born 1895-1942. Source: NES Cumulative File vcf0103, vcf0128, vcf0705, vcf 0707, and vc0f303.

The results presented in table 4.5 are very similar to those presented in table 4.4. Younger Catholics are generally less Democratic than their older counterparts. Pre-Vatican II Catholics are more Democratic than those Catholics who were raised in the post-Vatican II church. The differences, however, were much larger in the 1980s than they were during the 1990s.[19] There appears to be some convergence in electoral behavior between the three generations of Catholics, although the split between older Catholics and younger Catholics grew again in the 2000 elections (results not shown). While some differences do exist, it does not appear that Vatican II produced substantial differences in the electoral behavior among the three generations of Catholics examined here. Although Catholics raised before Vatican II came of age in a much different church than those who grew to adulthood after the council, the electoral behavior of the two groups looks relatively similar, and may be becoming more so. In addition, it is necessary to point out that Catholics, regardless of age cohort or indicator, were once again more supportive of the Democratic Party than were Protestants.

Hispanic Ethnicity

The final demographic variable to be examined in this chapter is Hispanic ethnicity. The Hispanic population in the United States has grown rapidly over the past twenty years, with the results of the 2000 U.S. Census placing the Hispanic percentage of the U.S. population at 12.5 percent.[20] The vast majority of these Hispanic immigrants to the United States come from what have been historically Catholic nations. Despite findings from those both inside and outside of the church that Hispanics have been leaving the Catholic faith in recent years,[21] an overwhelming majority of Hispanic Americans continue to identify themselves as Roman Catholics.[22] Thus the rapid increase in the Hispanic population in the United States is also producing an explosion in the number of Hispanic-American Catholics.[23] Various national estimates now place the Hispanic percentage of the American Catholic population from 13 percent[24] to 17 percent.[25] In the 1960s, the American Catholic population was largely of European ancestry. Now, that is no longer the case. Hispanics make up a substantial portion of the American Catholic population.[26] The sample of Catholics in the NES dataset reflects this development, as is shown in table 4.6. If current demographic trends continue, the time is not far off when Hispanics will comprise the largest single ethnic group in the American Catholic Church.[27]

Table 4.6: Percentage Hispanic and Non-Hispanic in NES Sample, Catholics and Protestants, Whites Only, 1980-1998

	Catholics		Protestants	
Year	Non-Hispanic	Hispanic	Non-Hispanic	Hispanic
1980	90	10	98	2
1982	91	9	98	2
1984	80	20	98	2
1986	87	13	97	3
1988	77	23	96	4
1990	78	22	95	5
1992	82	18	94	6
1994	82	18	95	5
1996	83	17	94	6
1998	76	24	96	4

Note: 1980 is the first year that Hispanics were reliably identified in the NES. Source: NES Cumulative File vcf0108 and vcf0128. This analysis is not relevant to the 2000 data in the 1948-2000 version of the NES Cumulative File. See endnote 32 in this chapter for an explanation.

The rapid rise in the Hispanic-American population in general, and in the Hispanic Catholic population in particular, has not gone unnoticed by scholars. However, the increase has happened so quickly that the academic community is in a sense playing catch-up as they begin to study this phenomenon. There is still much that we do not know about the fastest growing segment of the American population.[28] There are, however, a few things that we do know about Hispanic Catholics that are directly relevant to this study. The first is that Hispanic Catholics tend to have much lower family incomes than white, non-Hispanic Catholics.[29] We also know that, perhaps spurred by their lower incomes and recent immigrant status, Hispanic Catholics (except for Hispanics of Cuban ancestry) tend to support the Democratic Party at higher levels than do other white Catholics.[30]

Empirically examining the electoral behavior of Hispanics using the NES dataset is difficult. The NES provides only a very small subsample of Hispanics in its biennial surveys, rendering a statistically sound examination of Hispanic electoral behavior by year impossible. However the NES does allow a crude estimate of the electoral behavior of Hispanic Americans if respondents are pooled by decade. I have adopted this approach here in order to shed at least some light on Hispanic electoral behavior. Table 4.7 presents the Democratic percentages of presidential vote, House vote, and party identification for those Americans identified as both white *and* Hispanic by decade since 1980, the first year Hispanics were reliably identified in the NES. The table also separates Catholics from Protestants among the Hispanic sample. While the sample sizes are a vast improvement over those available when the analyses are conducted by year, they still remain relatively small and therefore these results too must be viewed with caution.[31]

Table 4.7: Democratic Presidential Vote, House Vote, and Party ID, Hispanic and White Catholics and Protestants, by Decade, 1980s-1990s

	Presidential Vote			House Vote			Party ID		
Dec.	Cath.	Prot.	Diff.	Cath.	Prot.	Diff.	Cath.	Prot.	Diff.
1980s	62	44	18	83	68	15	62	50	12
1990s	76	50	26	82	58	24	68	51	17

Source: NES Cumulative File vcf0108, vcf0128, vcf0705, vcf0707, and vcf0303.

The numbers presented in the above table, while they must be viewed critically, are nonetheless quite revealing. Hispanics, as a group, are more Democratic than white, non-Hispanics. This can be seen quite clearly by comparing table 4.7 with table 3.4 in chapter 3. Further comparison of these tables reveals that Hispanic Catholics are much more likely to support the Democratic Party than are white non-Hispanic Catholics.

Returning now to the central question of this analysis, what does this tendency of Hispanic Catholics to be highly supportive of the Democratic Party mean to the differences in support of the Democrats between white Catholics and white Protestants? At first glance, one might assume that it means nothing. Why would the behavior of Hispanics affect the reported behavior of whites? It does, however, have a potentially significant effect because of the way in which the NES recorded race and ethnicity until the administration of the 2000 National Election Study.[32] These procedures and their consequences are fully explained in endnote 32, below. Here in the text, suffice it to say that some Hispanics are included in the "whites only" category. Therefore, disproportionate support for the Democrats among Hispanic Catholics could have the effect of substantially increasing the differences in Democratic support between Catholics and Protestants, in much the same way that including African Americans diminished the differences that exist between the two religious groups. Logically then, the next step is to examine the levels of Democratic support exhibited by Catholics and Protestants after Hispanics are removed from the analysis. Tables 4.8 and 4.9 present these results.

Table 4.8: Democratic Presidential Vote, House Vote, and Party ID, Catholics and Protestants, White, Non-Hispanics Only, 1980-1998

	Presidential Vote			House Vote			Party ID		
Year	C	P	D	C	P	D	C	P	D
1980	39(40)	31	8(9)	57(58)	46	11(12)	54(54)	44	10(10)
1982	--	--	--	64(65)	48	16(17)	63(65)	45	18(20)
1984	42(44)	28	14(16)	57(59)	45	12(14)	52(52)	38	14(14)
1986	--	--	--	64(66)	49	15(16)	53(55)	39	14(15)
1988	46(51)	33	13(18)	61(66)	49	12(17)	45(49)	37	8(12)
1990	--	--	--	60(63)	55	5(7)	56(58)	40	16(17)
1992	45(48)	34	11(14)	58(61)	50	8(11)	52(55)	38	14(17)
1994	--	--	--	44(49)	35	9(13)	48(53)	34	14(19)
1996	50(54)	41	9(13)	44(49)	38	6(11)	52(55)	41	11(13)
1998	--	--	--	42(49)	33	9(14)	47(51)	40	7(11)

Source: NES Cumulative File vcf0108, vcf0128, vcf0705, vcf0707, and vcf0303.
Again, this analysis is not relevant to the 2000 data.

Table 4.9: Democratic Presidential Vote, House Vote, and Party ID, Catholics and Protestants, White, Non-Hispanics Only, by Decade, 1980s-1990s

	Presidential Vote			House Vote			Party ID		
Dec.	C	P	D	C	P	D	C	P	D
1980s	43 (46)	30	13 (15)	60 (63)	47	13 (15)	53 (54)	40	13 (14)
1990s	47 (51)	36	11 (14)	51 (55)	43	8 (11)	51 (55)	38	13 (16)

Source: NES Cumulative File vcf0108, vcf0128, vcf0705, vcf0707, and vcf0303.

Table 4.8 presents the Democratic percentages for presidential vote, House vote, and party identification for white, non-Hispanic Catholics and Protestants by year since 1980. Table 4.9 presents the same information by decade. The numbers in parentheses represent the results originally reported in tables 3.3 and 3.4, results that were obtained with Hispanics identified as white included in the sample. Once again, the results are quite clear. Strong Democratic support by Hispanic Catholics does increase the differences in Democratic support between Catholics and Protestants. This impact has been increasing over time. Hispanic Catholic electoral behavior factors significantly into the electoral behavior of American Catholics as a whole. Examinations of Catholic electoral behavior must take into account the growing Hispanic Catholic population.

We must, however, not make too much of the impact of Hispanic Catholics. As tables 4.8 and 4.9 show, the exclusion of Hispanic Catholics only has the effect of reducing differences in Democratic support between Catholics and Protestants, not eliminating them entirely. Sizeable differences still remain, even after controlling for Hispanic ethnicity. As table 4.7 shows, large differences in Democratic support also exist between Hispanic Catholics and Hispanic Protestants. According to evidence reported by Hunt, these differences cannot be explained away by differences in socioeconomic status.[33] It appears, then, that something about Catholic religious affiliation increases support for the Democratic Party in comparison to Protestantism.

The analyses in this chapter should not be taken as claims that the demographic characteristics examined here do not affect Catholic electoral behavior. Quite to the contrary, the analyses presented here show rather clearly that gender, age, and Hispanic ethnicity strongly affect the electoral behavior of American Catholics, as did family income in chapter 3. The point that needs to be stressed, however, is that significant differences in Democratic support between Catholics and Protestants remain even when controlling for these characteristics. These differences still need to be explained. Chapter 5 will continue the search for answers with an examination of church attendance, the importance of religion to individuals, and a denominational division of Protestants.

Notes

1. Paul Allen Beck, *Party Politics in America*, 8th ed. (New York: Longman, 1997), 144-45; Center for the American Woman and Politics, "The Gender Gap: Voting Choices, Party Identification, and Presidential Performance Ratings," *Fact Sheet* (Eagleton Institute of Politics, Rutgers University, July 1996); Warren E. Miller, "Party Identification, Realignment, and Party Voting: Back to the Basics," *American Political Science Review* 85, no. 2 (June 1991): 560, 562-63; Henry C. Kenski, "The Gender Factor in a Changing Electorate," in *The Politics of the Gender Gap: The Social Construction of Political Science*, ed. Carol M. Mueller (Newbury Park, Calif.: Sage Publications, 1988), 39.

2. Robert Booth Fowler, Allen D. Hertzke, and Laura R. Olson, *Religion and Politics in America*, 2d ed. (Boulder, Colo.: Westview Press, 1999), 95.

3. James D. Davidson, Andrea S. Williams, Richard A. Lamanna, Jan Stenftenagel, Kathleen Maas Weigert, William A. Whalen, and Patricia Wittberg, *The Search for Common Ground: What Unites and Divides Catholic Americans* (Huntington, Ind.: Our Sunday Visitor Publishing Division, 1997), 144.

4. The effects of church attendance in particular and religiosity in general will be examined in chapter 5.

5. In fact the gender gap may have had the effect of reducing the difference between the electoral behavior of Catholics and Protestants, at least in terms of results obtained using the NES dataset. Since the 1960s, the NES has consistently included more women than men in its total sample, as well as in its samples of presidential and House voters. Through the 1980s, the margin by which women outnumbered men was approximately equal among Catholics and Protestants (analysis not shown). However, in the 1990s women accounted for 51 percent of presidential voters, 49 percent of House voters, and 51 percent of the party ID sample among Catholics in the NES. The corresponding percentages for women among Protestants were 55, 56, and 57, respectively. If indeed the gender gap has been increasing in recent years, the higher percentage of women in the Protestant samples may have the effect of reducing overall differences in Democratic support between Catholics and Protestants that are obtained when using NES data.

6. For the original statement of generational effects see Karl Manheim, "The Problem of Generations," in Karl Mannheim, *Essays on the Sociology of Knowledge*, ed.

Paul Kecskemeti (New York: Oxford University Press, 1952), 276-320. For a brief description of each of these three types of effect see William Claggett, "Partisan Acquisition vs. Partisan Intensity: Life-Cycle, Generational, and Period Effects, 1952-1976," *American Journal of Political Science* 25, no. 2 (May 1981): 194.

7. William B. Prendergast, *The Catholic Voter in American Politics: The Passing of a Democratic Monolith* (Washington, D.C.: Georgetown University Press, 1999), 218; David C. Leege, "The Catholic Vote in '96: Can It Be Found in Church?" *Commonweal* 123 (Sept. 27, 1996): 11-18.

8. Claggett, "Partisan Acquisition," 193-214; W. Phillips Shively, "The Relationship between Age and Party Identification: A Cohort Analysis," *Political Methodology* 6, no. 4 (Fall 1979): 437-46; Angus Campbell, Philip E. Converse, Warren E. Miller, and Donald E. Stokes, *The American Voter* (New York: John Wiley & Sons, 1960), 161-65. For dissenting views, see: Paul R. Abramson, "Developing Party Identification: A Further Examination of Life-Cycle, Generational, and Period Effects," *American Journal of Political Science* 23, no. 1 (Feb. 1979): 78-96; Norval D. Glenn, "Sources of the Shifts to Political Independence: Some Evidence from a Cohort Analysis," *Social Science Quarterly* 53, no. 3 (Dec. 1972): 494-515.

9. Philip Gleason, "Catholicism and Cultural Change in the 1960's," *Review of Politics* 34, no. 4 (Oct. 1972): 94.

10. Many scholars have noted that while Vatican II did produce important changes in American Catholicism, it may have been more important in releasing many of the pressures for change that had been building up for some time in American Catholicism. Dean R. Hoge, "Interpreting Change in American Catholicism: The River and the Floodgate," *Review of Religious Research* 27, no. 4 (June 1986): 289-99; Gleason, "Catholicism and Cultural Change," 96; Thomas T. McAvoy, "American Catholicism and the Aggiornamento," *Review of Politics* 30, no. 3 (July 1968): 275-91.

11. For general discussions of the changes brought on by Vatican II, see William D'Antonio, James Davidson, Dean Hoge, and Ruth Wallace, *American Catholic Laity in a Changing Church* (Kansas City, Mo.: Sheed and Ward, 1989), 12-17; Jay P. Dolan, R. Scott Appleby, Patricia Byrne, and Debra Campbell, *Transforming Parish Ministry* (New York: The Crossroad Publishing Company, 1989); Jay P. Dolan, *The American Catholic Experience* (Notre Dame, Ind.: University of Notre Dame Press, 1992), 424-31; Andrew M. Greeley, *The American Catholic: A Social Portrait* (New York: Basic Books, 1977), 126-51.

12. Prendergast, *The Catholic Voter*, 19-20; Andrea S. Williams and James D. Davidson, "Catholic Conceptions of Faith: A Generational Analysis," *Sociology of Religion* 57, no. 3 (Fall 1996): 277; Robert Wuthnow, *The Restructuring of American Religion: Society and Faith since World War II* (Princeton, N.J.: Princeton University Press, 1988), 94-95. For the complete texts of the Vatican II documents see: Walter M. Abbott, ed., *The Documents of Vatican II* (New York: Guild Press, 1966).

13. Davidson, Williams, Lamanna, Stenftenagel, Weigert, Whalen, and Wittberg, *The Search for Common Ground*, 45.

14. Davidson, Williams, Lamanna, Stenftenagel, Weigert, Whalen, and Wittberg, *The Search for Common Ground*, 22; Williams and Davidson, "Catholic Conceptions of Faith," 277.

15. Davidson, Williams, Lamanna, Stenftenagel, Weigert, Whalen, and Wittberg, *The Search for Common Ground*, 116; Williams and Davidson, "Catholic Conceptions of Faith," 277-78.

16. This chapter focuses only on changes in electoral behavior that may have been produced by Vatican II. Much more will be said about the Second Vatican Council and the changes it produced in chapter 6.

17. Davidson, Williams, Lamanna, Stenftenagel, Weigert, Whalen, and Wittberg, *The Search for Common Ground*; Williams and Davidson, "Catholic Conceptions of Faith."

18. The age cohorts utilized by Davidson et al. are as follows: pre-Vatican II = born in or before 1940, Vatican II = born between 1941 and 1960, and post-Vatican II = born after 1960. Because of the limitations in the NES dataset, the age cohorts utilized here differ slightly from those used by Davidson et al. The cohorts used in this analysis are as follows: pre-Vatican II = born in or before 1942, Vatican II = born between 1943 and 1958, post-Vatican II = born after 1959.

19. Prendergast and Gallup and Castelli both claim that young Catholics were heavily drawn to the Republican Party during the 1980s by the personality and popularity of Ronald Reagan. Leege echoes this belief, further proposing that these Catholics may now be drifting away from the GOP because Reagan is no longer there. Prendergast, *The Catholic Voter*, 176-93; George Gallup, Jr., and Jim Castelli, *The American Catholic People: Their Beliefs, Practices, and Values* (Garden City, N.Y.: Doubleday and Co., 1987), 129-38; Leege, "The Catholic Vote in '96," 15.

20. United States Census Bureau, *United States Census 2000*. Available at http://www/census.gov/

21. For example, Greeley, in his 1990 book *The Catholic Myth*, claims that one in ten Hispanic-American Catholics were leaving the church (123). Greeley updated this figure to one in seven in 1997. Cited in Fowler, Hertzke, and Olson, *Religion and Politics in America*, 47. See also Allan Figueroa Deck, "The Challenge of Evangelical/Pentecostal Christianity to Hispanic Catholicism," in *Hispanic Catholic Culture in the U.S.: Issues and Concerns*, ed. Jay P. Dolan and Allan Figueroa Deck (Notre Dame, Ind.: University of Notre Dame Press, 1994), 409-39.

22. Hunt, utilizing 1984 data, reports that 77 percent of Hispanic Americans identify themselves as Catholic. Larry L. Hunt, "The Spirit of Hispanic Protestantism in the United States: National Survey Comparisons of Catholics and Non-Catholics," *Social Science Quarterly* 79, no. 4 (Dec. 1998): 832. A more recent national survey of Hispanics reports that 67 percent of Hispanics identified themselves as Catholics. Reported in Ana Maria Diaz-Stevens and Anthony M. Stevens-Arroyo, *Recognizing the Latino Resurgence in U.S. Religion* (Boulder, Colo.: Westview Press, 1998), 34-35.

23. Prendergast, *The Catholic Voter*, 7.

24. William D'Antonio, James D. Davidson, Dean R. Hoge, and Ruth A. Wallace, *Laity American and Catholic: Transforming the Church* (Kansas City, Mo.: Sheed and Ward, 1996), 179.

25. George Gallup, Jr., and Jim Castelli, *The People's Religion: American Faith in the 90's* (New York: Macmillan Publishing Company, 1989), 101.

26. Fowler, Hertzke, and Olson, *Religion and Politics in America*, 95.

27. Prendergast, *The Catholic Voter*, 7; Moises Sandoval, *On the Move: A History of the Hispanic Church in the United States* (Maryknoll, N.Y.: Orbis Books, 1990), 88.

28. Davidson, Williams, Lamanna, Stenftenagel, Weigert, Whalen, and Wittberg, *The Search for Common Ground*, 162-63. This lack of knowledge also applies to Hispanic Catholics and Hispanic Catholicism. Dolan and Deck, eds., *Hispanic Catholic Culture in the U.S.*, 1.

29. Diaz-Stevens and Stevens-Arroyo, *Recognizing the Latino Resurgence in U.S. Religion*, 22-32; Kenneth D. Wald, *Religion and Politics in the United States*, 3d ed., (Washington, D.C.: Congressional Quarterly Press, 1997), 31-32; Joan Moore, "The Social Fabric of the Hispanic Community since 1965," in *Hispanic Catholic Culture in the U.S.: Issues and Concerns*, ed. Jay P. Dolan and Allan Figueroa Deck (Notre Dame, Ind.: University of Notre Dame Press, 1994), 8; Dolan, Appleby, Byrne, and Campbell., *Transforming Parish Ministry*, 299, 311; John A. Coleman, "American Catholicism," in *World Catholicism in Transition*, ed. Thomas M. Gannon (New York: Macmillan Publishing Company, 1988), 238-39; Gallup and Castelli, *The American Catholic People*, 143.

30. Robert A. Jackson and Thomas A. Carsey, "Group Components of U.S. Presidential Voting across the States," *Political Behavior* 21, no. 2 (June 1999): 129; Fowler, Hertzke, and Olson, *Religion and Politics in America*, 95-96; Prendergast, *The Catholic Voter*, 203; Leege, "The Catholic Vote in '96," 12; Henry C. Kenski and William Lockwood, "Catholic Voting Behavior in 1988: A Critical Swing Vote," in *The Bible and the Ballot Box: Religion and Politics in the 1988 Election*, ed. James L. Guth and John C. Green (Boulder, Colo.: Westview Press, 1991), 174-75. Cain et al. present evidence showing that Hispanics as a group support the Democratic Party at substantially higher levels than do non-Hispanic whites. Bruce E. Cain, D. Roderick Kiewiet, and Carole J. Uhlaner, "The Acquisition of Partisanship by Latinos and Asian Americans," *American Journal of Political Science* 35, no. 2 (May 1991): 390-422.

31. The sample sizes are as follows: For the 1990s, Hispanic Catholics had an N of 86 for presidential vote, 153 for House vote, and 417 for party ID. For Hispanic Protestants, the N's were 50 for presidential vote, 78 for House vote, and 221 for party ID. For the 1980s, Hispanic Catholics had an N of 127 for presidential vote, 129 for House vote, and 336 for party ID. For Hispanic Protestants, the N's were 34 for presidential vote, 37 for House vote, and 117 for party ID.

32. From 1948 until 1998 the race of NES respondents was determined by interviewer observation. In other words, the person administering the survey instrument determined the race of the respondent by looking at the individual. The respondent was never asked his or her race. Beginning in 1972, the NES began asking a question that allowed respondents to self-identify their ethnicity. In all versions of the NES Cumulative File prior to the latest (2001) edition, race and ethnicity were separate variables, with race being coded as determined by interviewer observation. In the 2001 version of the Cumulative File, this practice has been changed. Respondents were asked for the first time in 2000 to self-identify their racial group as well as their ethnicity. This is certainly an advance in the administering of the NES. However, those in charge of the NES also chose to go back and alter the race data from prior years that had been included in previous versions of the Cumulative File. From 1972-1998, respondents who gave their ethnicity as Hispanic but who had previously been identified and coded as white for the race variable (vcf0106) have now been removed from the white category. This decision by the NES is at the very least problematic for researchers. The number of respondents classified as white in each year from 1972-1998 covered by the Cumulative File has declined (in many cases by over 100 respondents), thereby altering the dataset significantly from previous versions. This raises serious concerns about continuity and comparability of research using the latest version of the Cumulative File with research that utilized previous versions of the dataset. It is also somewhat questionable to remove a respondent from one category and place them in another when they were never asked the appropriate question in the first place. This is especially true given the muddled nature of the issue of race

with regard to Latinos. As discussed by Diaz-Stevens and Stevens Arroyo (1998), Hispanics may be of any race (including white), and generally respond in a number of different ways when asked to self-identify themselves racially. Would it be considered legitimate to remove any other ethnic group, for example Italians or Slovaks, from a racial category on the basis of their ethnic self-identification alone? I would argue no. Because of these issues and concerns, I have chosen to use the original race coding as available in all versions of the NES Cumulative File until 2001 when possible. This means the 2001 version of the Cumulative File will only be used when 2000 data are needed. My decision obviously has implications for this study. Given the fact that Hispanic whites tend to be more supportive of the Democratic Party than non-Hispanic whites and that approximately two-thirds of Hispanic Americans are Roman Catholic, including Hispanics in the "whites only" category has the potential to affect the results among Catholics that are presented in this study. The analyses presented in this chapter confirm that controlling for Hispanic ethnicity does reduce the Democratic support percentages among Catholics by two to four percentage points. However, the differences between Catholics and Protestants in their support of the Democratic Party do not disappear. The effects of Hispanic ethnicity are also controlled for in the multivariate tests conducted in chapter 7. This to me constitutes a sounder approach than relying on the recoded data in the 2001 version of the Cumulative File. Hopefully this matter will be addressed in the future by those in charge of the NES.

33. Hunt, "The Spirit of Hispanic Protestantism," 828-45.

Chapter Five

The Search Continued

Introduction

The previous two chapters have presented substantial empirical evidence that the electoral behavior of American Catholics differs significantly from the electoral behavior of American Protestants. Various social and demographic variables have been examined in an attempt to explain these differences. Chapter 3 showed that while family income levels do have significant impact on the electoral behavior of both Catholics and Protestants, they do not account for the differences in the electoral behavior of the two groups. Chapter 4 examined the effects of the key demographic variables of gender, age, and Hispanic ethnicity. Analyses showed that each of these variables has important effects on electoral behavior. However, in much the same way as family income levels, controlling for these characteristics does not eliminate the differences in electoral behavior that exist between Catholics and Protestants. The two groups remain distinct, with Catholics being more supportive of the Democratic Party than Protestants regardless of income, gender, or age. The removal of Hispanic Americans from the analyses reduces somewhat the magnitude of these differences, but does not eliminate them. This chapter continues the attempt to account for these differences with an examination of the impacts of religious salience and a denominational division of Protestants.

Religious Salience

Religious salience, also known as religiosity and religious commitment, refers to "the importance of religion to the individual."[1] Since the fundamental focus of this project is the electoral behavior of two religious groups in American society, it makes sense to examine the effects of religious salience on the behavior of these two groups. If Catholicism and Protestantism possess distinct qualities that produce differences in electoral behavior between their respective adherents, then it is possible that higher levels of religiosity will intensify these behavioral differences. In other words, Catholics' support of the Democratic Party may increase as their level of religious salience increases, while increases in religious salience among Protestants could lower their support of the Democrats. Along these same lines, lower levels of religiosity may result in decreased differences in electoral behavior between Catholics and Protestants. It might also be the case that Catholics and Protestants exhibit very different levels of religious salience, and that controlling for religious salience eliminates the differences in electoral behavior that exist between these two groups. Both of these possibilities will be examined in this chapter, beginning with the latter. Of course, it also possible that religious salience has no effect on the electoral behavior of Catholics and Protestants. This too will be investigated.

Defining religious salience is relatively straightforward. Operationalizing and effectively measuring this phenomenon is much more difficult. Religious salience has many dimensions, and may mean different things and manifest itself in different ways among different people.[2] Scholars therefore take varying tacks in the attempt to empirically capture religious salience. Although religious salience has been measured in multiple ways, two general approaches have come to dominate the scientific study of religion. The first is a behavioral measure of religiosity, which taps into activities related to religion that individuals may engage in. The simplest and most basic behavioral indicator is church attendance. It is also the most commonly used measure due to its nearly ubiquitous presence on national surveys. Ritual involvement and devotional activities (such as private prayer, bible reading, etc.) are also sometimes used as behavioral measures of religious salience. The second general approach is attitudinal in nature, utilizing questions that in some way attempt to gauge the importance of religion to individuals in their everyday lives. The utilization of an attitudinal approach is an attempt to tap into the psychological impact of religion on individuals.[3]

Both types of approaches have their strengths and weaknesses. Generally, it is safe to assume that those people who attend religious services on a regular basis have higher levels of religious salience than those who go infrequently or not at all. The effort undertaken in going to services indicates that the individual places at least some importance on religion. However, using church attendance as the only measure of religious salience may incorrectly portray some individuals as having low religious salience. For example, some believers may have difficulty in attending religious services due to old age, health problems, or lack of transportation. Some of these people may indeed be highly religious, but utilization of church attendance as an indicator would not reveal this fact. Similarly, the use of church attendance as the sole measure of religiosity has the potential to exclude individuals who do not attend services but engage in extensive religious activities in their homes or those who belong to religious movements that are not or have not yet organized institutionally. It is also possible that an individual may place a high level of psychological importance on religion but simply not attend services on a regular basis. In addition, it is possible that some individuals attend religious services for nonreligious reasons, such as to maintain a certain image in their community, establish business contacts, etc. Using church attendance as the only measure of religiosity would incorrectly characterize such individuals as possessing high religious salience. Each of these possibilities, along with others that may come to mind, is a weakness of church attendance as an indicator of religiosity.

Attitudinal measures have their weaknesses as well. Using importance of religion as the sole indicator of religious salience systematically devalues behavioral activities such as church attendance. As noted above, making the effort to attend services surely indicates at least some level of religious commitment above that possessed by those who do not attend. Furthermore, it is important to note that both behavioral and attitudinal measures of religious salience may be affected by social desirability effects. In a country widely noted for high levels of religious identification and attendance, respondents may be inclined to report higher levels of importance of religion, or of church attendance when answering survey questions on the subject.[4] The point is that measurement of religious salience is imperfect and difficult. Single indicators are problematic. As noted above, the concept of being religious may mean very different things to different people. For some, being religious may exclusively entail attending services on a regular basis, while for others being religious may mean taking religion into account in the conduct of their daily lives. Certainly, these ideas of what it means to be religious do not have to be exclusive of each other, and many individuals who consider themselves religious likely engage in both types of activity. However, the behavioral and attitudinal approaches to measuring religious salience entail different conceptions of what it means to be religious. The best approach, when possible, is to utilize multiple indicators (preferably a mix of attitudinal and behavioral) in the measurement of religious salience.[5]

The NES has traditionally been quite limited in the religious questions that it asks respondents. This is especially true with regard to possible indicators of religious salience. Until 1980, the only measure of religious salience included in the NES surveys was church attendance. The situation has improved somewhat since then. In 1980, the NES began including two questions that taken together provide a good attitudinal measure of religious salience. The first question asks respondents if religion is an important part of their life. Those who answer yes to this question are then asked a follow-up question about the amount of guidance they receive from religion in their everyday lives. Response options are "some," "quite a bit," or "a great deal." When combined with those respondents who said that religion is not important to them in the previous question, a four-point religious guidance scale is created. Therefore, while far from perfect for the measurement of religious salience, the NES does provide two reasonably good indicators. One is behavioral in nature and available since 1952, and the other is attitudinal in nature and available since 1980. As has been noted by other researchers, these measures are strongly correlated with one another, with a Pearson's r of .526 during the 1980s and .564 during the 1990s.[6] These results allow a fair amount of confidence that the variables are measuring the same phenomenon. However, the correlations are far from perfect, indicating the utility of using multiple measures. The next section of this chapter will use these variables to analyze the effects of religious salience on the three partisan support indicators for Catholics and Protestants. In keeping with the primary focus of this analysis, I will begin by examining the effect of religious salience on the levels of Democratic support exhibited by Catholics and Protestants, and on the differences in Democratic support between the two groups.

For reasons outlined in the above discussion, religious salience is best measured using multiple indicators, preferably a combination of behavioral and attitudinal variables. Unfortunately, this is not possible over this entire period under examination in this study. As noted earlier, the use of NES data only allows such an approach beginning in 1980, when the attitudinal measure guidance from religion is introduced. Therefore, all analyses involving religious salience before 1980 must rely solely on the behavioral measure of church attendance. In an effort to utilize the best indicator available, I have created a religious salience index that combines both variables (which will be explained when introduced) for use in analyses involving 1980 and the years following. Since it has been included in the NES for a longer period of time, I will begin my analyses with church attendance. Because the results are both valuable and interesting, analyses involving church attendance will be conducted over the entire 1952-2000 time period. After presenting these results, analyses utilizing the religious salience index will be conducted for the period from 1980-2000.

Church Attendance

Churches are the most common type of voluntary association in the United States. Approximately two-thirds of the adult population attend, on at least a monthly basis, one of the more than 300,000 on American soil.[7] Given that their members are "bound by strong affective ties and regular social interaction," churches are well positioned to create, transmit, and maintain group norms and attitudes among those who attend religious services.[8] Through their leadership of religious services and their presence at other church-related functions, clergy have ample opportunity to communicate to audiences that are large and likely to be relatively receptive, given the fact that religious institutions and leaders consistently garner high levels of respect, confidence, and trust among the American public.[9] In light of this information, it is clear that attendance at religious services has the potential to affect the political behavior of individuals.

In what ways does church attendance influence political behavior? We know that regular church attendance increases the likelihood of voting in elections.[10] Verba and his colleagues have also shown that church attendance can in some cases build civic skills and increase other forms of political participation.[11] This same study, along with others, has shown that political messages are disseminated from the pulpit on a relatively frequent basis.[12] It has clearly been determined that church attendance affects political behavior. The important question for this study is how church attendance affects the electoral behavior of Catholics and Protestants in the United States.

It is first necessary to examine the levels of church attendance for Catholics and Protestants. How do these groups compare in terms of church attendance? Because there is little yearly variation, the church attendance data are presented by decade since the 1950s in table 5.1. The attendance categories are explained in the note at the bottom of table 5.1.

Table 5.1: Church Attendance for Catholics and Protestants, Whites Only, by Decade, 1950s-1990s

Dec.	Regularly Cath.	Regularly Prot.	Diff.	Sometimes Cath.	Sometimes Prot.	Diff.	Rarely Cath.	Rarely Prot.	Diff.
1950s	68	35	33	14	19	-5	18	46	-28
1960s	69	37	32	13	18	-5	19	45	-26
1970s	53	38	15	11	13	-2	37	49	-8
1980s	46	39	7	14	12	2	41	48	-7
1990s	46	44	2	14	15	-1	40	41	-1

Note: Church attendance codes: 1960-1968: Regularly equals "regularly," Sometimes equals "often," and Rarely equals "seldom" and "never." 1970-2000: Regularly equals "every week" and "almost every week," Sometimes equals "once or twice a month," and Rarely equals "a few times a year" and "never." I realize that there are significant theoretical and substantive problems inherent in combining these responses. For example, there are important differences between attending services a few times a year and never. The same can be said for attending every week versus almost every week. However, in the interests of parsimony and greater sample sizes I have chosen to combine these responses in this analysis. I believe the benefits accrued from combining categories to be greater than those derived from keeping them separate. Church attendance was not asked in 1954. Source: NES Cumulative File vcf0128, vcf0131, and vcf0130.

One trend is clear from the data presented in these two tables. During the 1950s and 1960s, Catholics attended church at significantly higher levels than did Protestants. Beginning in the 1970s, however, attendance at Mass began to decline rather sharply among Catholics.[13] Although this trend appears to have leveled off, church attendance rates for Catholics are now almost indistinguishable from those of Protestants.[14]

This rather remarkable decline in church attendance among Catholics is an important phenomenon in its own right, one that demands the attention of scholars and Catholic officials alike. For this analysis, however, church attendance is only important in terms of how it affects the electoral behavior of Catholics and Protestants. What impact, if any, does attendance at religious services have on the vote choice and party identification patterns of members of these two religious groups? Tables 5.2-5.7 attempt to answer this question. Table 5.2 presents the Democratic presidential vote percentages for Catholics and Protestants by level of church attendance from 1952-2000. Table 5.3 presents this same information by decade from the 1950s-1990s. Tables 5.4 and 5.5 do the same for House vote, while tables 5.6 and 5.7 cover partisan identification.

Table 5.2: Democratic Presidential Vote for Catholics and Protestants, by Level of Church Attendance, Whites Only, 1952-2000

	Regularly			Sometimes			Rarely		
Year	Cath.	Prot.	Diff.	Cath.	Prot.	Diff.	Cath.	Prot.	Diff.
1952	55	29	**26**	50	26	**24**	41	39	**2**
1956	47	31	**16**	28	32	**-4**	45	38	**7**
1960	85	25	**60**	71	25	**46**	65	48	**17**
1964	78	53	**25**	76	54	**22**	81	64	**17**
1968	57	21	**36**	58	29	**29**	48	27	**21**
1972	38	18	**20**	21	25	**-4**	39	29	**10**
1976	55	34	**21**	56	49	**7**	55	43	**12**
1980	33	29	**4**	63	34	**29**	45	32	**13**
1984	45	22	**23**	53	32	**21**	40	33	**7**
1988	55	30	**25**	53	35	**18**	46	36	**10**
1992	42	27	**15**	55	30	**25**	55	43	**12**
1996	48	32	**16**	60	44	**16**	62	53	**9**
2000	45	29	**16**	48	47	**1**	48	53	**-5**

Source: NES Cumulative File vcf0128, vcf0131, vcf0130, and vcf0705.

Table 5.3: Democratic Presidential Vote for Catholics and Protestants, by Level of Church Attendance, Whites Only, by Decade, 1950s-1990s

	Regularly			Sometimes			Rarely		
Dec.	Cath.	Prot.	Diff.	Cath.	Prot.	Diff.	Cath.	Prot.	Diff.
1950s	51	30	**21**	40	29	**11**	42	38	**4**
1960s	74	34	**40**	70	36	**34**	64	46	**18**
1970s	45	25	**20**	37	38	**-1**	46	35	**11**
1980s	45	27	**18**	54	34	**20**	43	34	**9**
1990s	45	29	**16**	57	36	**21**	58	47	**11**

Source: NES Cumulative File vcf0128, vcf0131, vcf0130, and vcf0705.

Table 5.4: Democratic House Vote for Catholics and Protestants, by Level of Church Attendance, Whites Only, 1952-2000

	Regularly			Sometimes			Rarely		
Year	Cath.	Prot.	Diff.	Cath.	Prot.	Diff.	Cath.	Prot.	Diff.
1952	57	44	13	48	29	19	51	45	6
1956	64	49	15	48	39	9	51	47	4
1958	74	44	30	68	51	17	61	61	0
1960	79	38	41	89	37	52	63	53	10
1962	75	46	29	94	42	52	59	51	8
1964	70	54	16	77	55	22	76	63	13
1966	69	48	21	71	48	23	52	45	7
1968	59	40	19	76	40	36	57	45	12
1970	54	52	2	70	43	27	50	47	3
1972	65	43	22	58	52	6	69	49	20
1974	71	48	23	75	53	22	71	59	12
1976	59	45	14	67	50	17	63	48	15
1978	61	46	15	79	44	35	64	57	7
1980	57	40	17	62	46	16	60	52	8
1982	71	45	26	40	44	-4	59	53	6
1984	59	40	19	69	55	14	57	49	8
1986	70	51	19	59	56	3	61	46	15
1988	66	42	24	58	60	-2	69	54	15
1990	61	51	10	58	60	-2	70	63	7
1992	59	42	17	63	59	4	63	56	7
1994	44	31	13	52	32	20	54	44	10
1996	43	29	14	58	42	16	56	48	8
1998	43	29	14	65	34	31	52	45	7
2000	47	30	17	44	54	-10	62	48	14

Note: Neither House vote nor church attendance was asked in 1954. Source: NES Cumulative File vcf0128, vcf0131, vcf0130, and vcf0707.

Table 5.5: Democratic House Vote for Catholics and Protestants, by Level of Church Attendance, Whites Only, by Decade, 1950s-1990s

	Regularly			Sometimes			Rarely		
Dec.	Cath.	Prot.	Diff.	Cath.	Prot.	Diff.	Cath.	Prot.	Diff.
1950s	65	46	19	55	39	16	53	50	3
1960s	71	45	26	81	44	37	62	52	10
1970s	62	46	16	68	49	19	65	52	12
1980s	64	43	21	61	53	8	62	51	11
1990s	51	37	14	59	47	12	60	52	8

Source: NES Cumulative File vcf0128, vcf0131, vcf0130, and vcf0707.

Table 5.6: Democratic Party ID for Catholics and Protestants, by Level of Church Attendance, Whites Only, 1952-2000

	Regularly			Sometimes			Rarely		
Year	Cath.	Prot.	Diff.	Cath.	Prot.	Diff.	Cath.	Prot.	Diff.
1952	69	51	**18**	63	46	**17**	67	53	**14**
1956	61	44	**17**	51	43	**8**	57	46	**11**
1958	68	46	**22**	73	55	**18**	52	53	**-1**
1960	76	42	**34**	56	41	**13**	68	51	**17**
1962	68	44	**24**	77	43	**34**	59	50	**9**
1964	74	47	**27**	57	50	**7**	62	61	**1**
1966	63	50	**13**	67	47	**20**	61	45	**16**
1968	67	40	**27**	58	51	**7**	55	48	**7**
1970	60	44	**16**	77	45	**32**	64	48	**16**
1972	63	42	**21**	61	48	**13**	61	42	**19**
1974	62	38	**24**	68	40	**28**	58	48	**10**
1976	62	38	**24**	64	47	**17**	59	40	**19**
1978	70	38	**32**	57	42	**15**	61	46	**15**
1980	49	40	**9**	56	46	**10**	59	47	**12**
1982	70	43	**27**	61	44	**17**	59	48	**11**
1984	54	31	**23**	59	37	**22**	47	44	**3**
1986	60	37	**23**	53	43	**10**	49	41	**8**
1988	56	34	**22**	50	37	**13**	43	40	**3**
1990	61	40	**21**	52	40	**12**	56	43	**13**
1992	50	33	**17**	54	39	**15**	62	43	**19**
1994	51	30	**21**	55	37	**18**	55	38	**17**
1996	53	33	**20**	62	43	**19**	56	50	**6**
1998	46	33	**13**	59	46	**13**	54	47	**7**
2000	43	32	**11**	40	42	**-2**	52	49	**3**

Note: Church attendance was not asked in 1954. Source: NES Cumulative File vcf0128, vcf0131, vcf0130, and vcf0303.

Table 5.7: Democratic Party ID for Catholics and Protestants, by Level of Church Attendance, Whites Only, by Decade, 1950s-1990s

	Regularly			Sometimes			Rarely		
Dec.	Cath.	Prot.	Diff.	Cath.	Prot.	Diff.	Cath.	Prot.	Diff.
1950s	66	47	**19**	63	47	**16**	61	51	**10**
1960s	70	45	**25**	62	47	**15**	60	51	**9**
1970s	64	40	**24**	64	45	**19**	60	44	**16**
1980s	57	36	**21**	55	41	**14**	50	44	**6**
1990s	52	34	**18**	56	40	**16**	57	44	**13**

Source: NES Cumulative File vcf0128, vcf0131, vcf0130, and vcf0303.

In terms of the differences in levels of support for the Democratic Party, the results presented in the above tables are plain. Catholics remain more Democratic than Protestants regardless of the frequency of church attendance. This is true across all three party support indicators. With the exception of elections held during the early 1960s, these differences have remained large and relatively stable.[15] Once again, controlling for a key variable, Catholics remain more Democratic than their Protestant counterparts.

The Religious Salience Index

The above analyses have shown that levels of church attendance do not account for differences in partisan support between Catholics and Protestants. However, this does not mean that religious salience cannot explain these differences. It could be the case that church attendance is an incomplete measure of religiosity. The creation of a religious salience index allows investigation of this possibility. As noted earlier in this chapter, the NES first began asking two questions that together provide an attitudinal measure of religious salience in 1980. Table 5.8 presents the percentage of Catholics and Protestants who fall into each of these four categories. Because the yearly results for religious guidance show very little fluctuation for both Catholics and Protestants, the results are pooled and presented by decade.

Table 5.8: Amount of Guidance from Religion for Catholics and Protestants, Whites Only, by Decade, 1980s-1990s

	Great Deal			Quite a Bit			Some			None		
Dec.	C	P	D	C	P	D	C	P	D	C	P	D
80s	29	39	-10	28	22	6	26	20	6	18	19	-1
90s	30	41	-11	26	25	1	26	19	7	18	16	2

Source: NES Cumulative File vcf0128 and vcf0847.

The percentages of Catholics and Protestants who say that religion is not important to them are essentially the same. Catholics are somewhat more likely to respond that religion provides some guidance in their daily lives, while the two groups are about the same in the percentages who attribute quite a bit of guidance to religion. The most sizeable difference occurs among those who obtain a great deal of guidance from religion, with Protestants being the higher reporting group.

By combining the values obtained on the religious guidance scale with the responses to the query about church attendance, an index of religious salience was created.[16] Table 5.9 presents the percentage of Catholics and Protestants who possess high, medium, and low levels of religious salience by decade since the 1980s. Very little variation exists between Catholics and Protestants in terms of the percentages of each group within each level of religious salience.

Table 5.9: Level of Religious Salience for Catholics and Protestants, Whites Only, by Decade, 1980s-1990s

	High			Medium			Low		
Dec.	Cath.	Prot.	Diff.	Cath.	Prot.	Diff.	Cath.	Prot.	Diff.
1980s	35	35	0	48	45	3	17	21	-4
1990s	34	40	-6	45	41	4	21	20	1

Note: For an explanation of the religious salience level categories see endnote 16 in this chapter. Source: NES Cumulative File vcf0128, vcf0130, and vcf0847.

In an effort to attain a truer understanding of the impact of religious salience on the electoral behavior of Catholics and Protestants, analyses were conducted to determine the level of Democratic support among Catholics and Protestants by level of religious salience. Tables 5.10-5.15 present these results for all three support indicators by year and by decade since 1980.

Table 5.10: Democratic Presidential Vote for Catholics and Protestants, by Level of Religious Salience, Whites Only, 1980-2000

	High			Medium			Low		
Year	Cath.	Prot.	Diff.	Cath.	Prot.	Diff.	Cath.	Prot.	Diff.
1980	38	30	8	40	30	10	46	34	12
1984	48	23	25	45	31	14	32	30	2
1988	57	29	28	50	35	15	40	38	2
1992	42	25	17	52	41	11	51	43	8
1996	49	32	17	56	46	10	61	54	7
2000	47	26	21	43	47	-4	54	59	-5

Note: For an explanation of the religious salience level categories see endnote 16 in this chapter. Source: NES Cumulative File vcf0128, vcf0130, vcf0705, and vcf0847.

Table 5.11: Democratic Presidential Vote for Catholics and Protestants, by Level of Religious Salience, Whites Only, by Decade, 1980s-1990s

	High			Medium			Low		
Dec.	Cath.	Prot.	Diff.	Cath.	Prot.	Diff.	Cath.	Prot.	Diff.
1980s	48	27	21	45	32	13	39	34	5
1990s	45	28	17	54	44	10	55	47	8

Note: For an explanation of the religious salience level categories see endnote 16 in this chapter. Source: NES Cumulative File vcf0128, vcf0130, vcf0705, and vcf0847.

Table 5.12: Democratic House Vote for Catholics and Protestants, by Level of Religious Salience, Whites Only, 1980-2000

	High			Medium			Low		
Year	Cath.	Prot.	Diff.	Cath.	Prot.	Diff.	Cath.	Prot.	Diff.
1980	57	38	19	55	48	7	70	56	14
1984	62	44	18	58	46	12	55	49	6
1986	73	55	18	56	49	7	63	35	28
1988	67	42	25	63	54	9	72	57	15
1990	67	51	16	59	61	-2	64	60	4
1992	63	43	20	61	55	6	60	60	0
1994	45	30	15	48	39	9	56	45	11
1996	47	29	18	46	42	4	62	49	13
1998	38	28	10	59	40	19	48	38	10
2000	48	30	18	52	45	7	58	52	6

Note: For an explanation of the religious salience level categories see endnote 16 in this chapter. Source: NES Cumulative File vcf0128, vcf0130, vcf0707, and vcf0847.

Table 5.13: Democratic House Vote for Catholics and Protestants, by Level of Religious Salience, Whites Only, by Decade, 1980s-1990s

	High			Medium			Low		
Dec.	Cath.	Prot.	Diff.	Cath.	Prot.	Diff.	Cath.	Prot.	Diff.
1980s	64	44	20	59	49	10	65	52	13
1990s	53	37	16	55	48	7	59	53	6

Note: For an explanation of the religious salience level categories see endnote 16 in this chapter. Source: NES Cumulative File vcf0128, vcf0130, vcf0707, and vcf0847.

Table 5.14: Democratic Party ID for Catholics and Protestants, by Level of Religious Salience, Whites Only, 1980-2000

	High			Medium			Low		
Year	Cath.	Prot.	Diff.	Cath.	Prot.	Diff.	Cath.	Prot.	Diff.
1980	55	40	15	50	44	6	64	48	16
1984	54	33	11	53	41	12	44	37	7
1986	58	40	18	50	38	12	61	38	23
1988	56	34	22	50	41	9	44	38	6
1990	63	39	24	57	45	12	52	37	15
1992	54	33	21	54	44	10	59	40	19
1994	50	32	18	55	35	20	52	35	17
1996	50	33	17	59	47	12	55	47	8
1998	48	34	14	52	43	9	56	46	10
2000	45	32	13	46	44	2	49	50	-1

Note: For an explanation of the religious salience level categories see endnote 16 in this chapter. Source: NES Cumulative File vcf0128, vcf0130, vcf0303, and vcf0847.

Table 5.15: Democratic Party ID for Catholics and Protestants, by Level of Religious Salience, Whites Only, by Decade, 1980s-1990s

	High			Medium			Low		
Dec.	Cath.	Prot.	Diff.	Cath.	Prot.	Diff.	Cath.	Prot.	Diff.
1980s	55	36	**19**	51	41	**10**	51	40	**11**
1990s	53	34	**19**	56	43	**13**	55	40	**15**

Note: For an explanation of the religious salience level categories see endnote 16 in this chapter. Source: NES Cumulative File vcf0128, vcf0130, vcf0303, and vcf0847.

The most striking result presented in these tables is once again the distinctive nature of Catholic and Protestant electoral behavior. Regardless of the level of religious salience, Catholics are more Democratic than Protestants in terms of presidential vote, House vote, and party identification. The majority of the differences are quite large and fairly stable. Controlling for the level of religious salience people possess does not eliminate the differences in electoral behavior that exist between Catholics and Protestants.

The results presented in the above tables also lend substantial support to the hypothesis that higher levels of religious salience lead to increased differences in electoral behavior between Catholics and Protestants. Although the results are not monotonic, the general pattern in the previous analyses is quite clear, especially if one examines the results by decade. As levels of religious salience increase, differences in Democratic support between Catholics and Protestants also increase. As with all of the other results presented thus far in this study, it appears that there may be fundamental differences between Catholicism and Protestantism that affect the electoral behavior of members of these religious groups. That religious group differences in Democratic support are greatest between those Catholics and Protestants for whom religion is highly salient adds further support to this hypothesis.

Attentive readers may have noted one additional element of interest in tables 5.10-5.15. Specifically, what the data in these tables show with regard to what some have labeled the new religious cleavage in American electoral politics. Stated perhaps most prominently and eloquently by Wuthnow and Hunter, the claim is that a new religious cleavage based on religious salience has arisen in American politics, gradually displacing the traditional political divide that has existed between Catholics and Protestants. Simply put, the argument is that those individuals for whom religion is highly salient are also more likely to be conservative politically. Increasingly, these individuals are gravitating toward the Republican Party, regardless of denomination. Conversely, those individuals for whom religion is not particularly salient are more likely to be liberal, and are therefore moving into the Democratic Party.[17] This new cleavage now rivals and in some instances surpasses the old Catholic/Protestant split in terms of electoral behavior. Recent empirical analyses have presented findings supporting this claim.[18]

The data presented in the previous six tables certainly seem to support the development of a new electoral division based on religious salience. Throughout the 1990s, low salience individuals have been much more supportive of the Democratic Party than those for whom religion is highly salient. While not central to this analysis, this issue is important and will be examined further in chapter 7.

The Division of Protestants

Thus far in this study, all analyses have focused on differences in electoral behavior between Catholics and Protestants. This is a legitimate method of analysis, as these two groups constitute the two primary religious traditions in the United States, and a large and influential body of work in the study of both religion and politics concentrates on these groups and the differences between them.

This mode of analysis is not, however, without its drawbacks. Despite some recent evidence showing signs of internal divisions,[19] Catholicism represents a single, unified, religious denomination. Catholics are exposed to a single religious doctrine, a single set of teachings. All Catholics worship at services that are more or less the same. While their priests and bishops differ, all Catholics are part of the same organization, with the Vatican and the pope at its head. Catholicism and the Roman Catholic Church represent a single, institutional whole.

The same cannot be said for Protestantism. American Protestantism can be seen as single unit only on the grandest scale, if at all. Protestantism is marked by a staggering number of denominations and splinter groups. New ones arise relatively regularly. Each of these denominations is separate in and unto itself. They hold separate worship services, have separate organizational structures, have distinct doctrines of religious belief, and disseminate different religious teachings. Varying degrees of difference exist in these areas among the many Protestant denominations. These facts present difficulties to social scientists wishing to study the behavior of religious groups.

Fortunately, these difficulties can in large part be overcome. Despite their differences, Protestants have many characteristics in common. They are all intellectual, and more important, spiritual heirs of the Reformation. They hold in common the ideas that caused the original split from the Catholic Church, and thus see themselves as more similar to other Protestants than they are to Catholics. The degree of difference that exists between individual groups of Protestants varies widely. For some denominations, the divide may be quite small. Among others, the differences may be rather large. The key is to somehow group Protestant denominations into categories based on these similarities and differences.

Previous students of religion in the United States have developed such groupings. Based on religious beliefs, doctrines, and traditions, a number of scholars have developed schemas that categorize Protestant denominations into religious traditions or denominational families.[20] For the purposes of this study, the most useful of these schemas is the one that divides Protestants into mainline and evangelical categories.[21] This is the categorization utilized in the NES surveys, and therefore is applicable for use in this study.[22] Separating Protestants in mainline and evangelical traditions allows the researcher to escape many of the problems inherent in lumping all Protestants together into one group.[23]

The purpose of this analysis is not to discuss the differences that exist between mainline and evangelical Protestants. We know that such differences do exist, thus creating the utility of separating Protestants into these two groups. We also know that these differences sometimes produce variations in electoral behavior of these two groups of Protestants.[24] The important matter for this study is the impact that a division of Protestants into denominational families has on differences in electoral behavior between Catholics and Protestants. If, for example, one or the other of the two Protestant groupings was mostly responsible for the differences in electoral behavior observed between Catholics and Protestants, then much of the analysis presented in this study would need to be modified accordingly. If, on the other hand, Catholic electoral behavior is distinct from the behavior of both groups of Protestants, the underlying assumptions of the project remain sound and intact.

Before comparing the electoral behavior of these three religious groups, we first need to know what this behavior looks like. Table 5.16 presents the Democratic percentages on presidential vote, House vote, and party identification for Catholics, mainline Protestants, and evangelical Protestants by year since 1960, while table 5.17 presents this information by decade since the 1960s.[25]

The Democratic percentages shown here for Catholics are the same as those presented originally in chapter 3 and have already been discussed. Therefore, I will turn my attention to the percentages shown for the Protestant groups. Among mainline Protestants, the numbers for the most part present a picture of stability. Other than the 1996 presidential election, and perhaps House elections from 1988-1992, the Democratic support levels of mainline Protestants have remained essentially the same. Other analysts have reported a shift in the electoral behavior of mainliners in recent years, but the results presented here show little evidence of such a movement.[26] Evangelical Protestants, on the other hand, have undergone large-scale changes in their electoral behavior. During the 1960s and 1970s, evangelicals were much more Democratic than mainline Protestants, at least in House voting and party identification.[27] During the 1980s, the two groups became more similar in their electoral behavior. In the 1990s, evangelicals and mainliners have reversed their positions of the 1960s and 1970s. Evangelicals are now much less Democratic than their mainline coreligionists in both presidential and House elections. This development lends additional support to the claim of a realignment among evangelicals that has been reported by other analysts.[28]

Table 5.16: Democratic Presidential Vote, House Vote, and Party ID, Catholics, Mainline Protestants, and Evangelical Protestants, Whites Only, 1960-1996

	Presidential Vote			House Vote			Party ID		
Year	C	MP	EP	C	MP	EP	C	MP	EP
1960	82	33	38	79	40	55	73	39	60
1962	--	--	--	--	--	--	--	--	--
1964	78	54	65	72	52	71	69	47	67
1966	--	--	--	67	42	58	63	40	61
1968	55	27	24	60	39	56	63	43	51
1970	--	--	--	56	42	63	63	43	51
1972	36	26	19	65	43	55	62	39	48
1974	--	--	--	72	47	63	62	39	48
1976	55	37	46	61	42	57	61	36	48
1978	--	--	--	63	43	66	65	38	51
1980	40	29	34	58	46	49	54	39	52
1982	--	--	--	65	41	60	65	40	52
1984	44	28	27	59	45	45	52	38	38
1986	--	--	--	66	49	52	55	36	45
1988	51	36	29	66	51	48	49	36	39
1990	--	--	--	63	59	51	58	40	42
1992	48	36	30	61	52	46	55	36	40
1994	--	--	--	46	34	34	49	29	35
1996	54	47	36	49	39	38	55	40	43

Note: Protestants were not differentiated in 1962. Source: NES Cumulative File vcf0705, vcf0707, vcf0303, vcf0128A, and vcf0128B. The version of the NES Cumulative File utilized here does not contain any data allowing for the differentiation of Protestants in 1998 or 2000, at least not in the same manner as those groups were delineated in previous years.

Table 5.17: Democratic Presidential Vote, House Vote, and Party ID, Catholics, Mainline Protestants, and Evangelical Protestants, Whites Only, by Decade, 1960s-1990s

	Presidential Vote			House Vote			Party ID		
Dec.	C	MP	EP	C	MP	EP	C	MP	EP
1960s	72	38	42	69	43	60	67	43	60
1970s	45	31	32	64	43	60	63	39	49
1980s	46	31	30	63	47	50	54	38	45
1990s	51	40	32	56	48	43	55	38	41

Note: The 1990s do not include data for 1998. Source: NES Cumulative File vcf0705, vcf0707, vcf0303, vcf0128A, and vcf0128B.

82   *Chapter Five*

The growing divergence in electoral behavior between mainline and evangelical Protestants is important, and has captured the attention of numerous analysts. However, the main focus of this analysis is the differences in electoral behavior between Catholics and Protestants. What impact does separating Protestants into denominational families have on these differences? This information can be gleaned by examining the previous two tables. However, in an attempt to accommodate what I am certain are already weary readers, table 5.18 presents the differences in Democratic percentages between Catholics and mainline Protestants, Catholics and evangelical Protestants, and mainline Protestants and evangelical Protestants for all three partisan support indicators by decade since 1960. The results are quite clear. Regardless of support indicator, Catholics are much more Democratic than either mainline or evangelical Protestants. Once again, the differences are large and quite stable. The results also provide further support for a realignment of evangelical Protestants. They have clearly become less Democratic since the 1960s.

Table 5.18: Differences in Democratic Presidential Vote, House Vote, and Party ID, Catholics, Mainline Protestants, and Evangelical Protestants, Whites Only, by Decade, 1960s-1990s

	Presidential Vote		
Dec.	C minus MP	C minus EP	MP minus EP
1960s	34	30	-4
1970s	14	13	-1
1980s	15	16	1
1990s	11	19	8
	House Vote		
Decade			
1960s	26	9	-17
1970s	21	4	-17
1980s	16	13	-3
1990s	8	13	5
	Party ID		
Decade			
1960s	24	7	-17
1970s	24	14	-10
1980s	16	9	-7
1990s	17	14	-3

Note: The 1990s do not contain data for 1998. Source: NES Cumulative File vcf0128A, vcf0128B, vcf0705, vcf0707, and vcf0303.

The fact that differences in electoral behavior between Catholics and Protestants remain sizeable when Protestants are separated by denominational family is not surprising. The analyses contained in this chapter are consistent with the results produced by the analyses conducted in the previous two chapters. Regardless of the demographic characteristic or social variable controlled for, the electoral behavior of Catholics is different from the electoral behavior of Protestants. Thus far I have been unsuccessful in explaining this difference. At this point, it is my hypothesis that there is something inherent in the two religious traditions that causes the observed differences in electoral behavior. Chapter 6 will examine the religious traditions in more detail in the attempt to discover if there is something about them that can account for differences in electoral behavior between members of the two groups. Particular attention will be paid to Catholicism in an attempt to determine if there is something inherent in the religion that makes its members more supportive of the Democratic Party than are Protestants.

Notes

1. James L. Guth and John C. Green, "Salience: The Core Concept?" in *Rediscovering the Religious Factor in American Politics*, ed. David C. Leege and Lyman A. Kellstedt (Armonk, N.Y.: M. E. Sharpe, 1993), 157. See also Kenneth D. Wald and Corwin E. Smidt, "Measurement Strategies in the Study of Religion and Politics," in the same volume as above, pp. 28-37; Lyman A. Kellstedt, John C. Green, James L. Guth, and Corwin E. Smidt, "Grasping the Essentials: The Social Embodiment of Religion and Political Behavior," in *Religion and the Culture Wars: Dispatches from the Front*, ed. John C. Green, James L. Guth, Corwin E. Smidt, and Lyman A. Kellstedt (Lanham, Md.: Rowman & Littlefield Publishers, 1996), 177-78; Charles Y. Glock and Rodney Stark, *Religion and Society in Tension* (Chicago: Rand McNally and Company, 1965), 18-38.

2. Kellstedt, Green, Guth, and Smidt, "Grasping the Essentials," 177; Glock and Stark, *Religion and Society in Tension*, 19-23.

3. Guth and Green, "Salience: The Core Concept?" 158-62.

4. Kellstedt, Green, Guth, and Smidt, "Grasping the Essentials," 177-78; Wald and Smidt, "Measurement Strategies," 29-30.

5. Wald and Smidt, "Measurement Strategies," 41; Glock and Stark, *Religion and Society in Tension*, 29.

6. Both coefficients are significant at $p < .0001$. To obtain results by decade, all responses for a decade were pooled. Variables were recoded from the original NES Cumulative File format so that higher levels of church attendance and guidance from religion received higher scores. For church attendance (vcf0130), those who attended every week or almost every week received a code of 3, those who attended once or twice a month were coded 2, and those who attended a few times per year or never received a 1. For guidance from religion (vcf0847), those who answered a great deal were coded 4, those responding quite a bit received a 3, those responding some were coded 2, and those for whom religion was not important were given a code of 1.

7. The figure of 300,000 is taken from Kenneth D. Wald, Lyman A. Kellstedt, and David C. Leege, "Church Involvement and Political Behavior," in *Rediscovering the Religious Factor in American Politics*, ed. David C. Leege and Lyman A. Kellstedt (Armonk, N.Y.: M.E. Sharpe, 1993), 122. See also Kenneth D. Wald, *Religion and Politics in the United States*, 3rd ed., (Washington, D.C.: Congressional Quarterly Press, 1997), 9; Sidney Verba, Kay Lehman Schlozman, and Henry E. Brady, *Voice and Equality* (Cambridge, Mass.: Harvard University Press, 1995), 75.

8. Quote from Kenneth D. Wald, Dennis E. Owen, and Samuel S. Hill, Jr., "Churches as Political Communities," *American Political Science Review* 82, no. 2 (June 1988): 532. See also Wald, *Religion and Politics in the United States*, 35-38; Christopher P. Gilbert, *The Impact of Churches on Political Behavior* (Westport, Conn.: Greenwood Press, 1993), chapter 2; Kenneth D. Wald, Dennis E. Owen, and Samuel S. Hill, Jr., "Political Cohesion in Churches," *Journal of Politics* 52, no. 1 (Feb. 1990): 197-215; Richard H. White, "Toward a Theory of Religious Influence," *Pacific Sociological Review* 11, no. 1 (Spring 1968): 23-28; Glock and Stark, *Religion and Society in Tension*, 182-83.

9. Robert Booth Fowler, Allen D. Hertzke, and Laura R. Olson, *Religion and Politics in America*, 2d ed., (Boulder, Colo.: Westview Press, 1999), 30; Wald, *Religion and Politics in the United States*, 10, 37; Wald, Owen, and Hill, "Churches as Political Communities," 532-33.

10. For some examples of the many studies showing this fact, see Steven A. Peterson, "Church Participation and Political Participation: The Spillover Effect," *American Politics Quarterly* 20, no. 1 (Jan. 1992): 123-39; James M. Penning, "The Political Behavior of American Catholics: An Assessment of the Impact of Group Integration vs. Group Identification," *Western Political Quarterly* 41, no. 2 (June 1988): 289-308; Oscar B. Martinson and E. A. Wilkening, "Religious Participation and Involvement in Local Politics throughout the Life Cycle," *Sociological Focus* 20, no. 4 (Oct. 1987): 309-18; James G. Hougland, Jr., and James A. Christensen, "Religion and Politics: The Relationship of Religious Participation to Political Efficacy and Involvement," *Sociology and Social Research* 67, no. 4 (July 1983): 405-20; Theodore F. Macaluso and John Wanat, "Voting Turnout and Religiosity," *Polity* 12, no. 1 (Fall 1979): 158-69.

11. Verba, Schlozman, and Brady, *Voice and Equality*, 309-33.

12. Many different types of studies have borne out this claim. For studies based on survey results see Verba, Schlozman, and Brady, *Voice and Equality*, 372-75; Michael R. Welch, David C. Leege, Kenneth D. Wald, and Lyman A. Kellstedt, "Are the Sheep Hearing the Shepherds? Cue Perceptions, Congregational Responses, and Political Communications Processes," in *Rediscovering the Religious Factor in American Politics*, ed. David C. Leege and Lyman A. Kellstedt (Armonk, N.Y.: M.E. Sharpe, 1993), 235-54; Gilbert, *The Impact of Churches*, 171. Congregational analyses include Wald, Owen, and Hill, "Churches as Political Communities"; Wald, Owen, and Hill, "Political Cohesion in Churches"; Ted G. Jelen, *The Political Mobilization of Religious Beliefs* (New York: Praeger, 1991). For studies based on surveys of clergy, see James L. Guth, John C. Green, Corwin E. Smidt, Lyman A. Kellstedt, and Margaret M. Poloma, *The Bully Pulpit: The Politics of the Protestant Clergy* (Lawrence, Kans.: University of Kansas Press, 1997); Kathleen Murphy Beatty and Oliver Walter, "A Group Theory of Religion and Politics: The Clergy as Group Leaders," *Western Political Quarterly* 49, no. 1 (Mar. 1989): 129-46. For a recent example of the much neglected participant-observation method, see Mark D. Brewer, Rogan Kersh, and R. Eric Petersen, "Assessing Conventional Wisdom about Religion and Politics: A Preliminary View from the Pews," *Journal for the Scientific Study of Religion* 42, no. 1 (Mar. 2003): 125-36.

13. William D'Antonio, James Davidson, Dean Hoge, and Ruth Wallace, *American Catholic Laity in a Changing Church* (Kansas City, Mo.: Sheed and Ward, 1989), 41-45.

14. D. Paul Sullins, "Catholic/Protestant Trends on Abortion: Convergence and Polarity," *Journal for the Scientific Study of Religion* 38, no. 3 (Sept. 1999): 358-59.

15. For a discussion of the impact of the elections held in the 1960s on the magnitude of the differences in Democratic support between Catholics and Protestants, see chapter 3.

16. The religious salience index was created in the following manner. For church attendance, those attending every week were assigned a code of 3, those who attended almost every week or once or twice a month were coded 2, those who attended a few times per year were given a code of 1, and those who never went to services were coded 0. For guidance from religion, those who received a great deal were coded 3, those who responded quite a bit were given a 2, those who said some were coded 1, and those who said that religion was not important to them were given a 0. This results in a minimum religious salience score of 0 and a maximum score of 6. In the interests of parsimony and greater sample sizes, the religious salience score was further collapsed, with those who scored 5 or 6 coded as having a high level of religious salience, those with scores of 2, 3, and 4 coded as having a medium level of religious salience, and those who scored 0 or 1 coded as possessing a low level of religious salience. Altering the coding of scores to place scores of 4 in the high religious salience category and scores of 2 in the low category does not appreciably change the results generated using the religious salience index.

17. Robert Wuthnow, *The Restructuring of American Religion: Society and Faith since World War II* (Princeton, N.J.: Princeton University Press, 1988); James Davison Hunter, *Culture Wars: The Struggle to Define America* (New York: Basic Books, 1991).

18. Geoffrey Layman, *The Great Divide: Religious and Cultural Conflict in American Party Politics* (New York: Columbia University Press, 2001); Geoffrey C. Layman and Edward G. Carmines, "Cultural Conflict in American Politics: Religious Traditionalism, Postmaterialism, and U.S. Political Behavior," *Journal of Politics* 59, no. 3 (Aug. 1997): 751-77; Geoffrey C. Layman, "Religion and Political Behavior in the United States: The Impact of Beliefs, Affiliations, and Commitment from 1980-1994," *Public Opinion Quarterly* 61, no. 2 (Summer 1997): 288-316; Lyman A. Kellstedt, John C. Green, James L. Guth, and Corwin E. Smidt, "Religious Voting Blocs in the 1992 Elections: The Year of the Evangelical?" *Sociology of Religion* 55, no. 3 (Fall 1994): 307-26.

19. D'Antonio, Davidson, Hoge, and Wallace, *American Catholic Laity*.

20. For some of the more prominent and useful examples, see Glock and Stark, *Religion and Society in Tension*, chapter 5; Rodney Stark and Charles Y. Glock, *American Piety: The Nature of Religious Commitment* (Berkeley, Calif.: University of California Press, 1968), chapters 2-3; Paul Lopatto, *Religion and the Presidential Election* (New York: Praeger, 1985), chapter 2; Lyman A. Kellstedt and John C. Green, "Knowing God's Many People: Denominational Preference and Political Behavior," in *Rediscovering the Religious Factor in American Politics*, ed. David C. Leege and Lyman A. Kellstedt (Armonk, N.Y.: M.E. Sharpe, 1993), 53-71.

21. Many characteristics and beliefs serve to separate mainline and evangelical Protestants. Two of the major dividing points include the insistence among evangelicals that the Bible is the literal word of God and the emphasis of evangelicals on the necessity of a "born-again" experience for personal salvation. For a good discussion of the origins of the division of Protestants into mainline and evangelical camps, see Charles Howard Hopkins, *The Rise of the Social Gospel in American Protestantism, 1865-1915* (New Haven, Conn.: Yale University Press, 1967).

22. For a thorough discussion of this categorization schema, see Kellstedt and Green, "Knowing God's Many People."

23. Jeff Manza and Clem Brooks, "The Religious Factor in U.S. Presidential Elections, 1960-1992," *American Journal of Sociology* 103, no. 1 (July 1997): 42-45; Clem Brooks and Jeff Manza, "Social Cleavages and Political Alignments: U.S. Presidential Elections, 1960 to 1992," *American Sociological Review* 62, no. 6 (Dec. 1997): 939;

Lyman A. Kellstedt, "Evangelicals and Political Realignment," in *Contemporary Evangelical Political Involvement*, ed. Corwin E. Smidt (Lanham, Md.: University Press of America, 1989): 100.

24. For some examples, see Manza and Brooks, "The Religious Factor"; Lyman A. Kellstedt, John C. Green, James L. Guth, and Corwin E. Smidt, "Religious Voting Blocs in the 1992 Election: The Year of the Evangelical?", *Sociology of Religion* 55, no. 3 (Fall 1994): 307-26; Smidt, ed., *Contemporary Evangelical Political Involvement*.

25. The first year that Protestants were differentiated by denomination in the NES was 1960.

26. Manza and Brooks, "The Religious Factor," 44-45, 71.

27. This may be due in some part to the traditional Democratic allegiance of the American South during this time period. Evangelicals were (and continue to be) heavily concentrated in the South. In the 1960s, evangelical Protestants comprised 52 percent of the population in the South (11 states of the Confederacy), compared with only 17 percent in the rest of the nation. The figures for the 1970s were 51 percent and 18 percent, respectively. In the 1960s, the correlation between southern residence and evangelical affiliation was .335 ($p < .0001$), while the figure for the 1970s was .325 ($p < .0001$). It is highly likely that the partisan coloration of the South influenced the partisan allegiance of evangelicals in that region. Evangelicals continue to be heavily concentrated in the South, but the region is of course no longer solidly Democratic in its partisan support.

28. Layman, "Religion and Political Behavior"; Kellstedt, Green, Guth, and Smidt, "Religious Voting Blocs"; Kellstedt, "Evangelicals and Political Realignment"; A. James Reichley, "Religion and the Future of American Politics," *Political Science Quarterly* 101, no. 1 (1986): 23-47.

Chapter Six

Catholic/Protestant Division: A Religious Worldview Explanation

Introduction

At this point in the progression of this endeavor, it may be useful to pause for a moment and take stock of what has been accomplished thus far. First and foremost, it has been established that the traditional divide separating Catholics and Protestants in terms of their electoral behavior has not disappeared. Significant differences continue to exist between these two religious groups with regard to partisan preference in vote choice and identification, with Catholics being more likely than Protestants to support the Democratic Party. This remains true despite the rather dramatic ascent up the socioeconomic ladder Catholics have made since the 1950s. Increases in SES have not turned Catholics into a group that favors Republicans over Democrats, and family income levels do not account for the differences exhibited by the two groups in their support of the Democrats. The application of other demographic controls such as age, gender, Hispanic ethnicity, and religious salience also fail to explain the greater Democratic affinity of Catholics. Nor are the differences a product of increasing differentiation within American Protestantism. Although the electoral behavior of evangelical Protestants is increasingly divergent from that of mainline Protestants, Catholics remain substantially more Democratic than both Protestant groups.

The obvious question that remains to be answered is why. Why do Catholics remain more Democratic than Protestants? If demographic characteristics do not account for the differences in their electoral behavior, what is responsible? I hypothesize that fundamental differences between the two religious traditions account for the differences in electoral behavior that exist between the two groups. These differences result in Catholics and Protestants possessing different societal perspectives or worldviews. In other words, as Greeley so aptly put it,

"Catholics and Protestants see the world differently."[1] I claim that certain characteristics inherent in Catholicism and the worldview it produces, characteristics that are absent or less dominant in Protestantism and the Protestant worldview, result in Catholics being more supportive of the Democratic Party than Protestants. Specifically, I argue that Catholicism tends to promote a worldview that is communal in nature, with an emphasis on equality. On the other hand, Protestantism is marked by a more individualistic perspective, with greater stress placed on individual freedom and liberty.[2] Before investigating this hypothesis, it is first necessary to discuss the role social groups play in influencing individuals' worldviews.

Social Groups and Individual Worldviews

Early research on political behavior assigned a prominent, if not primary, role to social groups. Membership in particular social groups was found to play a key role in individuals' political behavior.[3] Beginning with the studies of the Michigan School, the role of social groups in the study of political behavior gradually began to diminish. The primary focus of political behavior studies shifted to the attitudes and psychological affects possessed by individuals. Social group memberships were relegated to a secondary role in political behavior research, used primarily to derive demographic categories for multivariate analyses.[4]

The Michigan School and the research agenda that it fostered showed conclusively that psychological variables such as affect toward political stimuli and issue positions did have a substantial impact on people's political behavior. However, despite this success scholars were largely unable to answer the perhaps more important question of how individuals developed their attitudes and issue stances.[5] From where did the political beliefs and opinions about public issues of individuals derive?

In an attempt to answer this important question, some academics renewed their interest in social groups. Building largely on the work of social psychologist Henri Tajfel, social scientists posited that perhaps individuals' attitudes and issue positions were derived at least in part from their social identities, defined by Tajfel as "that part of an individual's self-concept which derives from his knowledge of his membership [in] a social group (or groups) together with the value and emotional significance attached to that membership."[6] According to this theory of social categorization as developed by Tajfel and refined by Turner, human beings see themselves as belonging to some groups in society and not to others. This process of social categorization helps individuals to find their place in the world, to define their location in society.[7] At its foundation, social identity theory rests on the central claim that individuals use social group memberships to define themselves.[8] If indeed people define who they are at least in part through the groups they belong to, the claim that individuals' attitudes and issue positions derive at least in part from social group memberships is easy to make.[9]

How does membership in a social group affect individuals' attitudes and beliefs? To some degree, all social groups are marked by a set of norms, rules, and prescriptions about how one ought to think and act in certain situations.[10] Social groups also possess a distinct set of values, or beliefs about the desirability of certain outcomes or results over other possibilities.[11] By accepting membership in a particular social group, the individual also to a certain degree accepts the norms and the values of the group. Group members take these norms and values into consideration when thinking about a certain issue or situation.[12]

As in all areas of human interaction, this process applies to information and events in the political realm. Through this transmission of norms and values, social groups provide their members with a particular "cognitive structure" through which to view the political world, allowing members to simplify and understand the events happening around them.[13] As individuals identify with a particular social group, they increasingly adopt the group's perceptual lens through which to view things political.[14] To a certain degree, members of different groups possess different ways of looking at the political world, different perceptual viewpoints from which to evaluate political events.[15] In the same situation, it is possible that members of different groups will not see the same things as relevant and important, or even see the same reality. These differences in perception become the basis for diverging positions on political issues between groups.[16] In turn, these alternate views based on social identity provide the foundation for differences in political behavior between social groups.[17] When something in the political environment makes these differences relevant, members of different social groups will diverge politically.[18] Simply put, members of different social groups see the political world differently. These variations in perception result in different issue positions and, under the right circumstances, differences in political behavior.

Religious groups are well positioned to perform the cognitive function described above. Religion is fundamentally a group phenomenon.[19] Individuals choose whether or not to belong to a religious organization and, if they choose to do so, which particular denomination to affiliate with. Religious affiliation, signifying an important social group membership for many people, clearly has the potential to be an important component of one's social identity.

As Wilcox and his colleagues relate, religious identity comes primarily from the particular affiliation one chooses and the specific religious doctrine of one's chosen affiliation.[20] By affiliating with a religious group, the individual becomes a member of both a social institution and an interpersonal community, each of which is marked by an accepted set of teachings and a tradition of shared meanings.[21] Religious groups, perhaps more so than most other social groups, have a particular set of norms and values that they attempt to impose on their members.[22] As groups marked by voluntary membership (at least in the United States), churches are especially well suited to the transmission and maintenance of these norms and values.[23] Participation in religious rituals and practices, direct communications from religious elites, observation of environmental surroundings, and social interaction with other group members all contribute to the transmission of group norms and values.[24] Through various means, the importance of adherence to these norms and values is also reiterated and enforced on a regular basis.[25]

As discussed earlier, this transmission of group norms and values can under certain circumstances play a role in the political realm. Perhaps because of the nature of religion, religious groups have a unique ability to bring attention to a political matter or confer legitimacy on a specific political action.[26] Multiple studies have shown that religious identities do play a significant role in political attitudes and behaviors.[27] Certainly it is plausible—indeed highly possible—to claim that in some instances religious group membership influences the political attitudes and behaviors of individuals.

The above discussion raises two questions that are of fundamental importance to this analysis. First, do Catholicism and Protestantism significantly influence the worldviews of their members? Second, could these respective worldviews contribute to the observed differences between Catholic and Protestant electoral behavior?

A Catholic Ethic?

As social scientists, we are all familiar with the concept of the Protestant Ethic. As characterized by Weber, the Protestant Ethic places a heavy emphasis on the salvational qualities of work, elevating it to the status of a divine calling. In the course of pursuing this calling, the Protestant Ethic encourages the individual to be ambitious in seeking personal wealth and achievement. Independence and self-reliance are highly valued personal attributes.[28] Despite repeated references to elements of the Protestant Ethic that are lacking in other non-Protestant, notably Catholic, societies, Weber never offers a fully developed opposite or alternative to the Protestant Ethic.[29] Throughout the long, voluminous research tradition that Weber has spawned, very little scholarly effort has been devoted to the possible existence of the Protestant Ethic's alternative, an alternative that might be called the Catholic Ethic.[30]

One scholar however, has endeavored to explore the primary alternative to Weber's Protestant Ethic. In his book, *The Catholic Ethic in American Society*, John Tropman argues that a Catholic Ethic does indeed exist alongside its more familiar Protestant counterpart. Moreover, Tropman suggests that the values contained in the two ethics are in many instances fundamentally opposed.[31]

One of the primary areas in which the two ethics are opposed, according to Tropman, is the phenomenon of work. As noted above, the Protestant Ethic sees work as a divine calling. Work is a sacred duty, with important consequences for ultimate salvation. The Catholic Ethic too sees work as important, but for different reasons. Under the Catholic Ethic, work is important because it is human beings who are doing it. The person is special, not the work itself. Work is good because it provides the necessary means for fulfilling human needs, but it has no divine element. Work does not have "transformative" properties; it does not play a role in determining salvation. Work is the way to attain those things needed in order to exist; nothing more and nothing less.

The Protestant Ethic views work as an individual activity. Because of its salvational properties, work is to be engaged in by the individual for the benefit of the individual. The worker is entitled to keep whatever he or she makes, and the worker alone is entitled to make decisions about the use of the products of his or her work. Under the Catholic Ethic, work has important social aspects. Work is engaged in not only for oneself, but for others as well. The products of work do not belong to the worker alone; the worker's family and the worker's community also have valid claims on fruits of the worker's labor. Simply put, work is individualistic in the Protestant Ethic, communal in the Catholic Ethic.[32]

The characteristics that distinguish the Catholic Ethic from the Protestant Ethic with regard to work also serve to differentiate the two ethics in general. With its special emphasis on achievement, accomplishment, and self-reliance, the Protestant Ethic is at its foundation individualistic in nature. On the contrary, the Catholic Ethic has at its core a value Tropman terms "sharing." "What *sharing* means is not only the willingness to help others, but the obligation to do so. It conveys a sense of equality between sharers. As a culture of sharing, the Catholic Ethic contains a sense that sharing is part of a natural and expected exchange."[33] This sense of duty toward others results in a communal outlook being fostered under the Catholic Ethic.

Is Tropman correct? Does Catholicism promote a communal outlook among its adherents, while Protestantism tends to result in a more individualistic worldview among its followers? Certainly, this is not a new claim. It has long been recognized that a primary element of Protestantism is its individualistic view of society, a view that promotes the independence of the individual. At the same time, Catholicism tends to take a more collectivist or communal view of society, resulting in a more social outlook on human relations.[34] Greeley describes how Protestantism encourages people to relate to God as individuals, while Catholicism calls on its members to experience God as a member of a group.[35] Wuthnow too discusses the tendency of Protestantism to place more emphasis on the spiritual growth of individuals rather than communities. He also noted that Catholicism is much more likely to cultivate communal ties among its members than is Protestantism.[36] Along the same lines, Stark and Glock found that with regards to criteria for salvation, Catholics were more likely to emphasize behavior in relationships between human beings than were Protestants, while Protestants showed greater concern for the relationship of the individual to God.[37]

These signs all point to the existence of a fundamental difference between the worldviews of Catholicism and Protestantism. The Protestant worldview is at its heart individualistic, both in the manner it encourages its followers to relate to God and in the way it guides its adherents in the conduct of their everyday lives. And the Catholic worldview is at its foundation communal in nature, in both the way it instructs its members to relate with the divine and interact with their fellow human beings.

From its very onset, Catholic theology and practice have stressed the responsibility of human beings to assist those around them.[38] Followers of the Catholic worldview are constantly reminded that they have obligations to people other than themselves. In the words of Rembert G. Weakland, Archbishop of Milwaukee, "Self-interest cannot stand alone in Catholic thought. It cannot be dissociated from love of God and love of neighbor. In fact, love of neighbor becomes the first criterion for love of God. In this perspective, cooperation becomes as strong a motive as competition."[39] The Catholic worldview places a heavy emphasis on concern for others. This emphasis on concern for others is illustrated in the results of a 1978 survey conducted by Gallup. The survey asked respondents how they believed a person gained entrance to heaven. Forty-three percent of Catholics said that heaven was a reward for those who lived "a good life," as opposed to only twenty percent for Protestants. The same study found that 59 percent of Protestants believed the only way to enter heaven was through a "personal faith in Jesus Christ," double the percentage of Catholics who felt this way. As Gallup and Castelli stated, these findings clearly lend some credibility to the stereotype that Catholics believe salvation is achieved through good works while Protestants believe it is attained through faith.[40] These findings also point to the existence of a communal worldview produced by Catholicism and an individualistic worldview that results from Protestantism.

If a Catholic Ethic does indeed exist, where should one look to find the substance and specifics of this ethic? Certainly the Catholic Ethic can be found in the fundamental principles of the church itself. As McBrien relates in his classic text, Catholicism is in many ways characterized by three key principles. These principles also serve to separate Catholicism from Protestantism. The first of these principles is sacramentality. In the words of Pope Paul VI, a sacrament is "a reality imbued with the hidden presence of God."[41] Possession of such a sacramental perspective means that the presence of God exists in all things. For Catholics then, all reality is sacred because everything in the temporal world is marked by the presence of God. This view stands in stark opposition to the Protestant view of reality, which sees God and the sacred as separated from human existence. For Protestants, God is seen as "totally other," and therefore not present in the temporal world.

The second key principle of Catholicism is mediation. This principle holds that sacramental practices not only serve as symbols of God's presence, but that they also invoke God's presence. Performance of sacramental rites result in encounters with God that result in turn in God actually achieving some purpose for those participating in the sacrament. Again, this view sharply contrasts with the Protestant view, which holds that God can only be encountered through the inner-consciousness of individual believers.

The third, and perhaps most important key principle of Catholicism is communion. For Catholics, the only way to God is as part of a community of believers. Even when the individual relationship with God is at its most personal, such as individual biblical reflection or engaging in the sacrament of confession, the element of community is still present. In the case of biblical reflection, the individual is using the basis of the church's original faith as the focus of reflection. During confession, the individual is relating to God through the medium of an ordained priest, the local leader of his or her faith community, and a representative of the larger faith community to which the individual belongs. For Protestants, the individual engages in a one-on-one relationship with God. No participation from other elements or believers of the larger community is required.

These Catholic principles, and their differences from Protestant principles, all shed light on the existence of the Catholic Ethic, and its juxtaposition to the Protestant Ethic. For Catholics, God is present in everyday occurrences and encounters. Engaging in sacramental rites brings one in contact with God through relationships with other people. Under Catholic belief, God relates to the faithful, and the faithful to God, as members of a community of believers. Outside of this community, encounter with God is impossible. For Protestants, God is largely separate from the everyday world. Believers relate to God as individuals, and encounters with God necessarily do not involve the participation of others.[42] These distinctions serve as the basis for the different worldviews possessed by Catholics and Protestants.

A more specified account of the Catholic Ethic may be found in the social thought and teaching of the Catholic Church. As McBrien states, the social teaching of the church is perhaps the best expression of the fundamental perspective of Catholicism.[43] Disseminated primarily in the form of papal encyclicals and the documents of the Second Vatican Council, Catholic social teaching comprises a major component of the Catholic Ethic.[44] To many, the phrase "Catholic social teaching" immediately conjures thoughts of the church's pronouncements regarding human sexuality, particularly the issues of contraception and abortion.[45] While it is true that the church is very concerned with these issues, believing that they make up the sum of Catholic social teaching would be a mistake. There is more to Catholic social teaching than sex.[46] Catholic social thought covers a remarkably broad range of the issues confronting modern society. "Based on scripture, tradition, and reason," Catholic social teaching "carefully explain[s] a number of basic concepts as guides for understanding the relation between Christianity and the political order, and for rightly judging social, political, and economic phenomena."[47]

The use of the word "judging" in the above quotation is important. The Catholic Church promulgates its social thought in an attempt to provide its members with a basis for making decisions and taking actions. This alone makes the church's social teaching a key source to consult when discussing the Catholic worldview. There is, however, another reason why examining Catholic social thought can prove useful in delineating the Catholic Ethic. The images of how society is and how it should be that are presented in the body of Catholic teaching are the products of Catholic minds. These images therefore have the potential to provide substantial insight into the perspective from which Catholics view the world.[48] The next section of this chapter will provide an in-depth look at the

Catholic Church's social teaching with an eye toward what this teaching can reveal about the Catholic Ethic.

The Social Thought and Teaching of the Catholic Church

Papal encyclicals are letters written by the Pope for public dissemination. They have traditionally been directly addressed to all the bishops of the church, and indirectly to all Catholics worldwide.[49] Since the decision of Pope Benedict XIV in 1740 to devote greater attention to the promulgation of encyclicals, 290 letters by 17 popes have been issued.[50] While the encyclicals cover a very diverse array of topics, the principal concern of this discussion will be those encyclicals whose content focuses on social issues.

While Schuck found elements of social concern throughout the entirety of encyclical letters dating back to 1740,[51] modern Catholic social thought is generally acknowledged to have begun with the issuance of *Rerum Novarum (The Condition of Labor)* by Pope Leo XIII in 1891.[52] The world of the late nineteenth century had changed dramatically from the situation that existed at the beginning or even in the middle of the century. The industrial revolution was in full swing in Western Europe and the nonsouthern United States. The traditional agricultural economy was well into the process of being replaced by an economy driven by business and industry. The population distribution was rapidly shifting from rural to urban, as people left the farms en masse for the jobs and the economic possibilities offered by cities. Society was changing from traditional to modern.

All of these rapid changes resulted in a state of flux combined with high levels of uncertainty. People thrust into the midst of a new type of society were searching for answers and guidance. For those Catholics among the searchers, a natural place for them to turn for direction was their church. However, many members of the church hierarchy were equally unsure of where the church stood on many of the emerging issues of the day. These concerns were in many ways new ones to which the church had not yet given much thought. One of the primary areas of concern and uncertainty was labor and labor-related issues. Socialist movements were developing all across Europe. In the United States, labor unions were forming, with many Catholics in their ranks. Where did the church stand on these matters? Laity wanted to know from their clergy, the clergy wanted to know from their bishops, and the bishops wanted answers from the church hierarchy in the Vatican. Where did the church position herself in regards to workers and labor-related concerns that were arising in the midst of the new economy resulting from industrial capitalism?[53]

Pope Leo XIII attempted to answer these questions in *Rerum Novarum*. From the very outset of the encyclical, Leo made it clear that the church was placing itself on the side of the poor and the workers in society.[54] "Some remedy must be found, and quickly found, for the misery and wretchedness which press so heavily at this moment on the large majority of the very poor. . . . Workingmen have been given over, isolated and defenseless, to the callousness of employers and the greed of unrestrained competition."[55] Leo provided the stamp of church approval to labor unions, going so far as calling on the state to protect the right of workers to organize.[56] If employers would not provide fair labor hours, restrictions on child labor, and just wages for workers on their own, then the state was obligated to intervene on behalf of workers.[57] The Pope also assigned to the state the duty to intervene in society in the interests of the poor.[58] "Justice . . . demands that the interests of the poorer population be carefully watched over by the administration [the State], so that they who contribute so largely to the advantage of the community may themselves share in the benefits they create."[59] While staunchly defending the right to private property and condemning the socialist idea of all property held in common, Leo placed an important qualification on individuals' property rights. No person had the right to use private property against the common good of the community.[60] One must consider the situation of others when making decisions about the use of one's property. "No one is commanded to distribute to others that which is required for his own necessities and those of his household; nor even to give away what is reasonably required to keep up becomingly in his condition of life; 'for no one ought to live unbecomingly.' But when necessity has been supplied, and one's position fairly considered, it is a duty to give to the indigent out of that which is left over."[61]

Rerum Novarum presented a powerful, perhaps even radical message, especially when one considers the historical frame in which it was written.[62] In the words of Dorr, the encyclical represented a "strong protest against the prevailing order."[63] Leo asserted that the common good was the primary concern of any community, in terms of the organization of both social and economic relationships. Perhaps more important, Leo placed the obligation of establishing and protecting this common good squarely on the shoulders of government.[64] *Rerum Novarum* represented the beginning of modern Catholic social teaching, providing a solid and lasting foundation upon which later church social teaching could and would build.[65] A successor to Leo as pope, Pius XI, went so far as to call *Rerum Novarum* "the Magna Charta on which all Christian activities in social matters are ultimately based,"[66] a sentiment that more recent observers have consistently echoed.[67] An examination of how Catholic social teaching developed in the wake of this influential document, and of how this teaching relates to the Catholic Ethic, is now in order.

The next major official document of Catholic social teaching to appear was *Quadragesimo Anno (After Forty Years)*, issued by Pope Pius XI in 1931. Prepared in honor of the fortieth anniversary of *Rerum Novarum*, *Quadragesimo Anno* not only reiterated the important principles laid out in the previous social encyclical, it expanded on them and raised them to a higher plane. While *Rerum Novarum* did contain ideas that were quite radical for its day, its ultimate goal was the reform of society and its institutions. *Quadragesimo Anno*, on the other hand, was revolutionary in spirit, calling for a radical reordering of many aspects of society.[68] Although following in the footsteps of *Rerum Novarum* with a strong defense of private property, the overall theme of *Quadragesimo Anno* was a condemnation of laissez-faire capitalism.[69] It is helpful to quote Pius at length on this point:

> The proper ordering of economic affairs cannot be left to the free play of rugged competition. From this source as from a polluted spring have proceeded all the errors of the 'individualistic' school. This school, forgetful or ignorant of the social and moral aspect of economic activities, regarded these as completely free and immune from any intervention by public authority, for they would have in the market place and in unregulated competition a principle of self-direction more suitable for guiding them than any created intellect which might intervene. Free competition, however, though justified and quite useful within certain limits, cannot be an adequate controlling principle in economic affairs.[70]

By insisting that the proper ordering of economic life could not be left to free competition, Pius was rejecting one of the central tenets of capitalism.[71] Capitalism itself was not evil according to Pius, but became so when it ignored "the human dignity of the workers, the social character of economic life, social justice, and the common good."[72] Asserting the right and the duty of the church to speak authoritatively on economic and social issues,[73] Pius reiterated the call of Leo in placing the responsibility for ensuring that property was used for the common good on the government.[74] "Wealth . . . which is constantly being augmented by social and economic progress, must be distributed among the various individuals and classes of society that the common good of all . . . be thereby promoted. . . . Each class, then, must receive its due share, and the distribution of created goods must be brought into conformity with the demands of the common good and social justice."[75]

It is in the section of *Quadragesimo Anno* quoted above that the phrase "social justice" makes its first appearance in Vatican social teaching. Those even the least bit familiar with Catholic social thought are aware of the importance and emphasis the church currently assigns to the concept represented by this phrase. Its introduction, then, by Pius XI in *Quadragesimo Anno* stands as one of the most important accomplishments of both the Pope and his encyclical letter. What is the meaning of this concept? As Novak notes, what Pius means by "social justice" is never clearly defined in the course of *Quadragesimo Anno*.[76] Pius is, however, consistent throughout the encyclical in associating the concept with the responsibility of both individual citizens and the government to create a society in which the fostering of the common good is the primary goal.[77] These two ideas, the common good and social justice, are two of the most important concepts of the Catholic worldview, as further examination of Catholic social teaching will show.

The social teaching contained in *Rerum Novarum* and *Quadragesimo Anno* focused largely on the relationship between labor and capital in a capitalist economy, primarily in Europe and the United States.[78] This changed somewhat beginning with the social encyclicals of Pope John XXIII (1958-1963). The concepts of social justice and the common good retained their places of central importance, as did the concern with fair and just treatment of workers. But beginning with John, the scope of papal and church concern begins to widen.[79] Calls for political rights and civil liberties join economic rights as demands the church places on the state and society. Pope John XXIII begins his 1963 encyclical *Pacem in Terris (Peace on Earth)* with a detailed list of the rights of all human beings. Economic rights that had been spelled out in previous papal encyclicals such as the freedom to work, the right to a just wage, and the right to private property are joined on the Pope's list by political rights such as the right to participate in public affairs and the guarantee of legal protection of one's rights. Civil liberties such as freedoms of association and assembly and freedom of religion are also included.[80] Pope John Paul II reiterates and expands on these rights in the encyclical *Centesimus Annus (On the Hundredth Anniversary of Rerum Novarum)*.[81]

Another aspect of the church's broadened area of concern is the level of society to which its teachings are devoted. The obligation of constructing a society based on social justice and the common good, previously focused at the level of individual nations, expands and becomes international in scope.[82] National, and even local level concerns are still discussed and considered important, but they are now accompanied by pronouncements directed at how the nations of the world should relate to and interact with each other. In *Mater et Magistra (Christianity and Social Progress)* John XXIII devotes extensive attention to the obligation of the wealthy nations to provide assistance to the poor nations[83] and to the need for international cooperation in a world that was becoming more and more interdependent.[84] Pope Paul VI continues and expands upon John XXIII's international focus in *Populorum Progressio (On the Development of the Peoples)*, calling for greater aid from rich to poor nations, the development of a "World Fund" (which would use money saved from the reduction of the arms race to aid the poor of the world), and the establishment of fairness in world trade relations.[85] In celebration of the twentieth anniversary of *Populorum Progressio*, Pope John Paul II devotes considerable attention to the issue of international development in *Sollicitudo Rei Socialis (On Social Concern)*. In this document, John Paul cites the general lack of progress in the area of international development that has been made in the past twenty years along with the growing divide in wealth that exists between nations, specifically assigning a good portion of the blame to the more developed nations of the world.[86]

Perhaps the most important development in Catholic social teaching beginning with Pope John XXIII is a change in tone. Messages about the necessity of the common good become more strident. Calls for social justice are much more demanding. Consider the following evolution of Catholic social thought. In both *Rerum Novarum* and *Quadragesimo Anno*, the faithful were directed to assist the poor with their own resources.[87] However, the individual need only contribute out of what they do not need in order "to keep up becomingly his condition of life"[88] and "to live as becomes his station."[89] In *Gaudium et Spes (Pastoral Constitution on the Church in the Modern World)*, the church through the body of the Second Vatican Council issued a much more demanding teaching regarding assistance to the poor. "Men are obliged to come to the relief of the poor, and to do so not merely out of their superfluous goods." The document continues, "A man should regard his lawful possessions not merely as his own but also as common property in the sense that they should accrue to the benefit of not only himself but of others. . . . The right to have a share of earthly goods sufficient for oneself and one's family belongs to everyone.[90] Paul VI builds on this idea in *Populorum Progressio*: "Private property does not constitute for anyone an absolute and unconditioned right. No one is justified in keeping for his exclusive use what he does not need, when others lack necessities."[91]

Further examples of the church's more demanding calls for social justice and the common good abound in the Catholic social teaching of the last forty years. Governments are consistently reminded that the sole reason for their existence is the realization and fostering of the common good.[92] At both the national and international level, governments are called on to reduce the large disparities in wealth that exist between people and nations.[93] Paul VI goes so far as to call on rich nations to place their "superfluous wealth at the service of poor nations."[94] The primary work of governments must be to create a common good that can be shared by all people and by all nations.[95]

The laity too are urged to take action to promote social justice and the common good.[96] They are told to "conform their activity to the teachings and norms of the church in social matters,"[97] and to examine their own consciences with regard to these teachings when making decisions about public policy regarding social matters.[98] The church reminds its members that all private property has a "social mortgage," and that they have a duty to create a "preferential option for the poor" in their decisions and actions.[99] The laity are warned against possessing an individualistic morality, and told they are required to contribute to and work for the common good for all members of society.[100] In the words of Pope John Paul II: "Sacred scripture continually speaks to us of an active commitment to our neighbor and demands of us a shared responsibility for all of humanity. This duty is not limited to one's own family, nation or state, but extends progressively to all mankind, since no one can consider himself extraneous or indifferent to the lot of another member of the human family. No one can say that he is not responsible for the well-being of his brother or sister."[101] The person who ignores or neglects his or her duties towards others "jeopardizes his eternal salvation."[102] With regard to social issues, the collective mind of the Vatican is clearly focused on achieving social justice and the common good for all of humanity.

Some may wonder how aware individual Catholics are with regard to the social teaching emanating from the Vatican. Certainly it is not common practice for Catholics to spend their leisure time studying papal encyclicals. However, it is not only through papal and Vatican documents that American Catholics receive the social teaching of the church. The American Catholic bishops regularly issue statements dealing with particular policy areas and issues. In these statements, the bishops do not engage in the creation of new social thought, but rather seek to apply existing Catholic social teaching to specific areas of concern in American society. The American bishops have issued statements on such diverse matters as human rights in foreign nations, the military draft, nuclear weapons, the rights of farm workers, government aid to parochial schools, racism, and national health insurance.[103] In their statements, the bishops pay special attention to the idea of social justice, speaking often about social and economic equality. The bishops prepare these statements for the guidance of both individual Catholics and government policymakers.[104]

Perhaps the most familiar of the bishops' statements was the 1986 pastoral letter *Economic Justice for All*. This document offers what can only be called a scathing critique of the American economy and economic system, along with the society created by this system. The letter touches on almost every one of the aspects of Catholic social teaching discussed earlier in this section. The central importance of social justice and the common good are discussed throughout the letter, with the bishops making these concerns the primary basis on which an economy should be judged.[105] The bishops remind their audience that the most important function of government is the creation of the common good.[106] In the United States, the government is failing in this role. Wealth is too unevenly distributed.[107] There are far too many people in poverty for so rich a nation.[108] Many Americans are unable to even participate in the nation's economy.

The bishops also find fault with individual Americans. They are reminded that social justice and the common good require them to assist the poor in society. Citizens are called on to think and act differently, with the goal of improving the condition of life for all members of American society.[109] "The precarious economic situation of so many people and so many families calls for examination of U.S. economic arrangements. Christian conviction and the American promise of liberty and justice for all give the poor and the vulnerable a special claim on the nation's concern. They also challenge all members of the Church to help build a more just society."[110]

In addition to issuing collective letters, the individual bishops also write letters to the churches in their dioceses on a regular basis. These letters, often addressing some element of Catholic social teaching, are read by priests to parishioners during Mass. The bishops also compose pamphlets, such as *Faithful Citizenship*, which are distributed to churchgoers at services. Although this document will be discussed in the next chapter with regard to its emphasis on the issue of abortion, it also covers many other issues as well. Discussing such topics as the option for the poor, the rights of workers, and pursuing social justice, this document succinctly presents the fundamentals of Catholic social teachings to parishioners.[111] In addition, the priests who officiate at Mass each week are well schooled in Catholic social thought and teaching. Priests impart this knowledge to parishioners during the course of the homilies they deliver each week. Therefore, while it is quite likely that individual Catholics know very little about the key documents of Catholic social teaching, it is highly likely that they have been exposed to the teaching's basic principles on multiple occasions.

This examination of Catholic social thought has revealed that there is substantial evidence for asserting that Catholicism promotes a communal outlook among its adherents. The teaching of the church has consistently railed against unregulated capitalism and rampant individual self-interest in economic affairs.[112] Every pope since Leo XIII has insisted on the social nature of private property.[113] Using the words of Pope John Paul II: "Christian tradition has never upheld this right [to private property] as absolute and untouchable. On the contrary, it has always understood this right within the broader context of the right common to all to use the goods of the whole of creation: The right to private property is subordinated to the right to common use, to the fact that goods are meant for everyone."[114] In Catholic social teaching, the primary means for judging the justness of a society is the extent to which it provides and protects the rights of its citizens—not only political rights, but economic and social rights as well.[115]

The teachings of the church regarding social justice and the common good have become stronger and more intense since the pontificate of John XXIII, developing to the point where anyone with even limited knowledge of the ideological spectrum could correctly identify Catholic social teaching as extremely liberal.[116] In fact, the very first encyclical of John XXIII, *Mater et Magistra*, was so liberal that noted conservative (and Catholic) political commentator William F. Buckley responded "Mother, yes; teacher, no" to the encyclical's literal translation of "Mother and Teacher."[117] Since Vatican II, the church has placed increased importance on the connection of social justice to the mission it sees itself as having inherited from Jesus Christ.[118] More than other any ideas, concerns with social justice and the common good characterize Catholic social teaching, signifying the communal view of human society possessed by the Catholic Church.[119]

The Potential for Electoral Impact: American Political Parties and Concerns for Social Justice and the Common Good

The previous section examined in detail the tendency of Catholicism to promote a communal and egalitarian outlook, an outlook that is reflected in the emphasis Catholic social thought places on social justice and the common good. Given the earlier discussion of social group influences on individual behavior, it is possible that the social teaching of the church affects the electoral behavior of American Catholics. However, in order for Catholic social thought to produce an effect in the electoral arena, the major political parties must provide alternatives relating to the substance of Catholic teaching. Put simply, the parties must take differing positions in regard to issues relating to the broad themes of social justice and the common good. Indeed, the parties do differ in such a manner. On matters of social justice and the common good writ large, significant differences exist between the Democrats and the Republicans.

These differences are evident in many ways. Perhaps the most basic lies in the very different attitudes, beliefs, and sentiments that characterize each party. At their cores, the Democrats and Republicans possess political cultures that are quite distinct from one another.[120] Democrats present themselves as a party welcoming of all peoples and groups in American society, with a special emphasis on being the party of the common person.[121] The Democratic Party casts itself as the party of the outsiders, representing the interests of those on the periphery of American society. In the eyes of the Democrats, all Americans can find a political home under their banner. The Democratic Party is a party of groups, organized in a manner that is "pluralistic and polycentric." A sense of collectivism surrounds the party, both in the way it conducts its business and in the policies it promotes. Power is widely dispersed in the Democratic Party, with each of the many groups it includes having at least some opportunity to influence the direction and leadership of the party. In the party, power flows from the bottom up, theoretically at least enabling all of the diverse constituencies contained in the Democratic fold to have some input in the affairs and direction of the party.

The Republican Party, on the other hand, is not a party of groups, at least not in the sense that the Democrats are. The groups that make up the GOP are geographical units or ideological factions, not constituency groups based on sociodemographic characteristics. For Republicans, theirs is a party of individuals, not of groups. In the Republican Party power flows from the top down, with leadership dictating party positions and controlling party affairs. Whereas the Democrats see themselves as the voice of society's outsiders, Republicans view themselves as representing America's "insiders." They are the party of those at the center of American life and society.[122] Republicans pride themselves on being the party of true, responsible Americans, representing what Rossiter calls people of "standing and sobriety."[123]

Differences between the parties relating to concerns with social justice and the common good are also evident in the platforms that the parties put forth every four years at their national conventions. As Ginsberg states, party platforms represent "the principles, attitudes, appeals and concerns of the party as a whole."[124] Relying heavily on party platforms, Gerring in his impressive study of party ideologies from 1828 to 1996 finds that the two major American parties have consistently presented different values, beliefs, and issue positions to the American electorate.[125] For the majority of the twentieth century, these values, beliefs, and issue positions have been marked by consistent similarities within each party, and consistent differences between each party. For Republicans, the message presented has been first and foremost one of individualism.[126] In the words of Calvin Coolidge, the philosophy of the Republican Party was "protecting the freedom of the individual, of guarding his earnings, his home, his life."[127] In protecting this freedom, the Republican aim was to keep the individual free from government intervention and interference in all aspects of American life. Republicans view the state with suspicion, if not a touch of fear, ever wary of its encroachment into the lives of citizens.[128] For at least the last eighty years, individual initiative and freedom from government interference have been the watchwords of the Republican Party.

For the Democrats, the central message the party has conveyed to the electorate has been one of egalitarianism. Beginning with the first presidential campaign of William Jennings Bryan, the party has stressed the right of citizens to enjoy equality in economic matters. Over the last 100 years, Gerring finds that the Democratic Party has been strongly committed to social welfare policies and forms of wealth redistribution to assist the less fortunate classes in American society. Unlike the Republicans, Democrats were more than willing to use the coercive power of the state, particularly the national government, to advance their agenda for American society.[129] Beginning in the 1950s, the Democrats also added a call for inclusion to their overall message. In much the same manner as they had with immigrant groups in the early twentieth century, the Democrats gradually reached out to marginalized groups in society, attempting to bring these groups into the Democratic coalition by speaking to and representing their concerns. Democratic calls for equality came to mean more than economic equality, asking for social and political equality as well.[130] Again, the Democrats saw the power of the state as the primary means for achieving their goals.

Differences between the Democrats and the Republicans can also be detected in the public policies advocated by each party. The Democratic Party's emphasis on equality and fairness is evident in the party's calls for universal health care, higher taxes for the wealthy, increased spending on public education, and specific programs designed to assist minorities and the poor in society. The Republicans' fundamental concern of individualism can be seen in the party's consistent advocacy of decreased taxes, opposition to social welfare programs, and calls for more individual choice and less government involvement in many areas, including education and health care.[131] The identities of America's two major political parties, as defined by their internal cultures and political platforms, are also clearly present in the public policies they pursue.

Perhaps these differences between the parties can be best illustrated by examining each party's descriptions of who they are and what they stand for. The "Democratic Party Credo" states: "At the heart of our party lies a fundamental conviction, that Americans must not only be free, but they must live in a fair society. We believe it is the responsibility of government to help us achieve this fair society." Following this statement, the Credo lists a number of party beliefs related to the goals of equality and inclusion.[132] On the other hand, *The Republican Oath* contains the following statement: "I believe that good government is based on the individual and that each person's ability, dignity, freedom and responsibility must be honored and recognized. I believe that free enterprise and the encouragement of individual initiative and incentive have given this nation an economic system second to none."[133] In light of these statements, there is clearly some legitimacy in labeling the central message of the Republican Party one of "individual success" while describing the Democratic counterpart as one of "fairness."[134]

The above discussion shows that important differences exist between the parties on concerns relating to social justice and the common good. However, as important as these differences are, they will have no impact on electoral behavior unless they are perceived by the electorate. In the form of research relating to party images—substantive mental pictures an individual has about the political parties[135]—within the electorate, strong evidence exists that voters are in fact aware of these fundamental differences between the parties. As far back as the 1950s, the Democrats were firmly established in the public mind as the party of the common person and the party favoring government intervention in the economy. At the same time, the GOP was viewed as the party favorable to business, the wealthy, and free markets.[136] In his study of party images from 1952 to 1972, Trilling found that substantive party images did indeed exist within the electorate. Among other findings, Trilling reported that the Democrats were commonly seen by voters as the party of the common person, while the Republicans were identified as the party of business and the upper class.[137]

More recent research shows that these party images have only become stronger and more prevalent since the 1970s. Examining party images from 1976 to 1992, Baumer and Gold found that roughly two-thirds of voters possess substantive images of the two parties, a figure that has risen even higher over the last ten years. These images are also distinct, as very few respondents feel that the parties are similar to each other. The Democrats are seen as the party of the common people and the less affluent. They are more likely to promote social welfare spending and government intervention in the economy. In the eyes of the electorate, the Democratic Party is the party of equality, inclusiveness, social change, and liberalism. The electorate's image of the GOP is almost a complete opposite of the Democratic image. The Republicans are the party of individualism. They represent the interests of the affluent and business, and are more likely to protect property rights. The Republicans are against social welfare spending and government intervention in the economy, and for conservatism in general.[138] These images clearly correlate with the identities of the parties as expressed in their political cultures and platforms as described above. As stated by Baumer and Gold, the images of parties held by the electorate indicate that most voters clearly understand the different values and policies represented by the two parties.[139]

Do Differences between the Catholic and Protestant-Worldviews Matter for Issue Positions and Party Support? An Empirical Test

Thus far, this chapter has presented the argument that identification with the Catholic Church results in individuals possessing a different worldview than the one held by individuals who identify themselves as members of a Protestant church. The primary differences between these worldviews are a more communal outlook marked by a primary concern with equality for Catholics and an individualistic perspective focused on freedom for Protestants. I have hypothesized that these differences in worldviews produce different attitudes about public issues for Catholics and Protestants, resulting in differences in the electoral behavior between the two religious groups.

At this point these hypotheses are nothing more than informed conjecture. Only claims have been made. No evidence has been offered. In the final section of this chapter I will attempt to present such evidence. I do not expect to see extremely large differences between Catholics and Protestants on political issues. Certainly many factors other than religious affiliation affect individuals' political attitudes. Also, as Tropman makes clear, it is highly unlikely that any American possesses a "pure" Protestant or Catholic Ethic. It is almost certain that each person has a mixture of both.[140] I do however expect that Catholics and Protestants will tend to see issues somewhat differently, and that these differences will be substantial enough to produce some distinction in electoral behavior between the two groups.[141] With these caveats in mind, I turn to an empirical examination.

While in theory conducting an empirical test such as the one described above may sound simple and straightforward enough, the reality of carrying out such a task is far more difficult. The NES does not ask respondents about their perspectives on human society. Nor does it contain specific questions about social justice and the common good. However, while the NES does not contain questions on the exact subjects of interest here, it does include a few questions that may be construed as tapping into elements of social justice and the common good on a more general level. Since the NES is the best available source of Americans' attitudes on social and political issues over an extended period of time, I will conduct analyses using the few questions that are available in an effort to determine if Catholics and Protestants differ in their views on these matters.

One question that taps into concerns for social justice and the common good is whether government has the responsibility to provide its citizens with jobs and a decent standard of living. Such a question clearly relates to the earlier discussed positions of the church that it is government's responsibility to look out for the poor in society and promote the general welfare of all. It also relates nicely with Catholic teachings about work. Do Catholics and Protestants possess different views on this matter? Table 6.1 provides the answer to this question.

Table 6.1: Positions on Whether Government Should Guarantee Individuals Jobs and a Good Standard of Living, Catholics and Protestants, Whites Only, by Decade, 1950s-1990s

	Yes, Government Should			No, Government Should Not		
Dec.	Cath.	Prot.	Diff.	Cath.	Prot.	Diff.
1950s	73	62	11	27	38	-11
1960s	50	41	9	50	59	-9
1970s	28	21	7	49	55	-6
1980s	29	23	6	47	55	-8
1990s	30	24	6	46	53	-7

Note: In the 1950s and 1960s, respondents were asked if they agreed or disagreed that government should provide jobs for all who wanted to work. Beginning in 1970, respondents were asked to position themselves on a 7-point scale, with 1 being in favor of government seeing to it that everyone had a job and a good standard of living and 7 being in favor of government letting each person get ahead on his or her own. Those who responded 1, 2, or 3 were coded as supporting government guaranteeing jobs and a good standard of living, those who responded 4 were coded as neutral (not reported here), and those who responded 5, 6, or 7 were coded as opposed to government guaranteeing jobs and standards of living. Obviously, opinions on standards of living apply only from the 1970s-1990s. Chi-squares and significance levels (1950s and 1960s with 1 degree of freedom and 1970s, 1980s, and 1990s with 2 degrees of freedom) for each decade are as follows: 1950s = chi-square of 19.91 and p-value of <.0001. 1960s = chi-square of 18.08 and p-value of <.0001. 1970s = chi-square of 33.58 and p-value of <.0001. 1980s = chi-square of 34.91 and p-value of <.0001. 1990s = chi-square of 35.86 and p-value of <.0001. Source: NES Cumulative File, vcf0128, vcf0808, and vcf0809.

The results presented in table 6.1 show that Catholics and Protestants do indeed differ in their opinions on this issue. While since the 1960s, in neither religious group, does a majority believe that it is government's responsibility to provide citizens with jobs and good standards of living, Catholics are more likely than Protestants to agree that government should perform these functions. A similar pattern emerges when the opinions of Catholics and Protestants on whether or not government should provide health care to its citizens are examined. Table 6.2 presents these results.

106   Chapter Six

Table 6.2: Positions on Whether Government Should be Involved in Providing Health Care to Individuals, Catholics and Protestants, Whites Only, by Decade, 1950s-1990s

	Yes, Government Should			No, Government Should Not		
Decade	**Cath.**	**Prot.**	**Diff.**	**Cath.**	**Prot.**	**Diff.**
1950s	75	61	14	25	39	-14
1960s	73	61	12	27	39	-12
1970s	53	35	18	35	50	-15
1980s	43	35	8	37	45	-8
1990s	45	36	9	35	41	-6

Note: In the 1950s and 1960s, respondents were asked if they agreed or disagreed that government ought to help people get doctors and hospital care at low cost. Beginning in 1970, respondents were asked to position themselves on a 7-point scale, with 1 being in favor of a complete government insurance plan for healthcare and 7 being in favor of a completely private healthcare plan. Those who responded 1, 2, or 3 were coded as supporting government involvement in healthcare, those who responded 4 were coded as neutral (not reported here), and those who responded 5, 6, or 7 were coded as opposed to government involvement in providing healthcare. Chi-squares and significance levels (1950s and 1960s with 1 degree of freedom and 1970s, 1980s, and 1990s with 2 degrees of freedom) for each decade are as follows: 1950s = chi-square of 18.36 and p-value of <.0001. 1960s = chi-square of 42.61 and p-value of <.0001. 1970s = chi-square of 140.37 and p-value of <.0001. 1980s = chi-square of 12.69 and p-value of .0018. 1990s = chi-square of 27.54 and p-value of <.0001.
Source: NES Cumulative File, vcf0128, vcf0805, and vcf0806.

Once again, Catholics are more likely to adopt the position that shows a greater concern for the well-being of other human beings. Across all five decades, a higher percentage of Catholics than Protestants believes that government should be involved in providing healthcare to its citizens. This can be taken as indicative of a greater concern for the common good among Catholics than among Protestants. The results presented in the above two tables lend support, albeit limited, to the claim that Catholics view society through a more communal lens than do Protestants.

Catholic and Protestant attitudes relating to government services and spending provide further support for this claim. Table 6.3 presents the positions of Catholics and Protestants on the amount of spending and service provision that government should engage in, while table 6.4 does the same specifically for defense spending. Once again, the results are clear and in the hypothesized direction. Catholics are more likely to support increased government services and spending than are Protestants. In line with Catholic social teaching, Catholics are more willing to use the power and resources of the state to impact society. On defense, Catholics are more likely to favor reducing the amount of money spent by government. Although requiring extending the implications beyond the scope of the question, these results can be seen as an indication that Catholics believe that funds spent on defense could be better utilized elsewhere, especially when combined with the results contained in the previous table on overall government services and spending.

Table 6.3: Positions on Amount of Government Services and Spending, Catholics and Protestants, Whites Only, by Decade, 1980s-1990s

	Increase			Decrease		
Dec.	Cath.	Prot.	Diff.	Cath.	Prot.	Diff.
1980s	42	30	12	27	39	-12
1990s	37	30	7	32	40	-8

Note: Respondents were presented with a 7-point scale, with 1 representing the view that government should provide fewer services and cut spending, and 7 the position that government should provide more services and increase spending. Responses of 1, 2, and 3 were coded as favoring fewer services and reduced spending, 4 was coded neutral (not reported here), and responses of 5, 6, and 7 were coded as supporting more government services and increased spending. Chi-squares and significance levels (with 2 degrees of freedom) for each decade are as follows: 1980s = chi-square of 80.47 and p-value of <.0001. 1990s = chi-square of 42.22 and p-value of <.0001. Source: NES Cumulative File, vcf0128 and vcf0839.

Table 6.4: Positions on Amount of Government Spending on Defense, Catholics and Protestants, Whites Only, by Decade, 1980s-1990s

	Decrease			Increase		
Dec.	Cath.	Prot.	Diff.	Cath.	Prot.	Diff.
1980s	31	25	6	38	43	-5
1990s	43	34	9	22	28	-6

Note: Respondents were presented with a 7-point scale, with 1 representing the view that government should greatly reduce defense spending, and 7 the position that government should greatly increase defense spending. Responses of 1, 2, and 3 were coded as favoring decreased defense spending, 4 was coded neutral (not reported here), and responses of 5, 6, and 7 were coded as supporting increased government spending on defense. Chi-squares and significance levels (with 2 degrees of freedom) for each decade are as follows: 1980s = chi-square of 22.18 and p-value of <.0001. 1990s = chi-square of 47.39 and p-value of <.0001. Source: NES Cumulative File, vcf0128 and vcf0843.

The questions utilized in the above analyses effectively exhaust the indicators available in the NES Cumulative File that can be used to show differences in concern for social justice and the common good between Catholics and Protestants. Granted, these indicators are not totally satisfactory; they are however simply the best contained in the NES dataset. In an effort to provide greater support for the argument advanced in this chapter, the General Social Surveys (GSS) 1972-1998 Cumulative Data File was examined in the hope of locating indicators better suited to testing the possibility of differences between Catholics and Protestants in terms of concerns for social justice and the common good.[142] Although working with the GSS presents the drawbacks of a much shorter time period than the NES and a much lower degree of question consistency, it does provide more indicators relating to the themes of social justice and the common good. This examination of the GSS produced four questions that are particularly relevant to the matter at hand in this chapter.

The first question relates to the government services and spending indicators examined earlier. Respondents were asked if government should do more to solve the country's problems. The results of this question for Catholics and Protestants are presented in table 6.5 below. Catholics are more supportive of government solving the country's problems than are Protestants. These results are consistent with the previous analyses showing that Catholics are more likely to favor using government resources to affect situations in society. As noted earlier, support of government involvement in society is also consistent with Catholic social teaching.

Table 6.5: Positions on Whether Government Should Do More to Solve the Country's Problems, Catholics and Protestants, Whites Only, by Decade, 1980s-1990s

	Yes, Government Should			No, Government Should Not		
Dec.	Cath.	Prot.	Diff.	Cath.	Prot.	Diff.
1970s	43	31	12	28	36	-8
1980s	27	21	6	30	37	-7
1990s	27	21	6	32	40	-8

Note: Respondents were presented with a 5-point scale, with 1 representing the opinion that government should do more to solve the country's problems and 5 representing the view that this is not government's responsibility. Responses of 1 and 2 were coded as favoring government action, 3 was coded as neutral (not reported here), and responses of 4 and 5 were coded as being against government action. Chi-squares and significance levels (with 2 degrees of freedom) for each decade are as follows: 1970s = chi-square of 16 and p-value of .0003. 1980s = chi-square of 34.62 and p-value of <.0001. 1990s = 40.71 and p-value of <.0001. Source: GSS 1972-1998 Cumulative Data File, RELIG (104) and HELPNOT (310).

The additional three indicators selected from the GSS all relate in some way to the poor in society, a central concern of the Catholic Church and its social thought. The first question asks respondents their view on how much we should spend on assistance to the poor. The second question asks if government should do something to reduce income differences between the rich and the poor, and the final question asks whether or not government should act to improve the standard of living among the poor. The results of these questions for Catholics and Protestants are presented in tables 6.6-6.8 below.

Table 6.6: Positions on Amount Government Spends on Assistance to the Poor, Catholics and Protestants, Whites Only, by Decade, 1980s-1990s

	Too Little Spent on Poor			Too Much Spent on Poor		
Dec.	Cath.	Prot.	Diff.	Cath.	Prot.	Diff.
1980s	67	58	9	7	11	-4
1990s	57	52	5	11	16	-5

Note: Respondents were asked if they thought government spent too much, too little, or about the right amount (not reported here) on assistance to the poor. Chi-squares and significance levels (with 4 degrees of freedom) for each decade are as follows: 1980s = chi-square of 26.48 and p-value of <.0001. 1990s = chi-square of 20.89 and p-value of .0003. Source: General Social Surveys (GSS) 1972-1998 Cumulative Data File, variables RELIG (104) and NATFAREY (67k).

Table 6.7: Positions on Whether Government Should Do Something to Reduce Income Differences Between Rich and Poor, Catholics and Protestants, Whites Only, by Decade, 1980s-1990s

	Yes, Government Should			No, Government Should Not		
Dec.	Cath.	Prot.	Diff.	Cath.	Prot.	Diff.
1980s	48	43	5	32	37	-5
1990s	42	41	1	35	38	-3

Note: Respondents were presented with a 7-point scale, with 1 representing the opinion that government should do something to reduce income differences between rich and poor, and 7 representing the view that government should not be concerned with reducing these income differences. Responses of 1, 2, and 3 were coded as favoring government reducing income differences, 4 was coded as neutral (not reported here), and responses of 5, 6, and 7 were coded as against government action to reduce income differences. Chi-squares and significance levels (with 2 degrees of freedom) for each decade are as follows: 1980s = chi-square of 17.33 and p-value of .0002. 1990s = chi-square of 4.99 and p-value of .0823. Source: GSS 1972-1998 Cumulative Data File, RELIG (104) and EQWLTH (73a).

Table 6.8: Positions on Whether Government Should Do Something to Improve the Standard of Living of the Poor, Catholics and Protestants Whites Only, by Decade, 1980s-1990s

	Yes, Government Should			No, Government Should Not		
Decade	Cath.	Prot.	Diff.	Cath.	Prot.	Diff.
1970s	42	34	8	24	27	-3
1980s	32	24	6	23	29	-6
1990s	27	21	6	27	31	-4

Note: Respondents were presented with a 5-point scale, with 1 representing the opinion that government should do something to improve the standard of living among the poor and 5 representing the view that this is not government's responsibility. Responses of 1 and 2 were coded as favoring government action, 3 was coded as neutral (not reported here), and responses of 4 and 5 were coded as being against government action. Chi-squares and significance levels (with 2 degrees of freedom) for each decade are as follows: 1970s—chi-square of 6.70 and p-value of .0350. 1980s = 40.19 and p-value of <.0001. 1990s = chi-square of 23.97 and p-value of <.0001. Source: GSS 1972-1998 Cumulative Data File, RELIG (104) and HELPPOOR (309).

For the questions about spending on assistance to the poor and improving the standard of living of the poor, the results are consistent with those previously presented in this chapter. In other words, Catholics are more likely than Protestants to favor action aimed at helping society's less affluent members. Once again, Catholics exhibit a greater degree of concern for others than do Protestants. They are more supportive of measures designed to promote social justice and the common good. Only on the question of whether government should reduce income differences between the rich and the poor is there no real difference between the two religious groups.

Does the social teaching of the Catholic Church have an effect on the manner in which its members position themselves on social issues? The results presented in the final section of this chapter provide a qualified "yes" in response to this question. For seven of the eight indicators examined here, Catholics were more likely than Protestants to adopt the more liberal position. In keeping with the social teaching of their church, Catholics exhibited higher levels of concern with social justice and the common good than did their Protestant counterparts. These differences were not large, but they were consistent across both time and specific indicator. In the absence of better measures, the results shown here support the claim that Catholicism promotes a more communal worldview than does Protestantism, which tends to create a more individualistic perspective.

In addition to offering qualified support for my hypothesis, the results presented above also raise a concern that is more problematic for my argument. With the exception of attitudes about defense spending, the differences on issue positions between Catholics and Protestants have either declined or stayed flat over time. The declines point to the possibility that although there may indeed be some inherent differences between Catholicism and Protestantism that result in different views about political issues, the effect of these religious worldview differences may be diminishing. Even more interesting is the fact that this decline is occurring during the same period that the Catholic Church has become even more vocal and active concerning issues of the common good and social justice. This possibility is clearly important and in need of future study.

The final matter to be dealt with in this chapter is the connection of Catholic and Protestant positions on the above issues to their respective electoral behavior. How do the attitudes shown above relate to partisan support? This question can be answered in short order.

The relationship between issue position and party support was the same for both Catholics and Protestants. With the exception of a very few anomalies, the same relationship existed for all eight of the indicators examined in this chapter. Put simply, as issue positions moved from liberal to conservative, support for the Democratic Party declined among both religious groups. Table 6.9 demonstrates this relationship, using the NES question about whether or not government should guarantee individuals jobs and good standards of living as an example.

Table 6.9: Democratic Presidential Vote by Position on Whether Government Should Guarantee Individuals Jobs and a Good Standard of Living, Catholics and Protestants, Whites Only, by Decade, 1950s-1990s

Dec.	Gov't Should Cath.	Prot.	Neutral Cath.	Prot.	Gov't Should Not Cath.	Prot.
1950s	46	41	--	--	40	27
1960s	79	49	--	--	62	32
1970s	58	54	48	32	34	23
1980s	61	52	54	36	31	20
1990s	69	62	56	43	37	25

Note: In the 1950s and 1960s, respondents were asked if they agreed or disagreed that government should provide jobs for all who wanted to work. Beginning in 1970, respondents were asked to position themselves on a 7-point scale, with 1 being in favor of government seeing to it that everyone had a job and a good standard of living and 7 being in favor government letting each person get ahead on his or her own. Those who responded 1, 2, or 3 were coded as supporting government guaranteeing jobs and a good standard of living, those who responded 4 were coded as neutral, and those who responded 5, 6, or 7 were coded as opposed to government guaranteeing jobs and standards of living. Obviously, opinions on standards of living apply only from the 1970s-1990s. Source: NES Cumulative File, vcf0128, vcf0705, vcf0808, and vcf0809.

As respondents become less supportive of government guaranteeing jobs and a good standard of living support for the Democrats declines, regardless of religious affiliation. The above results illustrate that as respondents move from liberal to conservative on the issue, Democratic support decreased. As noted above, this same trend is evident for all of the indicators analyzed in this chapter. Although additional variables need to be controlled for, these results demonstrate that issue positions are linked to electoral behavior, for both Catholics and Protestants.

Two additional observations can be made by examining table 6.9. The first is that regardless of issue position, Catholics are more likely than Protestants to vote Democratic. This comes as no surprise given the material contained in the previous chapters. For those adopting the liberal position, the difference between Catholics and Protestants is not that large. Among those taking moderate and conservative stances, however, the gap between the two religious groups becomes much wider. Among moderates and conservatives, Catholics are much more likely to vote Democratic than are Protestants. This indicates the possibility of an interaction effect among Catholics, with religious affiliation working to reduce the impact of issue position on vote choice. This is a very intriguing possibility, deserving of future scholarly attention.

The task of this chapter however, is complete. It has been shown that the worldview produced by the Catholic Church contributes to Catholics taking different positions than Protestants on issues relating to social justice and the common good. These differences on issues, in turn, have been shown to affect electoral behavior. The next chapter will attempt to determine how large the impact of religion on electoral behavior is through a detailed multivariate analysis.

Notes

1. Andrew M. Greeley, "Protestant and Catholic: Is the Analogical Imagination Extinct?" *American Sociological Review* 54, no. 4 (Aug. 1989): 486.
2. Greeley, "Protestant and Catholic," 485-502. For discussion of individualistic and communal religious worldviews, see: David C. Leege and Michael R. Welch, "Religious Roots of Political Orientations: Variations among American Catholic Parishioners," *Journal of Politics* 51, no. 1 (Feb. 1989): 137-62; David C. Leege, "Catholics and the Civic Order: Parish Participation, Politics, and Civic Participation," *Review of Politics* 50, no. 4 (Fall 1988): 704-36; Michael R. Welch and David C. Leege, "Religious Predictors of Catholic Parishioners Sociopolitical Attitudes: Devotional Style, Closeness to God, Imagery, and Agentic/Communal Religious Identity," *Journal for the Scientific Study of Religion* 27, no. 4 (Dec. 1988): 536-52; Peter L. Benson and Dorothy L. Williams, *Religion on Capitol Hill: Myths and Realities* (San Francisco: Harper and Row Publishers, 1982).
3. Paul F. Lazarsfeld, Bernard Berelson, and Hazel Gaudet, *The People's Choice: How the Voter Makes Up His Mind in a Presidential Campaign*, 2d ed. (New York: Columbia University Press, 1948); Bernard R. Berelson, Paul F. Lazarsfeld, and William N. McPhee, *Voting: A Study of Opinion Formation in a Presidential Campaign* (Chicago: University of Chicago Press, 1954).
4. Pamela Johnston Conover, "The Influence of Group Identifications on Political Perception and Evaluation," *Journal of Politics* 46, no. 3 (Aug. 1984): 760-61.
5. Conover, "The Influence of Group Identification," 761; Pamela Johnston Conover and Stanley Feldman, "Group Identifications, Values, and the Nature of Political Beliefs," *American Politics Quarterly* 12, no. 2 (Apr. 1984): 151.
6. Henri Tajfel, *Human Groups and Social Categories* (New York: Cambridge University Press, 1981), 255.

7. Tajfel, *Human Groups*; John C. Turner, "Towards a Cognitive Redefinition of the Social Group," in *Social Identity and Intergroup Relations*, ed. Henri Tajfel (New York: Cambridge University Press, 1982), 15-40; John C. Turner with Michael A. Hogg, Penelope J. Oakes, Stephen D. Reicher, and Margaret S. Wetherell, *Rediscovering the Social Group: A Self-Categorization Theory* (New York: Basil Blackwell, 1987).

8. Tom R. Tyler, Roderick M. Kramer, and Oliver P. John, "What Does Studying the Psychology of the Social Self Have to Offer to Psychologists?" in *The Psychology of the Social Self*, ed. Tom Tyler, Roderick M. Kramer, and Oliver P. John (Manweh, N.J.: Lawrence Erlbaum Associates, 1999), 2.

9. Many scholars call attention to the important distinction between group membership and group identification. Group membership requires only a person's awareness of meeting the objective criteria for belonging to a group (e.g. female, Hispanic, Episcopalian, etc.). Group identification, on the other hand, requires the self-awareness of membership plus a feeling of psychological attachment or "closeness" to the group in question. I too agree that this is an important distinction. Unfortunately, the NES Cumulative File offers no completely satisfactory way by which to measure the psychological attachments of individuals to the religious groups in which they claim membership. As far as I can determine, the "closeness" question that Conover used in her 1984 article does not appear in the Cumulative File. In a 1988 article, Penning used the "feeling thermometer" question about Catholics to measure Catholics' attachment to their religious group. Although potentially useful, this is also not a feasible option for this study. Neither the Protestant feeling thermometer nor the Catholic feeling thermometer are asked over the entire length of the time period under consideration here. The Protestant thermometer was only asked five times, beginning in 1964 and ending in 1976. The Catholic thermometer was asked eight times, last in 1992. By pooling the results from all years in which the respective religious group feeling thermometers were asked, it is clear that both Catholics and Protestants feel "warmly" toward their own group. In these pooled analyses Catholics received a mean rating of 79.33 among Catholics and Protestants gave themselves a rating of 76.84. In comparison, Protestants gave Catholics a rating of 60.63 and Catholics gave Protestants a 71.35 rating. In light of these results and the limitations discussed above, I choose to use the terms "group membership" and "group identification" interchangeably. In addition, one could argue that volunteering "Catholic" or "Protestant" in response to a question about one's religious affiliation qualifies as at least a weak measure of group identification. After all, as Deaux and her colleagues point out, respondents could have just as easily chose not to claim membership in these religious groups when asked by the interviewer. For more on this point, see Kay Deaux, Anne Reid, Kim Mirrahi, and Dave Cotting, "Connecting the Person to the Social: The Functions of Social Identification," in *The Psychology of the Social Self*, ed. Tyler, Kramer, and John, 92. For discussions of the distinction between group membership and group identification, see John C. Turner, *Social Influence* (Pacific Grove, Calif.: Brooks/Cole Publishing, 1991), 5; James M. Penning, "The Political Behavior of American Catholics: An Assessment of the Impact of Group Integration vs. Group Identification," *Western Political Quarterly* 41, no. 2 (June 1988): 289-308; Turner with Hogg, Oakes, Reicher, and Wetherell, *Rediscovering the Social Group*, 1-2; Conover and Feldman, "Group Identifications, Values," 154-55; Conover, "The Influence of Group Identifications," 761-62; Tajfel, *Human Groups*; Patricia Gurin, Arthur H. Miller, and Gerald Gurin, "Stratum Identification and Consciousness," *Social Psychology Quarterly* 43, no. 1 (Mar. 1980): 30.

10. Turner, *Social Influence*, 3.

11. Conover and Feldman, "Group Identifications, Values," 173. The definition of values is taken from Milton Rokeach, *The Nature of Human Values* (New York: The Free Press, 1973), 5.

12. John C. Turner and Rina S. Ororato, "Social Identity, Personality, and the Self-Concept: A Self-Categorization Perspective," in *The Psychology of the Social Self*, ed. Tyler, Kramer, and John, 27; Turner with Hogg, Oakes, Reicher, and Wetherell, *Rediscovering the Social Group*, 1-2.

13. Ted G. Jelen, "The Political Consequences of Religious Group Attitudes," *Journal of Politics* 55, no. 1 (Feb. 1993): 178.

14. Conover and Feldman, "Group Identifications, Values," 155.

15. Conover, "The Influence of Group Identifications," 765.

16. Conover, "The Influence of Group Identifications," 763-64.

17. Turner, *Social Influence*, 155; John C. Turner and Penelope J. Oakes, "Self-Categorization Theory and Social Influence," in *Psychology of Group Influence*, 2d ed., ed. Paul B. Paulus (Hillsdale, N.J.: Lawrence Erlbaum Associates, 1989), 238-40; Turner with Hogg, Oakes, Reicher, and Wetherell, *Rediscovering the Social Group*, 203.

18. Conover, "The Influence of Group Identifications," 778, 782; Turner, "Towards a Cognitive Redefinition," 21.

19. Richard H. White, "Toward a Theory of Religious Influence," *Pacific Sociological Review* 11, no. 1 (Spring 1968): 25.

20. Clyde Wilcox, Ted G. Jelen, and David C. Leege, "Religious Group Identifications: Towards a Cognitive Theory of Religious Mobilization," in *Rediscovering the Religious Factor in American Politics*, ed. David C. Leege and Lyman A. Kellstedt (Armonk, N.Y.: M.E. Sharpe, 1993), 86.

21. David Tracy, *The Analogical Imagination: Christian Theology and the Culture of Pluralism* (New York: Crossroad Publishing Company, 1981), 22.

22. White, "Toward a Theory of Religious Influence," 25.

23. Kenneth D. Wald, Dennis E. Owen, and Samuel S. Hill, Jr., "Churches as Political Communities," *American Political Science Review* 82, no. 2 (June 1988): 532.

24. While each of these mechanisms no doubt add to a sense of group identification, Turner and his colleagues have shown in laboratory experiments that these conditions are not necessary to foster group identification. The perception by an individual that they belong to a group is enough to promote identification with the group on the part of the individual, without any personal interaction. Turner and Oakes, "Self-Categorization Theory," 238; Turner with Hogg, Oakes, Reicher, and Wetherell, *Rediscovering the Social Group*, 115; Turner, "Towards a Cognitive Redefinition," 15, 23.

25. Ted G. Jelen, "Political Christianity: A Contextual Analysis," *American Journal of Political Science* 36, no. 3 (Aug. 1992): 692-714; Christopher P. Gilbert, *The Impact of Churches on Political Behavior* (Westport, Conn.: Greenwood Press, 1993): 18-24; Kenneth D. Wald, Dennis E. Owen, and Samuel S. Hill, Jr., "Political Cohesion in Churches," *Journal of Politics* 52, no. 1 (Feb. 1990): 203; Wald, Owen, and Hill, "Churches as Political Communities," 533; White, "Toward a Theory of Religious Influence," 23-28.

26. Jeffrey K. Hadden, "Religion and the Construction of Social Problems," in *Religion and Religiosity in America*, ed. Jeffrey K. Hadden and Theodore E. Long (New York: Crossroad Publishing Company, 1983), 25-26.

27. Wilcox, Jelen, and Leege, "Religious Group Identifications"; Gilbert, *The Impact of Churches*; Wald, Owen, and Hill, "Churches as Political Communities."

28. Max Weber, *The Protestant Ethic and the Spirit of Capitalism*, translated by Talcott Parsons (London: George Allen & Unwin LTD, 1930).

29. G. H. Mueller, "The Protestant and the Catholic Ethic," *Annual Review of the Social Sciences of Religion* 2 (1978): 148.

30. John E. Tropman, "The 'Catholic Ethic' vs. the 'Protestant Ethic': Catholic Social Service and the Welfare State," *Social Thought* 12, no. 1 (Winter 1985): 13.

31. John E. Tropman, *The Catholic Ethic in American Society: An Exploration of Values* (San Francisco: Jossey-Bass Publishers, 1995).

32. Tropman, *The Catholic Ethic*, chapters 2 and 3.

33. Tropman, *The Catholic Ethic*, 8.

34. Mueller, "The Protestant and the Catholic Ethic," 155.

35. Greeley, "Protestant and Catholic," 485.

36. Robert Wuthnow, *The Restructuring of American Religion: Society and Faith since World War II* (Princeton, N.J.: Princeton University Press, 1988), 55.

37. Rodney Stark and Charles Y. Glock, *American Piety: The Nature of Religious Commitment* (Berkeley, Calif.: University of California Press, 1968), 70-72.

38. Tropman, *The Catholic Ethic*, 125.

39. Rembert G. Weakland, "Foreword," in Tropman, *The Catholic Ethic*, x. This teaching is presented in the Catholic Church's Pastoral Constitution. Second Vatican Council, *Gaudium et Spes*, no. 24, in *Catholic Social Thought: The Documentary Heritage*, ed. David J. O'Brien and Thomas A. Shannon (Maryknoll, N.Y.: Orbis Books, 1992), 180.

40. George Gallup, Jr., and Jim Castelli, *The American Catholic People: Their Beliefs, Practices, and Values* (Garden City, N.Y.: Doubleday and Co., 1987), 18.

41. From Pope Paul VI's opening address at the second session of Vatican II. Quoted in Richard P. McBrien, *Catholicism*, Rev. ed. (San Francisco: HarperCollins Publishers, 1994), 9.

42. McBrien, *Catholicism*, chapter I.

43. McBrien, *Catholicism*, 10.

44. Michael J. Schuck, *That They Be One: The Social Teaching of the Papal Encyclicals, 1740-1989* (Washington, D.C.: Georgetown University Press, 1991), ix; J. Brian Benestad, *The Pursuit of a Just Social Order: Policy Statements of the U.S. Catholic Bishops, 1966-1980* (Washington, D.C.: Ethics and Public Policy Center, 1982), 8.

45. Michael J. Schultheis, Edward P. DeBerri, and Peter J. Henriot, *Our Best Kept Secret: The Rich Heritage of Catholic Social Teaching* (Washington, D.C.: Center of Concern, 1987), 8.

46. Andrew Greeley, *The Catholic Imagination* (Berkeley, Calif.: University of California Press, 2000), 186.

47. Benestad, *The Pursuit of a Just Social Order*, 8.

48. Greeley, *The Catholic Imagination*, 125.

49. Recently, papal encyclicals have been addressed to a much wider audience, including "all men and women (or people) of good will." This is another indication of the broadened concern of the church in social matters, a development that will be discussed later in this chapter.

50. Total of 284 encyclicals from 1740-1989 taken from Schuck, *That They Be One*, ix. Six encyclicals have been issued since 1989, resulting in a total of 290. Information on the encyclicals issued since 1989 was obtained from the Vatican website, http://www.vatican.va/

51. Schuck, *That They Be One*, see especially chapter 4.

52. John A. Coleman, "Introduction: A Tradition Celebrated, Reevaluated, and Applied," in *One Hundred Years of Catholic Social Thought*, ed. John A. Coleman (Maryknoll, N.Y.: Orbis Books, 1991), 2; Jean-Yves Calvez, "Economic Policy Issues in Roman Catholic Social Teaching," in *The Catholic Challenge to the American Economy*, ed. Thomas M. Gannon (New York: Macmillan, 1987), 17.

53. Aaron I. Abell, *American Catholicism and Social Action: A Search for Social Justice, 1865-1950* (Notre Dame, Ind.: University of Notre Dame Press, 1963), chapter 3.

54. David A. Boileau, "Introduction," in *Principles of Catholic Social Teaching*, ed. David A. Boileau (Milwaukee, Wis.: Marquette University Press, 1998), 15; Donal Dorr, *Option for the Poor: A Hundred Years of Vatican Social Teaching* (Maryknoll, N.Y.: Orbis Books, 1983), 12.

55. Pope Leo XIII, *Rerum Novarum*, 1891, no. 2 in *Catholic Social Thought: The Documentary Heritage*, ed. David J. O'Brien and Thomas A. Shannon (Maryknoll, N.Y.: Orbis Books, 1992), 15. All future references to the text of papal encyclicals in this book, unless otherwise noted, are taken from this volume edited by O'Brien and Shannon. Thus the citation to the volume will be omitted.

56. Pope Leo XIII, *Rerum Novarum*, nos. 36-38, pp. 32-34. See also Franz H. Mueller, *The Church and the Social Question* (Washington, D.C.: American Enterprise Institute, 1984), 79.

57. Pope Leo XIII, *Rerum Novarum*, nos. 33-34, pp. 30-31

58. Dorr, *Option for the Poor*, 14-18; David J. O'Brien, *American Catholics and Social Reform* (New York: Oxford University Press, 1968), 14.

59. Pope Leo XIII, *Rerum Novarum*, nos. 27-28, pp. 27-28.

60. David J. O'Brien and Thomas A. Shannon, "Introduction to *Rerum Novarum*," in *Catholic Social Thought: The Documentary Heritage*, ed. David J. O'Brien and Thomas A. Shannon (Maryknoll, N.Y.: Orbis Books, 1992), 13.

61. Pope Leo XIII, *Rerum Novarum*, no. 19, pp. 22-23.

62. O'Brien and Shannon, "Introduction to *Rerum Novarum*," 12; Dorr, *Option for the Poor*, 12.

63. Dorr, *Option for the Poor*, 12.

64. Fred Crosson, "Catholic Social Teaching and American Society," in *Principles of Catholic Social Teaching*, ed. David A. Boileau (Milwaukee, Wis.: Marquette University Press, 1998), 169; Calvez, "Economic Policy Issues," 17-18; Abell, *American Catholicism and Social Action*, 75.

65. Dorr, *Option for the Poor*, 11.

66. Pope Pius XI, *Quadragesimo Anno*, 1931, no. 39, p. 50.

67. Michael Novak, *The Catholic Ethic and the Spirit of Capitalism* (New York: The Free Press, 1993), 37; Coleman, "Introduction: A Tradition Celebrated," 4; Schultheis, DeBerri, and Henriot, *Our Best Kept Secret*, 11

68. Boileau, "Introduction," 16; David J. O'Brien, "A Century of Catholic Social Teaching: Contexts and Comments," in *One Hundred Years of Catholic Social Thought*, ed. John A. Coleman (Maryknoll, N.Y.: Orbis Books, 1991), 19.

69. George Q. Flynn, *American Catholics & the Roosevelt Presidency, 1932-1936* (Lexington, Ky.: University of Kentucky Press, 1968), 24.

70. Pope Pius XI, *Quadragesimo Anno*, no. 88, p. 62.

71. Dorr, *Option for the Poor*, 63.

72. Pope Pius XI, *Quadragesimo Anno*, no. 101, p. 64.

73. Pope Pius XI, *Quadragesimo Anno*, no. 41, pp. 50-51.

74. Pope Pius XI, *Quadragesimo Anno*, no. 49, pp. 52-53.

75. Pope Pius XI, *Quadragesimo Anno*, nos. 56-58, pp. 55-56.
76. Novak, *The Catholic Ethic and the Spirit of Capitalism*, 73.
77. Gerard Beigel, *Faith and Social Justice in the Teaching of Pope John Paul II* (New York: Peter Lang Publishing, 1997), 88-89; O'Brien, "A Century of Catholic Social Teaching," 19-20.
78. B. Kettern, "Social Justice: The Development of the Concept of 'iustitia' from St. Thomas Aquinas through the Social Encyclicals," in *Principles of Catholic Social Teaching*, ed. David A. Boileau (Milwaukee, Wis.: Marquette University Press, 1998), 95; Beigel, *Faith and Social Justice*, 83.
79. Schuck, *That They Be One*, 122.
80. Pope John XXIII, *Pacem in Terris*, 1963, nos. 8-27, pp. 132-35.
81. Pope John Paul II, *Centesimus Annus*, 1991, pp. 439-88.
82. Kettern, "Social Justice: The Development," 83.
83. Pope John XXIII, *Mater et Magistra*, 1961, nos. 157-77, pp. 110-13.
84. Pope John XXIII, *Mater et Magistra*, nos. 200-11, pp. 116-18.
85. Pope Paul VI, *Populorum Progressio*, 1967, nos. 45-65, pp. 250-55.
86. Pope John Paul II, *Sollicitudo Rei Socialis*, 1987, nos. 11-25, pp. 401-10.
87. For further discussion of this evolution in Catholic social thought, see Dorr, *Option for the Poor*, 128.
88. Pope Leo XIII, *Rerum Novarum*, no. 19, pp. 22-23.
89. Pope Pius XI, *Quadragesimo Anno*, no. 50, p. 53.
90. Second Vatican Council, *Gaudium et Spes*, 1965, no, 69, pp. 213-14.
91. Pope Paul VI, *Populorum Progressio*, no. 23, p. 245.
92. Pope John XXIII, *Pacem in Terris*, no. 54, p. 140; Second Vatican Council, *Gaudium et Spes*, no. 74, p. 216; Pope Paul VI, *Octogesimo Adveniens*, 1971, no. 46, p. 282; and Pope John Paul II, *Centesimus Annus*, no. 11, p. 447.
93. Pope John XIII, *Mater et Magistra*, no. 73, p. 96; Second Vatican Council, *Gaudium et Spes*, no. 63, p. 209; Paul VI, *Octogesima Adveniens*, no. 43, p. 281; and Pope John Paul II, *Sollicitudo Rei Socialis*, no. 8, p. 399.
94. Pope Paul VI, *Populorum Progressio*, no. 49, p. 251.
95. Pope John XXIII, *Pacem in Terris*, 1963, no. 56, p. 140.
96. Pope John XXIII, *Mater et Magistra*, nos. 233-41, pp. 121-23 and Pope John XXIII, *Pacem in Terris*, no. 146, pp. 154-55.
97. Pope John XXIII, *Mater et Magistra*, no. 241, pp. 122-23.
98. Pope Paul VI, *Populorum Progressio*, no. 47, p. 251.
99. Pope John Paul II, *Sollicitudo Rei Socialis*, no. 42, pp. 425-26.
100. Pope John XXIII, *Pacem in Terris*, no. 53, pp. 139-40; Second Vatican Council, *Gaudium et Spes*, no. 30, p. 183; Pope John Paul II, *Sollicitudo Rei Socialis*, no. 32, p. 416; and Pope John Paul II, *Centesimus Annus*, no. 49, p. 476.
101. Pope John Paul II, *Centesimus Annus*, no. 51, p. 478.
102. Second Vatican Council, *Gaudium et Spes*, no. 43, p. 192.
103. Benestad, *The Pursuit of a Just Social Order*, 3-4.
104. Benestad, *The Pursuit of a Just Social Order*, 62.
105. National Conference of Catholic Bishops (NCCB), *Economic Justice for All* (Washington, D.C.: United States Catholic Conference, 1986).
106. NCCB, *Economic Justice for All*, no. 122, p. 60.
107. NCCB, *Economic Justice for All*, nos. 70-76, pp. 36-39.
108. NCCB, *Economic Justice for All*, no. 16, p. 8.
109. NCCB, *Economic Justice for All*, no. 25, p. xiv-xv.

110. NCCB, *Economic Justice for All*, no. 19, p. 9.
111. Administrative Board of the U.S. Catholic Bishops, *Faithful Citizenship: Responsibility for a New Millennium* (Washington, D.C.: United States Catholic Conference, 1999).
112. Mary E. Hobgood, *Catholic Social Teaching and Economic Theory* (Philadelphia: Temple University Press, 1991), 5.
113. Philip S. Land, *Catholic Social Teaching: As I Have Lived, Loathed, and Loved It* (Chicago: Loyola University Press, 1991), 89; Schuck, *That They Be One*, 184-85.
114. Pope John Paul II, *Laborem Exercens*, 1981, no. 14, p. 371.
115. Charles E. Curran, "Catholic Social Teaching and Human Morality," in *One Hundred Years of Catholic Social Thought*, ed. John A. Coleman (Maryknoll, N.Y.: Orbis Books, 1991), 79.
116. Again, this is with the exception of church teaching on matters involving human sexuality and reproduction.
117. David J. O'Brien and Thomas A. Shannon, "Introduction to *Mater et Magistra*," in *Catholic Social Thought: The Documentary Heritage*, ed. O'Brien and Shannon, 83.
118. Beigel, *Faith and Social Justice*, 84-85; Marie Augusta Neal, "Faith and Social Ministry: A Catholic Perspective," in *Faith and Social Ministry: Ten Christian Perspectives*, ed. James D. Davidson, C. Lincoln Johnson, and Alan K. Mock (Chicago: Loyola University Press, 1990), 206-11.
119. Kettern, "Social Justice: The Development," 98; Schuck, *That They Be One*, see especially chapter 4.
120. Jo Freeman, "The Political Culture of the Democratic and Republican Party," *Political Science Quarterly* 101, no. 3 (1986): 327.
121. Clinton Rossiter, *Parties and Politics in America* (Ithaca, N.Y.: Cornell University Press, 1960), 110.
122. Freeman, "The Political Culture," 328-30, 336-37.
123. Rossiter, *Parties and Politics in America*, 114-15.
124. Benjamin Ginsberg, "Critical Elections and the Substance of Party Conflict," *Midwest Journal of Political Science* 16, no. 4 (Nov. 1972): 607.
125. John Gerring, *Party Ideologies in America, 1828-1996* (New York: Cambridge University Press, 1998).
126. Gerring, *Party Ideologies in America*, 125-58.
127. Gerring, *Party Ideologies in America*, 134.
128. Gerring, *Party Ideologies in America*, 125-58; Freeman, "The Political Culture," 336-37.
129. Gerring, *Party Ideologies in America*, 187-253. For more on the willingness of the Democratic Party to use the power of the state, see Freeman, "The Political Culture," 336-37.
130. Gerring, *Party Ideologies in America*, 232-53.
131. For a good discussion of the differences between the Democrats and Republicans in both their central concerns and policy objectives, see Jeffrey M. Stonecash, *Class and Party in American Politics* (Boulder, Colo.: Westview Press, 2000), 43-86.
132. Democratic National Committee, "Democratic Party Credo," in *The Charter and Bylaws of the Democratic Party of the United States*, 8-9. Available at http://www.democrats.org/
133. Republican National Committee, *The Republican Oath*. Available at: http://www.rnc.org/2000/gopoath

134. Freeman," The Political Culture," 338.
135. Richard J. Trilling, *Party Image and Electoral Behavior* (New York: John Wiley & Sons, 1976), 2.
136. Rossiter, *Parties and Politics in America*, 89-93, 109-18.
137. Trilling, *Party Image*, 74-78. See also Arthur Sanders, "The Meaning of Party Images," *Western Political Quarterly* 41, no. 3 (Sept. 1988): 583-99.
138. Donald C. Baumer and Howard J. Gold, "Party Images after the Clinton Years" (paper presented at the annual meeting of the New England Political Science Association, Portland, Maine, May 2002); Donald C. Baumer and Howard J. Gold, "Party Images and the American Electorate," *American Politics Quarterly* 23, no. 1 (Jan. 1995): 33-61; Mark D. Brewer, "A Divided Public? Party Images and Mass Polarization in the United States" (paper presented at the annual meeting of the American Political Science Association, Boston, Mass., Aug. 2002); Marc J. Hetherington, "Resurgent Mass Partisanship: The Role of Elite Polarization," *American Political Science Review*, 95, no. 3 (Sept. 2001): 619-31.
139. Baumer and Gold, "Party Images and the American Electorate," 53.
140. Tropman, *The Catholic Ethic*, xv; Tropman, "The 'Catholic Ethic' vs. the 'Protestant Ethic,'" 20.
141. Greeley, *The Catholic Imagination*, 20; Greeley, "Protestant and Catholic," 488.
142. James Allan Davis and Tom W. Smith, *General Social Surveys, 1972-1998*, (machine-readable data file). Principal Investigator, James A. Davis; Director and Co-Principal Investigator, Tom W. Smith; Co-Principal Investigator, Peter V. Marsden, NORC ed. (Chicago: National Opinion Research Center, producer, 1998; Storrs, Conn.: The Roper Center for Public Opinion Research, University of Connecticut, distributor).

Chapter Seven

A Final Test: Multivariate Analyses

Introduction

The analyses conducted thus far in this study cast serious doubt on the conventional wisdom regarding the electoral behavior of American Catholics. Catholics as a group have not left the Democratic Party. They continue to vote for and identify with the Democrats at higher levels than they do the Republicans, although the margin has declined some over the last thirty years. More important, Catholic electoral behavior remains distinct from that of Protestants. In terms of presidential vote, House vote, and party identification Catholics are more Democratic than Protestants. Except for the period from 1960-1964, these differences in Democratic support between Catholics and Protestants have remained remarkably stable since the 1950s. Many researchers have portrayed the last forty years as a period of great change in the electoral behavior of American Catholics. Quite contrary to such analyses, the findings presented here make a strong case for continuity in Catholic electoral behavior.

While all of the results presented to this point have clearly shown that Catholics are both more likely to support the Democrats than the Republicans and much more likely to support the Democrats than Protestants, some may find the evidence insufficient or unconvincing. While all of the simple cross-tabulations have consistently shown that Catholics are more Democratic than Protestants, there is the possibility that the differences in electoral behavior shown to exist between Catholics and Protestants are spurious. That is, the differences could be accounted for by some variable or variables that have been excluded from the analyses. The final set of analyses to be conducted here will attempt to account for this possibility.

Multivariate Analyses

In order to more fully determine the effect of Catholic affiliation on electoral behavior, multivariate analyses were conducted with the three partisan support indicators—presidential vote choice, House vote choice, and party identification—as the dependent variables. Because each of these dependent variables is nominal in nature, logistic regression (specifically, logit) was chosen as the method of analysis. The variables previously examined in this study—age, family income, gender, church attendance, religious salience, and Hispanic ethnicity—have been included along with Catholic religious affiliation (as opposed to Protestant affiliation) as independent variables in the analyses. Two additional independent variables, residence in a union household and residence in the South, have also been included in the subsequent analyses because of their known impact on electoral behavior during some or all of the time period under examination here. Because two of these independent variables are available only since 1980, two separate sets of models have been created. The first, covering the period from 1952-2000, includes Catholic affiliation, age, family income, female gender, church attendance, residence in a union household, and residence in the South as independent variables. The second set of models, covering the period from 1980-2000, utilizes the same independent variables as the first set, with the religious salience index (introduced in chapter 5) substituted for church attendance and the addition of a variable measuring Hispanic ethnicity.[1]

Tables 7.1-7.6 present the results of these multivariate analyses. The figures reported in each table are unstandardized logit coefficients and percentage increases in the odds of Democratic support as a result of each independent variable included in the model equation. As will be discussed further below, the results of the multivariate analyses summarized in these six rather long tables strongly support the previously discussed findings that were based on cross-tabular analyses. Those readers with little interest in or knowledge of multivariate logistic regression can safely pass over these tables.

A Final Test: Multivariate Analyses

Table 7.1: Logit Estimates and Odds Increases for Catholic Affiliation, Age, Family Income, Gender, Church Attendance, Union Household, and Southern Residence on Presidential Vote, Whites Only, 1952-2000

	Cath	Age	Inc	Fem	Ch Att	Union	South
Year							
1952	.88***	-.09*	-.22***	-.02	-.09	.91***	1.06***
	(59%)	(-10%)	(-25%)	(-2%)	(-9%)	(60%)	(66%)
1956	.84***	.01	-.14*	-.27*	-.17*	.70***	1.14***
	(57%)	(1%)	(-15%)	(-31%)	(-19%)	(50%)	(68%)
1960	2.66***	-.13*	-.20*	-.26	-.37***	.68***	.97***
	(93%)	(-14%)	(-22%)	(-29%)	(-45%)	(50%)	(62%)
1964	1.16***	-.17***	-.40***	.21	-.19*	1.27***	.19
	(69%)	(-19%)	(49%)	(19%)	(-21%)	(72%)	(18%)
1968	1.32***	.05	-.04	.20	-.07	.32	-.11
	(73%)	(5%)	(-4%)	(18%)	(-7%)	(27%)	(-11%)
1972	.53***	-.12**	-.23***	.36**	-.17**	.52***	-.38*
	(41%)	(-13%)	(27%)	(30%)	(-19%)	(40%)	(-47%)
1976	.68***	-.06	-.34***	-.08	-.01	.77***	.45**
	(49%)	(-6%)	(-41%)	(-8%)	(-2%)	(54%)	(36%)
1980	.42*	.07	-.25**	.40*	-.23**	.84***	.36
	(34%)	(6%)	(-28%)	(33%)	(-26%)	(57%)	(30%)
1984	.70***	.05	-.42***	.21	-.12	.96***	.07
	(50%)	(4%)	(-53%)	(19%)	(-13%)	(62%)	(6%)
1988	.73***	.01	-.29***	.30*	-.05	.82***	.17
	(52%)	(1%)	(-33%)	(26%)	(-5%)	(56%)	(15%)
1992	.69***	.11**	-.33***	.24	-.36***	.51**	.28
	(50%)	(11%)	(-39%)	(21%)	(-44%)	(40%)	(25%)
1996	.71***	.01	-.36***	.57***	-.39***	.85***	-.03
	(51%)	(1%)	(-43%)	(43%)	(-47%)	(58%)	(-3%)
2000	.26	.14**	-.15	.39*	-.33***	.66**	-.48*
	(23%)	(13%)	(-16%)	(33%)	(-39%)	(49%)	(-62)

*p ≤ .05   **p ≤ .01   ***p ≤ .001

Note: A positive value for the logit coefficient indicates an increased likelihood of supporting the Democratic Party, while a negative sign indicates a reduced likelihood of Democratic support. The figures in parentheses beneath each logit coefficient represent the percentage change in the odds of an individual voting Democratic for president due to a one-unit increase in the independent variable in question, with all other independent variables held constant at their sample means. Presidential vote was coded 1 if Democrat and 0 if otherwise. Catholic affiliation was coded 1 if Catholic and 0 if Protestant. For gender, female was coded 1 and male 0. For church attendance from 1952-1968 "regular" attendance was coded 3, "often" was coded 2, "seldom" was coded 1, and "never" was coded 0. For 1970-2000 "every week" was coded 3, "almost every week" and "once or twice a month" were coded 2, "a few times a year" was coded 1, and "never" was coded 0. Union household is coded 1 if someone in the household belongs to a labor union and 0 if otherwise. South, defined here as the 11 states of the former Confederacy, is coded 1 if applicable and 0 if not. Codes for age and family income are taken without alteration from the original NES Cumulative File. Source: NES Cumulative File, vcf0705, vcf0128, vcf0102, vcf0114, vcf0104, vcf0131, vcf0130, vcf0127, and vcf0113.

Chapter Seven

Table 7.2: Logit Estimates and Odds Increases for Catholic Affiliation, Age, Family Income, Gender, Church Attendance, Union Household, and Southern Residence on House Vote, Whites Only, 1952-2000

Year	Cath	Age	Inc	Fem	Ch Att	Union	South
1952	.94***	-.13*	-.24**	.11	-.13	1.09***	4.10***
	(61%)	(-14%)	(27%)	(11%)	(-14%)	(66%)	(98%)
1956	1.06***	-.06	-.17**	-.37**	-.10	.58***	2.24***
	(65%)	(-7%)	(-18%)	(-45%)	(-11%)	(44%)	(89%)
1958	1.38***	-.07	-.24**	.02	-.31**	1.07***	2.49***
	(75%)	(-7%)	(-27%)	(2%)	(-37%)	(66%)	(92%)
1960	2.11***	-.12	-.18*	.06	-.27**	.83***	1.93***
	(88%)	(-12%)	(-20%)	(6%)	(-31%)	(57%)	(85%)
1964	1.02***	-.12*	-.32***	.08	-.23**	1.25***	1.39***
	(64%)	(-13%)	(-37%)	(7%)	(-25%)	(71%)	(75%)
1966	.97***	-.07	-.10	-.49**	.16	.74***	1.24***
	(62%)	(-7%)	(-11%)	(-63%)	(15%)	(52%)	(71%)
1968	1.11***	.00	-.23**	-.05	-.10	.60**	1.50***
	(67%)	(0%)	(-26%)	(-6%)	(-11%)	(45%)	(78%)
1970	.35	-.12	-.27**	.16	.06	.77***	.90***
	(30%)	(-13%)	(-31%)	(15%)	(6%)	(54%)	(59%)
1972	.90***	-.07	-.26***	-.13	-.09	.45**	1.07***
	(59%)	(-7%)	(-30%)	(-14%)	(-9%)	(36%)	(66%)
1974	.95***	-.03	-.28**	.06	-.19*	.64**	.84***
	(62%)	(-3%)	(-32%)	(6%)	(-20%)	(48%)	(57%)
1976	.76***	-.01	-.26***	-.10	-.04	.93***	1.20***
	(53%)	(-1%)	(-30%)	(-11%)	(-4%)	(60%)	(70%)
1978	.78***	.00	-.26***	-.09	-.13	.97***	1.57***
	(54%)	(0%)	(-29%)	(-10%)	(-14%)	(62%)	(79%)
1980	.61**	-.05	-.15	-.03	-.24**	.78***	.83***
	(46%)	(-5%)	(-16%)	(-3%)	(-27%)	(54%)	(56%)
1982	.72**	.01	-.35***	.06	-.04	.86***	.35
	(51%)	(1%)	(-42%)	(6%)	(-4%)	(58%)	(29%)
1984	.64***	-.01	-.30***	.06	-.10	.53**	.47**
	(47%)	(-1%)	(-35%)	(6%)	(-11%)	(41%)	(38%)
1986	.77***	.09	-.21*	.14	.07	.41*	.97***
	(54%)	(8%)	(-24%)	(13%)	(7%)	(34%)	(62%)
1988	.90***	-.04	-.25**	.09	-.25**	.68***	1.02***
	(59%)	(-4%)	(-29%)	(9%)	(-28%)	(49%)	(64%)
1990	.44*	-.03	-.52***	.36	-.23**	.67**	.14
	(35%)	(-3%)	(-68%)	(30%)	(-26%)	(49%)	(13%)
1992	.48**	.04	-.38***	.05	-.21***	.37*	.00
	(38%)	(4%)	(-47%)	(5%)	(23%)	(31%)	(0%)
1994	.65***	.13*	-.42***	.07	-.33***	.86***	-.12
	(48%)	(12%)	(-52%)	(7%)	(-39%)	(58%)	(-13%)
1996	.52**	-.01	-.44***	.27	-.36***	.75***	-.17
	(41%)	(-1%)	(-56%)	(23%)	(-44%)	(53%)	(-19%)

Continued on next page

Table 7.2—Continued

	Cath	Age	Inc	Fem	Ch Att	Union	South
Year							
1998	.69**	.08	-.16	.38	-.33**	.46	-.28
	(50%)	(8%)	(-17%)	(32%)	(-39%)	(37%)	(-32%)
2000	.40*	.02	-.24**	.40*	-.24**	.62*	-.53*
	(33%)	(2%)	(-28%)	(33%)	(-28%)	(46%)	(-70%)

*p ≤ .05   **p ≤ .01   ***p ≤ .001

Note: A positive value for the logit coefficient indicates an increased likelihood of supporting the Democratic Party, while a negative sign indicates a reduced likelihood of Democratic support. The figures in parentheses beneath each logit coefficient represent the percentage change in the odds of an individual voting Democratic for House due to a one-unit increase in the independent variable in question, with all other independent variables held constant at their sample means. House vote was coded 1 if Democrat and 0 if otherwise. For coding of all other variables see table 7.1. House vote was not asked in 1954. Union household not asked in 1962. Source: NES Cumulative File, vcf0707, vcf0128, vcf0102, vcf0114, vcf0104, vcf0131, vcf0130, vcf0127, and vcf0113.

Table 7.3: Logit Estimates and Odds Increases for Catholic Affiliation, Age, Family Income, Gender, Church Attendance, Union Household, and Southern Residence on Party ID, Whites Only, 1952-2000

	Cath	Age	Inc	Fem	Ch Att	Union	South
Year							
1952	1.11***	-.10*	-.16**	-.10	-.10	.76***	2.25***
	(67%)	(-10%)	(-18%)	(-11%)	(-10%)	(53%)	(89%)
1956	1.13***	-.04	-.15**	-.34**	-.14*	.59***	1.67***
	(68%)	(-4%)	(-16%)	(-40%)	(-15%)	(45%)	(81%)
1958	1.02***	-.12**	-.10	.00	-.18**	.81***	1.46***
	(64%)	(-13%)	(-11%)	(0%)	(-20%)	(56%)	(77%)
1960	1.62***	-.09	-.21**	-.09	-.15	.68***	1.58***
	(80%)	(-9%)	(-23%)	(-9%)	(-16%)	(50%)	(79%)
1964	.95***	-.10*	-.28***	.12	-.14*	1.13***	1.10***
	(61%)	(-10%)	(-32%)	(11%)	(-15%)	(68%)	(67%)
1966	.72***	-.02	-.12	.14	.10	.80***	.83***
	(51%)	(-2%)	(-13%)	(13%)	(10%)	(55%)	(57%)
1968	.99***	.01	-.15**	.15	-.08	.35*	.86***
	(63%)	(1%)	(-17%)	(14%)	(-8%)	(30%)	(58%)
1970	.82***	.01	-.14*	.07	-.04	.78***	.36*
	(56%)	(1%)	(-15%)	(6%)	(-4%)	(54%)	(30%)
1972	.91***	.05	-.15***	.22*	-.03	.56***	.71***
	(60%)	(5%)	(-17%)	(20%)	(-3%)	(43%)	(51%)
1974	.94***	-.01	-.24***	.14	-.13*	.47**	.75***
	(61%)	(-1%)	(-27%)	(14%)	(-14%)	(37%)	(53%)
1976	1.00***	.04	-.26***	.01	.02	.77***	.74***
	(63%)	(4%)	(-30%)	(1%)	(2%)	(54%)	(52%)

Continued on next page

Table 7.3—Continued

	Cath	Age	Inc	Fem	Ch Att	Union	South
Year							
1978	1.05***	.04	-.25***	.14	-.07	.65***	.41**
	(65%)	(4%)	(-28%)	(13%)	(-7%)	(48%)	(34%)
1980	.57***	.09*	-.27***	.40**	-.21***	.58***	.59***
	(43%)	(8%)	(-31%)	(33%)	(-23%)	(44%)	(44%)
1982	.89***	.07	-.30***	.25	-.10	.90***	.56***
	(59%)	(6%)	(-35%)	(22%)	(-11%)	(59%)	(43%)
1984	.64***	.05	-.28***	.10	-.13*	.58***	.28*
	(47%)	(4%)	(-32%)	(9%)	(-14%)	(44%)	(24%)
1986	.77***	.13***	-.15**	.23*	-.05	.54***	.54***
	(54%)	(12%)	(-17%)	(21%)	(-5%)	(42%)	(42%)
1988	.61***	.12***	-.19**	.23	-.05	.69***	.70***
	(46%)	(11%)	(-20%)	(21%)	(-5%)	(50%)	(50%)
1990	.84***	.12***	-.20***	.12	-.07	.92***	.42**
	(57%)	(11%)	(-22%)	(11%)	(-7%)	(60%)	(34%)
1992	.87***	.09**	-.30***	.37***	-.24***	.89***	.26*
	(58%)	(9%)	(-35%)	(31%)	(-27%)	(59%)	(23%)
1994	1.01***	.04	-.46***	.37**	-.14*	.74***	.09
	(64%)	(4%)	(-58%)	(31%)	(-15%)	(52%)	(9%)
1996	.66***	-.01	-.38***	.47***	-.22***	.79***	.10
	(48%)	(-1%)	(-46%)	(38%)	(-25%)	(55%)	(10%)
1998	.53***	.11**	-.13*	.20	-.20**	.22	-.02
	(41%)	(11%)	(-14%)	(18%)	(-22%)	(20%)	(-2%)
2000	.18	.11*	-.25***	.40**	-.25***	.88***	-.24
	(17%)	(10%)	(-28%)	(33%)	(-28%)	(58%)	(-27%)

*p ≤ .05   **p ≤ .01   ***p ≤ .001

Note: A positive value for the logit coefficient indicates an increased likelihood of supporting the Democratic Party, while a negative sign indicates a reduced likelihood of Democratic support. The figures in parentheses beneath each logit coefficient represent the percentage change in the odds of an individual identifying with the Democratic Party due to a one-unit increase in the independent variable in question, with all other independent variables held constant at their sample means. Party ID was coded 1 if Democrat and 0 if otherwise. For coding of all other variables see table 7.1. Church attendance and southern residence not asked in 1954. Union household not asked in 1962. Source: NES Cumulative File, vcf0303, vcf0128, vcf0102, vcf0114, vcf0104, vcf0131, vcf0130, vcf0127, and vcf0113.

Table 7.4: Logit Estimates and Odds Increases for Catholic Affiliation, Age, Family Income, Gender, Hispanic Ethnicity, Religious Salience, Union Household, and Southern Residence on Presidential Vote, Whites Only, 1980-2000

Year	Cath	Age	Inc	Fem	Hisp	RelSal	Union	South
1980	.36.	.07	-.25**	.41*	.21	-.24	.86***	.34
	(31%)	(6%)	(-28%)	(34%)	(19%)	(-27%)	(58%)	(29%)
1984	.61***	.06	-.42***	.20	.52	-.14	.98***	-.02
	(46%)	(6%)	(-52%)	(18%)	(41%)	(-15%)	(62%)	(-2%)
1988	.55***	.02	-.25**	.31*	.85**	-.13	.81***	.03
	(43%)	(2%)	(-29%)	(27%)	(57%)	(-14%)	(55%)	(2%)
1992	.56***	.13**	-.33***	.25	.59*	-.53***	.52**	.18
	(43%)	(12%)	(-39%)	(23%)	(45%)	(-71%)	(40%)	(17%)
1996	.48**	.03	-.33***	.59***	1.24***	-.58***	.90***	-.17
	(38%)	(3%)	(-39%)	(45%)	(71%)	(78%)	(59%)	(-18%)
2000	.25	.17**	-.16*	.42*	n/a	-.65***	.69**	-.40*
	(22%)	(16%)	(-18%)	(34%)		(92%)	(50%)	(-49%)

*p ≤ .05   **p ≤ .01   ***p ≤ .001

Note: A positive value for the logit coefficient indicates an increased likelihood of supporting the Democratic Party, while a negative sign indicates a reduced likelihood of Democratic support. The figures in parentheses beneath each logit coefficient represent the percentage change in the odds of an individual voting Democratic for president due to a one-unit increase in the independent variable in question, with all other independent variables held constant at their sample means. Presidential vote was coded 1 if Democrat and 0 if otherwise. Catholic affiliation was coded 1 if Catholic and 0 if Protestant. For gender, female was coded 1 and male 0. Hispanic ethnicity was coded 1 if present and 0 if otherwise. Union household is coded 1 if someone in the household belongs to a labor union and 0 if otherwise. South, defined here as the 11 states of the former Confederacy, is coded 1 if applicable and 0 if not. For the coding procedure used to create the religious salience index, see endnote 16 in chapter 5. Codes for age and family income are taken without alteration from the original NES Cumulative File. Source: NES Cumulative File, vcf0705, vcf0128, vcf0102, vcf0114, vcf0104, vcf0108, vcf0130, vcf0847, vcf0127, and vcf0113.

Table 7.5: Logit Estimates and Odds Increases for Catholic Affiliation, Age, Family Income, Gender, Hispanic Ethnicity, Religious Salience, Union Household, and Southern Residence on House Vote, Whites Only, 1980-2000

	Cath	Age	Inc	Fem	Hisp	RelSal	Union	South
Year								
1980	.54**	-.04	-.15	.02	.13	-.38**	.77***	.84***
	(42%)	(-4%)	(-17%)	(2%)	(12%)	(-46%)	(47%)	(43%)
1984	.49**	.00	-.30***	.04	.72	-.07	.54**	.40*
	(39%)	(0%)	(-35%)	(4%)	(52%)	(-7%)	(41%)	(33%)
1986	.61*	.10	-.15	.14	n/a	.28	.27	1.02***
	(46%)	(10%)	(-16%)	(13%)		(25%)	(24%)	(64%)
1988	.76***	-.04	-.22**	.16	.82*	-.39***	.71***	1.00***
	(53%)	(-4%)	(-25%)	(14%)	(56%)	(-48%)	(51%)	(63%)
1990	.26	-.01	-.50***	.40*	1.11*	-.21	.66**	-.07
	(23%)	(-1%)	(-65%)	(33%)	(67%)	(-23%)	(49%)	(-7%)
1992	.38*	.05	-.39***	.07	.78*	-.33***	.36*	-.06
	(32%)	(5%)	(-47%)	(7%)	(54%)	(-39%)	(30%)	(-6%)
1994	.44*	.15**	-.39***	.07	1.21**	-.47***	.90***	-.24
	(36%)	(14%)	(-48%)	(7%)	(70%)	(-60%)	(59%)	(-27%)
1996	.32	.00	-.42***	.30	1.05**	-.55***	.79***	-.27
	(27%)	(0%)	(-53%)	(26%)	(65%)	(-74%)	(55%)	(-32%)
1998	.37	.11	-.12	.37	2.33***	-.44**	.48	-.51
	(31%)	(11%)	(-13%)	(31%)	(90%)	(-55%)	(38%)	(-66%)
2000	.38	.03	-.26**	.43*	n/a	-.43**	.64*	-.47*
	(32%)	(3%)	(-30%)	(35%)		(-54%)	(47%)	(-60%)

*p ≤ .05   **p ≤ .01   ***p ≤ .001

Note: A positive value for the logit coefficient indicates an increased likelihood of supporting the Democratic Party, while a negative sign indicates a reduced likelihood of Democratic support. The figures in parentheses beneath each logit coefficient represent the percentage change in the odds of an individual voting Democratic for House due to a one-unit increase in the independent variable in question, with all other independent variables held constant at their sample means. House vote was coded 1 if Democrat and 0 if otherwise. Catholic affiliation was coded 1 if Catholic and 0 if Protestant. For gender, female was coded 1 and male 0. Hispanic ethnicity was coded 1 if present and 0 if otherwise. Union household is coded 1 if someone in the household belongs to a labor union and 0 if otherwise. South, defined here as the 11 states of the former Confederacy, is coded 1 if applicable and 0 if not. For the coding procedure used to create the religious salience index, see endnote 16 in chapter 5. Codes for age and family income are taken without alteration from the original NES Cumulative File. The religious salience index is unable to be computed in 1982, thus that year is not included here. There is a problem with the Hispanic ethnicity data for 1986 and thus no coefficient can be generated for that year. Source: NES Cumulative File, vcf0707, vcf0128, vcf0102, vcf0114, vcf0104, vcf0108, vcf0130, vcf0847, vcf0127, and vcf0113.

A Final Test: Multivariate Analyses

Table 7.6: Logit Estimates and Odds Increases for Catholic Affiliation, Age, Family Income, Gender, Hispanic Ethnicity, Religious Salience, Union Household, and Southern Residence on Party Identification, Whites Only, 1980-2000

Year	Cath	Age	Inc	Fem	Hisp	RelSal	Union	South
1980	.55***	.07	-.29***	.38**	.51	-.26**	.53**	.62***
	(42%)	(6%)	(-34%)	(31%)	(40%)	(-30%)	(41%)	(46%)
1984	.60***	.03	-.29***	.04	.35	-.11	.58***	.33*
	(45%)	(3%)	(-34%)	(4%)	(29%)	(-11%)	(44%)	(28%)
1986	.77***	.19***	-.08	.26	.44	-.14	.51*	.64***
	(54%)	(17%)	(-8%)	(23%)	(36%)	(-15%)	(40%)	(48%)
1988	.54***	.12**	-.17**	.23	.57	-.16	.70***	.74***
	(42%)	(11%)	(-18%)	(21%)	(44%)	(-17%)	(51%)	(52%)
1990	.78***	.12***	-.19***	.11	.33	-.03	.92***	.38**
	(54%)	(11%)	(-21%)	(10%)	(28%)	(-3%)	(60%)	(32%)
1992	.75***	.10**	-.31***	.38***	.46*	-.32***	.93***	.22
	(53%)	(9%)	(-36%)	(32%)	(37%)	(-38%)	(61%)	(20%)
1994	.94***	.04	-.45***	.38**	.59*	-.13	.73***	.05
	(61%)	(4%)	(-56%)	(32%)	(44%)	(-14%)	(52%)	(5%)
1996	.53***	.01	-.37***	.50***	.63**	-.38***	.81***	.03
	(41%)	(1%)	(-45%)	(39%)	(47%)	(-46%)	(56%)	(3%)
1998	.35*	.14**	-.11	.19	1.01***	-.29**	.24	-.11
	(30%)	(13%)	(-12%)	(17%)	(64%)	(-34%)	(22%)	(-12%)
2000	.15	.12**	-.26***	.42**	n/a	-.43***	.89***	-.19
	(14%)	(12%)	(-29%)	(34%)		(-54%)	(59%)	(-21%)

*p ≤ .05 **p ≤ .01 ***p ≤ .001

Note: A positive value for the logit coefficient indicates an increased likelihood of supporting the Democratic Party, while a negative sign indicates a reduced likelihood of Democratic support. The figures in parentheses beneath each logit coefficient represent the percentage change in the odds of an individual identifying with the Democratic Party due to a one-unit increase in the independent variable in question, with all other independent variables held constant at their sample means. Party identification was coded 1 if Democrat and 0 otherwise. Catholic affiliation was coded 1 if Catholic and 0 if Protestant. For gender, female was coded 1 and male 0. Hispanic ethnicity was coded 1 if present and 0 if otherwise. Union household is coded 1 if someone in the household belongs to a labor union and 0 if otherwise. South, defined here as the 11 states of the former Confederacy, is coded 1 if applicable and 0 if not. For the coding procedure used to create the religious salience index, see endnote 16 in chapter 5. Codes for age and family income are taken without alteration from the original NES Cumulative File. The religious salience index is unable to be computed in 1982, thus that year is not included here. Source: NES Cumulative File, vcf0303, vcf0128, vcf0102, vcf0114, vcf0104, vcf0108, vcf0130, vcf0847, vcf0127, and vcf0113.

The results of the multivariate logistic analyses support the findings presented in the previous cross tabulations. Examining first the models for 1952-2000 (tables 7.1-7.3), the coefficients for Catholic affiliation demonstrate a strong relationship between Catholic affiliation and affinity for the Democratic Party. For all years and across all three partisan support indicators Catholic affiliation increases the likelihood of an individual supporting the Democratic

Party. Only three times out of a possible fifty-nine (presidential vote in 2000, House vote in 1970, and party identification in 2000) does the logit coefficient for Catholic affiliation fail to achieve statistical significance at the .05 level, in the majority of cases reaching the .001 level or better. In the results presented above, being Catholic (as opposed to begin Protestant) substantially increases the odds of voting for or identifying with the Democratic Party across the board. The results of the multivariate analyses confirm that the differences in partisan support that were found to exist between Catholics and Protestants are not spurious. Put simply, Catholics are more Democratic than Protestants.

Examining the coefficients of the remaining independent variables also results in some interesting findings. Not surprisingly, family income levels and membership in a union household strongly affect individuals' electoral behavior. Union membership produces increased likelihood of Democratic support. This relationship remains much the same today as it was in the 1950s, and has been extremely consistent over time (statistically significant at the .05 level in fifty-six out of fifty-nine instances). As family income increases, the likelihood of voting for or identifying with the Democratic Party decreases for all years. Failing to achieve significance at the .05 level just seven times, family income has consistently affected individuals' electoral behavior. The impact of family income also appears to have increased since the mid-1970s on all three support indicators, bolstering the earlier finding of a growing class cleavage within American Catholicism in terms of electoral behavior. The results presented above also reinforce the recent findings by Stonecash that social class has become an increasingly powerful force in Americans' electoral behavior over the last twenty to thirty years.[2]

Southern residence has also had a strong impact on electoral behavior over time, but the nature of its impact has changed dramatically. For much of the past fifty years, living in the South made an individual much more likely to vote for or identify with the Democratic Party. The strength of this relationship diminished over time, and in recent years has undergone a complete reversal. In the 1990s, living in the South makes Americans less likely to support the Democrats. This finding, much the same as those reported for family income and residence in a union household, coincides with much of the recent research on electoral behavior in the United States.

The results obtained for age and female gender present much more of a mixed bag, so to speak. The impact of age on electoral behavior achieves statistical significance at the .05 level in only nineteen instances. The odds increases for this variable are generally quite small, and exhibit fluctuations in the direction of impact. The estimates for female gender are significant at the .05 level in only seventeen out of a possible fifty-nine instances, a figure that is certainly smaller than anticipated given the considerable attention devoted to the gender gap in American electoral politics. However, the effects of gender have been increasing in recent years.

Examination of the coefficients for church attendance also produces some interesting findings. With only five exceptions, higher levels of church attendance have resulted in decreased support of the Democratic Party. However, from 1952-1986 the impact of church attendance is usually very small, reaching statistical significance at the .05 level only sixteen out of a possible forty-one times. Since 1986, the effect of church attendance on vote choice and party identification has grown considerably. In fifteen out of a possible eighteen instances church attendance is significant at the .05 level, and the odds increases in these cases are quite large. Religious salience, at least as measured by church attendance, does appear to be having a greater effect on electoral behavior over the last decade.

The results of the second set of models covering the period from 1980-2000 (tables 7.4-7.6) for the most part reinforce the findings discussed above. Catholic affiliation still results in an increased likelihood of supporting the Democrats. Catholic affiliation achieves significance at the .05 level in nineteen of twenty-six instances, and six of the seven failures to reach this level were by very slim margins. The magnitudes of the odds increases for Catholic affiliation do decline a small amount from those reported in tables 7.1-7.3, but this is to be expected with the inclusion of additional independent variables. Family income and living in a union household remain important determinants of vote choice and party identification, while age and female gender retain the somewhat mixed patterns presented in the first set of models. The results for southern residence are very similar as well.

The most interesting aspects of the second set of models involve the two newly introduced dependent variables—Hispanic ethnicity and religious salience. Hispanic ethnicity has had a consistent and relatively strong effect on individuals' electoral behavior, with the result being that Hispanics are more likely to support the Democratic Party. This comes as no surprise, given the Latino preference for the Democrats that previous researchers have found. More important for the purposes of this project is the fact the Catholic affiliation remains significant when Hispanic ethnicity is included in the multivariate models. This result supports the earlier claim that Catholic electoral behavior remains distinct from that of Protestants even when Hispanic ethnicity is controlled for. The continued difference between the electoral behavior of Catholics and Protestants is not just a result of the rapidly increasing number of Hispanic Catholics in the United States.

The results generated for religious salience are intriguing. Until 1992 (with the exception of 1980), the effect of religious salience was either very small, as in the cases of presidential vote and party identification, or marked by rather wild fluctuations, as is the case for House vote. Since 1992 this has changed. Over the last ten years, religious salience level has come to have a significant impact on electoral behavior. Those with low levels of salience are strongly and consistently more supportive of the Democratic Party than are those with high levels of religious salience. These results support the claims made by previous researchers about the increasing importance of religious salience in American electoral behavior.[3] Based on these results, it certainly appears that a new religious cleavage based on salience has developed alongside the more traditional denomination divisions. Both are now relevant in determining Americans' electoral behavior.

Given the rise in ideological polarization American politics has witnessed in recent years,[4] the idea of a new political cleavage based on religious salience is very plausible. The multivariate results presented above do indeed point to the existence of such an electoral division. These results also raise an important question. If there is in fact something inherent in Catholicism that produces an increased likelihood of supporting the Democratic Party, why have those Catholics for whom religion is highly salient become more likely to support the GOP during the 1990s? This was certainly not the case in 1950s, 1960s (using church attendance as the measure of religious salience), or even in the 1980s. What happened?

At this point I can offer only somewhat informed speculation. It is possible that the high level of emphasis that the church places on the issue of abortion (some would say at the expense of other issues supposedly important to the Catholic Church) has resulted in decreased Democratic support among those Catholics for whom religion is highly salient. A recent example of the church's high level of concern is contained in the pamphlet *Faithful Citizenship: Civic Responsibility for a New Millennium*. As noted, this publication was prepared by the church as a guide for parishioners regarding the political responsibility of Catholics, and was widely distributed during Masses leading up to the 2000 elections. In the three sections of this pamphlet explicitly focused on the political responsibility of Catholics ("Challenges for Believers," "A Call to Faithful Citizenship," and "Moral Priorities for Public Life"), abortion is the first issue discussed.[5] Highly committed Catholics could be receiving the message that abortion is the most important political issue in the eyes of the church. If this is the case, then the recent move of high salience Catholics to the Republican Party makes sense. Very preliminary analyses of this possibility have been conducted and the results have been mixed and not easily interpreted. Further examination is needed to explain this recent but important shift in Catholic electoral behavior.

What is clear from the results reported in this chapter is that the electoral behavior of Catholics in the United States continues to differ from that of Protestants. Catholics remain much more likely than Protestants to support the Democratic Party, a phenomenon that cannot be accounted for by the effects of other social characteristics such as family income levels, gender, or levels of religious salience. As has been the case at least since the introduction of reliable survey data in the 1930s, and quite likely long before that, white American Catholics are more Democratic in the partisan tendencies than white American Protestants. And religious affiliation appears to be the driving force behind this partisan difference.

Notes

1. For complete information on the coding of each of the variables included in the analyses, see the notes at the bottom of each table.

2. Jeffrey M. Stonecash, *Class and Party in American Politics* (Boulder, Colo.: Westview Press, 2000).

3. John R. Petrocik, "Reformulating the Party Coalitions: The 'Christian Democratic' Republicans" (paper presented at the annual meeting of the American Political Science Association, Boston, Mass., Sept. 1998); Geoffrey C. Layman, "Religion and Political Behavior in the United States: The Impact of Beliefs, Affiliations, and Commitment from 1980-1994," *Public Opinion Quarterly* 61, no. 2 (Summer 1997): 288-316; Lyman A. Kellstedt, John C. Green, James L. Guth, and Corwin E. Smidt, "Religious Voting Blocs in the 1992 Election: The Year of the Evangelical?" *Sociology of Religion* 55, no. 3 (Fall 1994): 307-26.

4. Alan I. Abramowitz and Kyle A. Saunders, "Ideological Realignment in the U.S. Electorate," *Journal of Politics* 60, no. 3 (Aug. 1998): 634-52; Alan I. Abramowitz, "Issue Evolution Reconsidered: Racial Attitudes and Partisanship in the U.S. Electorate," *American Journal of Political Science* 38, no. 1 (Feb. 1994): 1-24.

5. Administrative Board of the U.S. Catholic Bishops, *Faithful Citizenship: Civic Responsibility for a New Millennium* (Washington, D.C.: United States Catholic Conference, 1999).

Conclusion

Questions Answered

Now that much ink has been spilled and a seemingly endless number of data analyses have been completed, it is time to return to the questions posed at the outset of this examination in an effort to provide some answers. First, have American Catholics abandoned the Democratic Party? The answer to this question is clearly no. Certainly, there has been some decline in Catholic support for the Democrats over the last thirty years, as many analysts have noted.[1] However, Catholics have most certainly not abandoned or deserted the party. As Bendyna and Jelen note, a majority of Catholics still support the Democratic Party. Given the dramatic increases in family income, education levels, and suburban residence experienced by Catholics over the last sixty years combined with the disappearance of overt anti-Catholic prejudice and the assimilation of Catholics into the mainstream of American society, an increase in Republican support among Catholics is not surprising. What is surprising is that the movement by Catholics toward the GOP and away from the Democrats has been so small, especially when compared to other segments of the American population.[2] In terms of their presidential vote, House vote, and party identification American Catholics remain more Democratic than Republican, although the margin by which this is the case certainly has decreased somewhat from past years.

The second key question asked at the beginning of this project involved Catholic electoral behavior as compared to that of Protestants. Marked by large differences for well over 100 years, the question was did these differences between Catholics and Protestants remain significant in contemporary American electoral politics. The conventional wisdom response to this question has been no. For example, Kosmin and Lachman argued that "the partisan differences between Catholics and Protestants are marginal today."[3] Hunter claimed that the political relevance of differences between Catholics and Protestants "has largely become defunct."[4] Accurately summing up the thoughts of many political analysts, Prendergast characterized the current state of Catholic electoral behavior in comparison to Protestant electoral behavior in the following manner: "The hefty Democratic margins of old are not found in the voting behavior of Catholics in the 1990s. The new pattern shows a Catholic vote that has lost much of its distinctiveness."[5]

The findings presented in this analysis clearly establish that claims such as those made above are incorrect. The electoral behavior of Catholics clearly remains distinct from that of Protestants. Catholics are much more supportive of the Democratic Party than are Protestants. These differences are quite large, generally about 10-20 percentage points, and remarkably consistent, with the exception of the years from 1960-1964. Despite convergence with Protestants on a wide array of social and demographic characteristics, Catholics remain much more Democratic than their Protestant counterparts. Catholics still constitute a distinct group in American electoral politics.

This study has produced several other interesting findings regarding Catholic electoral behavior. One such finding is the development of a rather substantial class cleavage within the Catholic electorate. Since the 1970s Catholics in the upper third of the income distribution have been significantly more Republican in their vote choice and party identification than Catholics in the middle and lower thirds of the distribution. The gap has grown in the 1980s and 1990s, and shows no signs of disappearing. Future analyses will need to devote more attention to this development.

Age and gender were also shown to affect Catholic electoral behavior. Mirroring trends within the American electorate as a whole, Catholic women were found to be more Democratic than Catholic men since the 1970s. Also since the 1970s, older Catholics were shown to be more Democratic than younger Catholics. However, the differences in Democratic support by age among Catholics declined in the 1990s, raising the possibility that age differences are becoming less relevant to Catholic electoral behavior. This too bears watching.

Finally, Hispanic Catholics were shown to be more Democratic than white, non-Hispanic Catholics. Given the fact that Hispanics make up an increasing percentage of the American Catholic population, this finding certainly merits the attention of future scholars examining Catholic electoral behavior.

Future Directions

The evidence presented here clearly establishes two facts about the electoral behavior of Roman Catholics in the United States. First, Catholics are more likely to support the Democratic Party than the Republican Party. Second, Catholics are much more supportive of the Democrats than are Protestants. These are important findings. However, it is more important to understand the reasons behind these phenomena. Why are Catholics more likely than Protestants to vote for and identify with the Democratic Party?

Chapter 6 of this book attempted to answer this question. Taking a cue from the work of scholars such as Benson and Williams and Leege and Welch, I attempted to examine religious worldviews as the possible source of differences in electoral behavior between Catholics and Protestants. Specifically, I adopted their use of communal versus individualistic worldviews and applied it to Catholics and Protestants.[6] Borrowing heavily from the work of Greeley and Tropman, I hypothesized that Catholicism imparts a worldview to its adherents that is more communal in nature and focused more on equality than does Protestantism, which tends to inculcate in its followers a worldview that is more concerned with individualism and freedom.[7] I advanced the claim that these distinct worldviews could account for the observed differences in electoral behavior between Catholics and Protestants.

The empirical evidence presented in chapter 6 provides some support for my hypothesis. On selected political issues, Catholics were shown to be more likely than Protestants to support the "communal" position. However the differences in issue positions between Catholics and Protestants were not large, and thus the support for my hypothesis was by no means overwhelming. This lack of strong empirical support does not however, exclude the possibility that religious worldviews account for the differences in the electoral behavior of Catholics and Protestants. As Greeley relates, religion (for some individuals) provides meaning to the events and experiences that individuals encounter.[8] It is a lens, although perhaps one of many, through which a person views the world. If Durkheim is correct in his belief that religion's true function is to assist individuals in living their lives and to provide reasons for their actions (or non-actions), then it is not surprising that religion can have a powerful impact on political behavior.[9] The reason why social scientists have yet to produce strong evidence for the impact of religious worldviews on electoral behavior may be because we have yet to recognize exactly how religion can affect political behavior.[10] Those of us who study electoral behavior empirically are at a particular disadvantage in that two of the primary tools we use to carry out our work—the NES and GSS datasets—do not provide any data to properly examine the role of religious worldviews in electoral behavior.[11] Future research needs to devise a way in which to better examine religious worldviews and their impact on individuals' political behavior. Until a more complete understanding of the political role of religious worldviews is achieved, we are unlikely to fully comprehend the role religion plays in electoral behavior.

Even without such a complete understanding, it is still abundantly clear that when examining American electoral behavior, religion matters. If the findings presented in this study do nothing else, they should serve to substantiate the importance of religion for political behavior. Religion plays a significant role in individuals' vote choice and party identification. The role of religion is potentially of equal importance to the role played by other social group characteristics such as social class, gender, ethnicity, and race. Echoing the sentiments of Leege and Kellstedt, a full understanding of American elections and the electoral behavior of Americans is impossible without examining the role of religion.[12]

Notes

1. See chapters 2 and 3 for examples of this work.
2. Mary E. Bendyna and Ted G. Jelen, "Catholic Political Behavior in the United States: An Overview and Agenda" (paper presented at the annual meeting of the American Political Science Association, Boston, Mass., Sept. 1998), 6-7.
3. Barry A. Kosmin and Seymour P. Lachman, *One Nation under God: Religion in Contemporary American Society* (New York: Harmony Books, 1993), 191.
4. James Davison Hunter, *Culture Wars: The Struggle to Define America* (New York: Basic Books, 1991), 105.
5. William B. Prendergast, *The Catholic Voter in American Politics: The Passing of a Democratic Monolith* (Washington, D.C.: Georgetown University Press, 1999), 203.
6. These scholars have successfully utilized the concept of individualistic and communal worldviews to account for a number of differences in political attitudes and behaviors. For examples of this work, see: Peter L. Benson and Dorothy L. Williams, *Religion on Capitol Hill: Myths and Realities* (San Francisco: Harper and Row Publishers, 1982); Michael R. Welch and David C. Leege, "Religious Predictors of Catholic Parishioners Sociopolitical Attitudes: Devotional Style, Closeness to God, Imagery, and Agentic/Communal Religious Identity," *Journal for the Scientific Study of Religion* 27, no. 4 (Dec. 1988): 536-53; David C. Leege, "Catholics and the Civic Order: Parish Participation, Politics, and Civic Participation," *Review of Politics* 50, no. 4 (Fall 1988): 704-36; David C. Leege and Michael R. Welch, "Religious Roots of Political Orientations: Variations among American Catholic Parishioners," *Journal of Politics* 51, no. 1 (Feb. 1989): 137-62.
7. Andrew M. Greeley, "Protestant and Catholic: Is the Analogical Imagination Extinct?" *American Sociological Review* 54, no. 4 (Aug. 1989): 485-502; John E. Tropman, *The Catholic Ethic in American Society: An Exploration of Values* (San Francisco: Jossey-Bass Publishers, 1995); Andrew M. Greeley, *The Catholic Imagination* (Berkeley, Calif.: University of California Press, 2000).
8. Andrew M. Greeley, *The Religious Imagination* (New York: Sadlier, 1981), 5.
9. Emile Durkheim, *The Elementary Forms of Religious Life*, translated by Karen E. Fields, (New York: The Free Press, 1995), 419.
10. David C. Leege and Lyman A. Kellstedt, "Religious Worldviews and Political Philosophies: Capturing Theory in the Grand Manner through Empirical Data," in *Rediscovering the Religious Factor in American Politics*, ed. David C. Leege and Lyman A. Kellstedt (Armonk, N.Y.: M.E. Sharpe, 1993), 228.
11. Leege and Kellstedt, "Religious Worldviews," 220.
12. David C. Leege and Lyman A. Kellstedt, Preface to *Rediscovering the Religious Factor in American Politics*, ed. David C. Leege and Lyman A. Kellstedt (Armonk, N.Y.: M.E. Sharpe, 1993), xi.

Bibliography

Abbott, Walter M., ed. *The Documents of Vatican II*. New York: Guild Press, 1966.

Abell, Aaron I. *American Catholicism and Social Action: A Search for Social Justice, 1865-1950*. Notre Dame, Ind.: University of Notre Dame Press, 1963.

Abramowitz, Alan I. "Issue Evolution Reconsidered: Racial Attitudes and Partisanship in the U.S. Electorate." *American Journal of Political Science* 38, no. 1 (Feb. 1994): 1-24.

Abramowitz, Alan I., and Kyle A. Saunders. "Ideological Realignment in the U.S. Electorate." *Journal of Politics* 60, no. 3 (Aug. 1998): 634-52.

Abramson, Paul R. "Developing Party Identification: A Further Examination of Life-Cycle, Generational, and Period Effects." *American Journal of Political Science* 23, no. 1 (Feb. 1979): 78-96.

Abramson, Paul R., John H. Aldrich, and David W. Rohde. *Change and Continuity in the 1992 Elections*. Washington, D.C.: Congressional Quarterly Press, 1995.

Administrative Board of the U.S. Catholic Bishops. *Faithful Citizenship: Civic Responsibility for a New Millennium*. Washington, D.C.: United States Catholic Conference, 1999.

Allinsmith, Wesley, and Beverly Allinsmith. "Religious Affiliation and Politico-Economic Attitudes: A Study of Eight Major U.S. Religious Groups." *Public Opinion Quarterly* 12, no. 3 (Fall 1948): 377-89.

Allit, Patrick. *Catholic Intellectuals and Conservative Politics in America, 1950-1985*. Ithaca, N.Y.: Cornell University Press, 1993.

Allswang, John M. *A House for All Peoples: Ethnic Politics in Chicago, 1890-1936*. Lexington, Ky.: University Press of Kentucky, 1971.

———. *The New Deal and American Politics: A Study in Political Change*. New York: John Wiley & Sons, 1978.

Anbinder, Tyler. *Nativism and Slavery: The Northern Know Nothings and the Politics of the 1850's.* New York: Oxford University Press, 1992.

Axelrod, Robert. "Where the Votes Come From: An Analysis of Electoral Coalitions, 1952-1968." *American Political Science Review* 66, no. 1 (Mar. 1972): 11-20.

Baumer, Donald C., and Howard J. Gold. "Party Images and the American Electorate." *American Politics Quarterly* 23, no. 1 (Jan. 1995): 33-61.

―――. "Party Images after the Clinton Years." Paper presented at the annual meeting of the New England Political Science Association, Portland, Maine, May 2002.

Beatty, Kathleen Murphy, and Oliver Walter. "A Group Theory of Religion and Politics: The Clergy as Group Leaders." *Western Political Quarterly* 49, no. 1 (Mar. 1989): 129-46.

Beck, Paul Allen. *Party Politics in America.* 8th ed. New York: Longman, 1997.

Beigel, Gerard. *Faith and Social Justice in the Teaching of Pope John Paul II.* New York: Peter Lang Publishing, 1997.

Bendyna, Mary E., and Ted G. Jelen. "Catholic Political Behavior in the United States: An Overview and Agenda." Paper presented at the annual meeting of the American Political Science Association, Boston, Mass., Sept. 1998.

Benestad, J. Brian. *The Pursuit of a Just Social Order: Policy Statements of the U.S. Catholic Bishops, 1966-1980.* Washington, D.C.: Ethics and Public Policy Center, 1982.

Bensen, Lee. *The Concept of Jacksonian Democracy: New York as a Test Case.* Princeton, N.J.: Princeton University Press, 1961.

Benson, Peter L., and Dorothy L. Williams. *Religion on Capitol Hill: Myths and Realities.* San Francisco: Harper and Row Publishers, 1982.

Berelson, Bernard R., Paul F. Lazarsfeld, and William N. McPhee. *Voting: A Study of Opinion Formation in a Presidential Campaign.* Chicago: University of Chicago Press, 1954.

Bianchi, Eugene C. *John XXIII and American Protestants.* Washington, D.C.: Corpus Books, 1968.

Billington, Ray Allen. *The Protestant Crusade, 1800-1860: A Study of the Origins of American Nativism.* New York: Macmillan, 1938.

Boileau, David A. "Introduction." Pp. 9-24 in *Principles of Catholic Social Teaching*, edited by David A. Boileau. Milwaukee, Wis.: Marquette University Press, 1998.

Brewer, Mark D. "A Divided Public? Party Images and Mass Polarization in the United States." Paper presented at the annual meeting of the American Political Science Association, Boston, Mass., Aug. 2002.

Brewer, Mark D., Rogan Kersh, and R. Eric Petersen. "Assessing Conventional Wisdom about Religion and Politics: A Preliminary View from the Pews." *Journal for the Scientific Study of Religion* 42, no. 1 (Mar. 2003): 125-36.

Brewer, Mark D., and Jeffrey M. Stonecash. "Class, Race Issues, and Declining White Support for the Democratic Party in the South." *Political Behavior* 23, no. 2 (June 2001): 131-55.

Brooks, Clem, and Jeff Manza. "Social Cleavages and Political Alignments: U.S. Presidential Elections, 1960 to 1992." *American Sociological Review* 62, no. 6 (Dec. 1997): 937-46.

Buchanan, Patrick. *The Conservative Choice.* New York: Quadrangle, 1975.

Burner, David. *The Politics of Provincialism: The Democratic Party in Transition, 1918-1932.* New York: Alfred A. Knopf, 1968.

Burnham, Walter Dean. "The Changing Shape of the American Political Universe." *American Political Science Review* 59, no. 1 (Mar. 1965): 7-28.

Byrnes, Timothy A. *Catholic Bishops in American Politics.* Princeton, N.J.: Princeton University Press, 1991.

———. "The Politics of the American Catholic Hierarchy." *Political Science Quarterly* 108, no. 3 (Fall 1993): 497-514.

Cain, Bruce E., D. Roderick Kiewiet, and Carole J. Uhlaner. "The Acquisition of Partisanship by Latinos and Asian Americans." *American Journal of Political Science* 35, no. 2 (May 1991): 390-422.

Calvez, Jean-Yves. "Economic Policy Issues in Roman Catholic Social Thought." Pp. 15-26 in *The Catholic Challenge to the American Economy,* edited by Thomas M. Gannon. New York: Macmillan, 1987.

Campbell, Angus, Philip E. Converse, Warren E. Miller, and Donald E. Stokes. *The American Voter.* New York: John Wiley and Sons, 1960.

Carey, Patrick W. *The Roman Catholics.* Westport, Conn.: Greenwood Press, 1993.

Carmines, Edward G., and James A. Stimson. *Issue Evolution: Race and the Transformation of American Politics.* Princeton, N.J.: Princeton University Press, 1989.

Carmines, Edward G., and Geoffrey C. Layman. "Issue Evolution in Postwar American Politics: Old Certainties and Fresh Tensions." Pp. 89-134 in *Present Discontents: American Politics in the Very Late Twentieth Century,* edited by Byron E. Shafer. Chatham, N.J.: Chatham House Publishers, Inc., 1997.

Center for the American Woman and Politics. "The Gender Gap: Voting Choices, Party Identification, and Presidential Performance Ratings." *Fact Sheet*. Eagleton Institute of Politics, Rutgers University, July 1996.

Claggett, William. "Partisan Acquisition vs. Partisan Intensity: Life-Cycle, Generational, and Period Effects, 1952-1976." *American Journal of Political Science* 25, no. 2 (May 1981): 193-214.

Clubb, Jerome M. "Party Coalitions in the Early Twentieth Century." Pp. 107-26 in *Party Coalitions in the 1980s*, edited by Seymour Martin Lipset. San Francisco: Institute for Contemporary Studies, 1981.

Clubb, Jerome M., and Howard W. Allen. "The Cities and the Election of 1928: Partisan Realignment?" *American Historical Review* 74, no. 4 (Apr. 1969): 1205-20.

Cochran, Clarke E., Jerry D. Perkins, and Murray Clark Havens. "Public Policy & the Emergence of Religious Politics." *Polity* 19, no. 4 (Summer 1987): 595-612.

Cogley, John. *Catholic America*. New York: The Dial Press, 1973.

Coleman, John A. "American Catholicism." Pp. 232-49 in *World Catholicism in Transition*, edited by Thomas M. Gannon. New York: Macmillan Publishing Company, 1988.

———. "Introduction: A Tradition Celebrated, Reevaluated, and Applied." Pp. 1-10 in *One Hundred Years of Catholic Social Thought*, edited by John A. Coleman. Maryknoll, N.Y.: Orbis Books, 1991.

Conover, Pamela Johnston. "The Influence of Group Identifications on Political Participation and Evaluation." *Journal of Politics* 46, no. 3 (Aug. 1984): 760-85.

Conover, Pamela Johnston, and Stanley Feldman. "Group Identifications, Values, and the Nature of Political Beliefs." *American Politics Quarterly* 12, no. 2 (Apr. 1984): 151-75.

Converse, Philip E. "Religion and Politics: The 1960 Election." Pp. 96-124 in *Elections and the Political Order*, edited by Angus Campbell, Philip E. Converse, Warren E. Miller, and Donald E. Stokes. New York: John Wiley and Sons, 1966.

Crosson, Fred. "Catholic Social Teaching and American Society." Pp. 165-76 in *Principles of Catholic Social Teaching*, edited by David A. Boileau. Milwaukee, Wis.: Marquette University Press, 1998.

Curran, Charles E. "Catholic Social Teaching and Human Morality." Pp. 72-87 in *One Hundred Years of Catholic Social Thought*, edited by John A. Coleman. Maryknoll, N.Y.: Orbis Books, 1991.

D'Antonio, William, James Davidson, Dean Hoge, and Ruth Wallace. *American Catholic Laity in a Changing Church*. Kansas City, Mo.: Sheed and Ward, 1989.

———. *Laity American and Catholic: Transforming the Church*. Kansas City, Mo.: Sheed and Ward, 1996.

Davidson, James D., and Andrea S. Williams. "Megatrends in 20th-century American Catholicism." *Social Compass* 44, no. 4 (Dec. 1997): 507-27.

Davidson, James D., Andrea S. Williams, Richard A. Lamanna, Jan Stenftenagel, Kathleen Maas Weigert, William A. Whalen, and Patricia Wittberg. *The Search for Common Ground: What Unites and Divides Catholic Americans.* Huntington, Ind.: Our Sunday Visitor Publishing Division, 1997.

Davis, James Allan, and Tom W. Smith. *General Social Survey, 1972-1998* (machine readable data file). Principal Investigator, James A. Davis; Director and Co-Principal Investigator, Tom W. Smith; Co-Principal Investigator, Peter V. Marsden, NORC ed. Chicago: National Opinion Research Center, producer, 1998; Storrs, Conn.: The Roper Center for Public Opinion Research, University of Connecticut, distributor.

De Santis, Vincent P. "Catholicism and Presidential Elections, 1865-1900." *Mid-America* 42, no. 2 (Apr. 1960): 67-79.

Deaux, Kay, Anne Reid, Kim Mirrahi, and Dave Cotting. "Connecting the Person to the Social: The Functions of Social Identification." Pp. 91-113 in *The Psychology of the Social Self*, edited by Tom R. Tyler, Roderick M. Kramer, and Oliver P. John. Manweh, N.J.: Lawrence Erlbaum Associates, 1999.

Deck, Allan Figueroa. "The Challenge of Evangelical/Pentecostal Christianity to Hispanic Catholicism." Pp. 409-39 in *Hispanic Catholic Culture in the U.S.: Issues and Concerns*, edited by Jay P. Dolan and Allan Figueroa Deck. Notre Dame, Ind.: University of Notre Dame Press, 1994.

Democratic National Committee. "Democratic Party Credo," in *The Charter and Bylaws of the Democratic Party of the United States.*

Diaz-Stevens, Ana Maria, and Anthony M. Stevens Arroyo. *Recognizing the Latino Resurgence in U.S. Religion.* Boulder, Colo.: Westview Press, 1998.

Dionne, E. J., Jr. "Catholics and the Democrats: Estrangement but Not Desertion." Pp. 307-25 in *Party Coalitions in the 1980s*, edited by Seymour Martin Lipset. San Francisco: Institute for Contemporary Studies, 1981.

Dolan, Jay P. *The American Catholic Experience.* Notre Dame, Ind.: University of Notre Dame Press, 1992.

Dolan, Jay P., R. Scott Appleby, Patricia Byrne, and Debra Campbell. *Transforming Parish Ministry.* New York: The Crossroad Publishing Company, 1989.

Dorr, Donal. *Option for the Poor: One Hundred Years of Vatican Social Teaching.* Maryknoll, N.Y.: Orbis Books, 1983.

Dulce, Berton, and Edward J. Richter. *Religion and the Presidency: A Recurring American Problem.* New York: Macmillan, 1962.

Durkheim, Emile. *The Elementary Forms of Religious Life*. Translated by Karen E. Fields. New York: The Free Press, 1995.

Ellis, John Tracy. *American Catholicism*. 2d ed., rev. Chicago: University of Chicago Press, 1969.

Erikson, Robert S., Thomas D. Lancaster, and David W. Romero. "Group Components of the Presidential Vote, 1952-1984." *Journal of Politics* 51, no. 2 (May 1989): 337-46.

Fee, Joan L. "Party Identification among American Catholics, 1972, 1973." *Ethnicity* 3, no. 1 (Mar. 1976): 53-69.

Flynn, George Q. *American Catholics & the Roosevelt Presidency, 1932-1936*. Lexington, Ky.: University of Kentucky Press, 1968.

Fowler, Robert Booth, Allen D. Hertzke, and Laura R. Olson. *Religion and Politics in America*. 2d ed. Boulder, Colo.: Westview Press, 1999.

Freedman, Samuel G. *The Inheritance*. New York: Simon & Schuster, 1996.

Freeman, Jo. "The Political Culture of the Democratic and Republican Party." *Political Science Quarterly* 101, no. 3 (1986): 327-56.

Fuchs, Lawrence H. *John F. Kennedy and American Catholicism*. New York: Meredith Press, 1967.

Gallup, George, Jr., and Jim Castelli. *The American Catholic People: Their Beliefs, Practices, and Values*. Garden City, N.Y.: Doubleday and Co., 1987.

———. *The People's Religion: American Faith in the 90's*. New York: Macmillan, 1989.

Gerring, John. *Party Ideologies in America, 1828-1996*. New York: Cambridge University Press, 1998.

Gienapp, William. "Politics Seem to Enter into Everything: Political Culture in the North, 1840-1860." Pp. 15-69 in *Essays on American Antebellum Politics, 1840-1860*, edited by Stephen E. Maizlish and John J. Kushma. College Station, Tex.: Texas A&M University Press, 1982.

Gilbert, Christopher P. *The Impact of Churches on Political Behavior*. Westport, Conn.: Greenwood Press, 1993.

Ginsberg, Benjamin. "Critical Elections and the Substance of Party Conflict." *Midwest Journal of Political Science* 16, no. 4 (Nov. 1972): 603-25.

Gleason, Philip. "Catholicism and Cultural Change in the 1960's." *Review of Politics* 34, no. 4 (Oct. 1972): 91-107.

———. "Pluralism, Democracy, and Catholicism in the Era of World War II." *Review of Politics* 49, no. 2 (Spring 1987): 208-30.

———. *Keeping the Faith: American Catholicism Past and Present.* Notre Dame, Ind.: University of Notre Dame Press, 1987.

Glenn, Norval D. "Sources of the Shifts to Political Independence: Some Evidence from a Cohort Analysis." *Social Science Quarterly* 53, no. 3 (Dec. 1972): 494-515.

Glenn, Norval D., and Ruth Hyland. "Religious Preference and Worldly Success: Some Evidence from National Surveys." *American Sociological Review* 32, no. 1 (Feb. 1967): 73-85.

Glock, Charles Y., and Rodney Stark. *Religion and Society in Tension.* Chicago: Rand McNally and Company, 1965.

Greeley, Andrew M. *The American Catholic: A Social Portrait.* New York: Basic Books, 1977.

———. "How Conservative Are American Catholics?" *Political Science Quarterly* 92, no. 2 (Summer 1977): 199-218.

———. "Catholics and Coalition: Where Should They Go?" Pp. 271-95 in *Emerging Coalitions in American Politics*, edited by Seymour Martin Lipset. San Francisco: Institute for Contemporary Studies, 1978.

———. *The Religious Imagination.* New York: Sadlier, 1981.

———. *Religious Change in America.* Cambridge, Mass.: Harvard University Press, 1989.

———. "Protestant and Catholic: Is the Analogical Imagination Extinct?" *American Sociological Review* 54, no. 4 (Aug. 1989): 485-502.

———. *The Catholic Myth: The Behavior and Beliefs of American Catholics.* New York: Charles Scribner's Sons, 1990.

———. *The Catholic Imagination.* Berkeley, Calif.: University of California Press, 2000.

Green, John C., and James L. Guth. "Religion, Representatives, and Roll Calls." *Legislative Studies Quarterly* 16, no. 4 (Nov. 1991): 571-84.

Greer, Scott. "Catholic Voters and the Democratic Party." *Public Opinion Quarterly* 25, no. 4 (Winter 1961): 611-25.

Gurin, Patricia, Arthur H. Miller, and Gerald Gurin. "Stratum Identification and Consciousness." *Social Psychology Quarterly* 43, no. 1 (Mar. 1980): 30-47.

Guth, James L., and John C. Green. "Salience: The Core Concept?" Pp. 157-74 in *Rediscovering the Religious Factor in American Politics*, edited by David C. Leege and Lyman A. Kellstedt. Armonk, N.Y.: M. E. Sharpe, 1993.

Guth, James L., John C. Green, Corwin E. Smidt, Lyman A. Kellstedt, and Margaret M. Poloma. *The Bully Pulpit: The Politics of Protestant Clergy*. Lawrence, Kans.: University Press of Kansas, 1997.

Hadden, Jeffrey K. "Religion and the Construction of Social Problems." Pp. 17-30 in *Religion and Religiosity in America*, edited by Jeffrey K. Hadden and Theodore E. Long. New York: Crossroad Publishing Company, 1983.

Hanna, Mary T. *Catholics and American Politics*. Cambridge, Mass.: Harvard University Press, 1979.

Hennesey, James. *American Catholics*. New York: Oxford University Press, 1981.

Herberg, Will. *Protestant-Catholic-Jew*. Rev. ed. Garden City, N.Y.: Anchor Books, 1960.

Hetherington, Marc J. "Resurgent Mass Partisanship: The Role of Elite Polarization." *American Political Science Review* 95, no. 3 (Sept. 2001): 619-31.

Himmelstein, Jerome L., and James A. McRae, Jr. "Social Issues and Socioeconomic Status." *Public Opinion Quarterly* 52, no. 4 (Winter 1988): 492-512.

Hobgood, Mary E. *Catholic Social Teaching and Economic Theory*. Philadelphia: Temple University Press, 1991.

Hoge, Dean R. "Interpreting Change in American Catholicism: The River and the Floodgate." *Review of Religious Research* 27, no. 4 (June 1986): 289-99.

Hopkins, Charles Howard. *The Rise of the Social Gospel in American Protestantism, 1865-1915*. New Haven, Conn.: Yale University Press, 1967.

Hougland, James G., Jr., and James A. Christensen. "Religion and Politics: The Relationship of Religious Participation to Political Efficacy and Involvement." *Sociology and Social Research* 67, no. 4 (July 1983): 405-20.

Hunt, Larry L. "The Spirit of Hispanic Protestantism in the United States: National Survey Comparisons of Catholics and Non-Catholics." *Social Science Quarterly* 79, no. 4 (Dec. 1998): 828-45.

Hunter, James Davison. *Culture Wars: The Struggle to Define America*. New York: Basic Books, 1991.

Huthmacher, J. Joseph. *Massachusetts People and Politics, 1919-1933*. Cambridge, Mass.: Belknap Press, 1959.

Jackson, Robert A., and Thomas A. Carsey. "Group Components of U.S. Presidential Voting Across the States." *Political Behavior* 21, no. 2 (June 1999): 123-51.

Jelen, Ted G. *The Political Mobilization of Religious Beliefs*. New York: Praeger, 1991.

———. "Political Christianity: A Contextual Analysis." *American Journal of Political Science* 36, no. 3 (Aug. 1992): 692-714.

———. "The Political Consequences of Religious Group Attitudes." *Journal of Politics* 55, no. 1 (Feb. 1993): 178-90.

Jensen, Richard. *The Winning of the Midwest*. Chicago: University of Chicago Press, 1971.

———. "Party Coalitions and the Search for Modern Values: 1820-1970." Pp. 55-85 in *Party Coalitions in the 1980s*, edited by Seymour Martin Lipset. San Francisco: Institute for Contemporary Studies, 1981.

Johnson, Stephen D. "What Relates to Vote for Three Religious Categories." *Sociology of Religion* 55, no. 3 (Fall 1994): 263-75.

Keith, Bruce E., David B. Magleby, Candice J. Nelson, Elizabeth Orr, Mark C. Westlye, and Raymond E. Wolfinger. *The Myth of the Independent Voter*. Berkeley, Calif.: University of California Press, 1992.

Kellstedt, Lyman A. "Evangelicals and Political Realignment." Pp. 99-117 in *Contemporary Evangelical Political Involvement*, edited by Corwin E. Smidt. Lanham, Md.: University Press of America, 1989.

Kellstedt, Lyman A., and John C. Green. "Knowing God's Many People: Denominational Preference and Political Behavior." Pp. 53-71 in *Rediscovering the Religious Factor in American Politics*, edited by David C. Leege and Lyman A. Kellstedt. Armonk, N.Y.: M. E. Sharpe, 1993.

Kellstedt, Lyman A., John C. Green, James L. Guth, and Corwin E. Smidt. "Grasping the Essentials: The Social Embodiment of Religion and Political Behavior." Pp. 174-92 in *Religion and the Culture Wars: Dispatches from the Front*, edited by John C. Green, James L. Guth, Corwin E. Smidt, and Lyman A. Kellstedt. Lanham, Md.: Rowman & Littlefield, 1996.

———. "Religious Voting Blocs in the 1992 Elections: The Year of the Evangelical?" *Sociology of Religion* 55, no. 3 (Fall 1994): 307-26.

Kellstedt, Lyman A., and Mark A. Noll. "Religion, Voting for President, and Party Identification." Pp. 355-79 in *Religion and American Politics: From the Colonial Period to the 1980s*, edited by Mark A. Noll. New York: Oxford University Press, 1990.

Kellstedt, Lyman A., Corwin E. Smidt, and Paul M. Kellstedt. "Religious Tradition, Denomination, and Commitment: White Protestants and the 1988 Election." Pp. 139-58 in

The Bible and the Ballot Box: Religion and Politics in the 1988 Election, edited by James L. Guth and John C. Green. Boulder, Colo.: Westview Press, 1991.

Kenski, Henry C. "The Gender Factor in a Changing Electorate." Pp. 38-60 in *The Politics of the Gender Gap: The Social Construction of Political Science*, edited by Carol M. Mueller. Newbury Park, Calif.: Sage Publications, 1988.

Kenski, Henry C., and William Lockwood. "The Catholic Vote from 1980 to 1986: Continuity or Change?" Pp. 109-37 in *Religion and Political Behavior in the United States*, edited by Ted G. Jelen. New York: Praeger, 1989.

―――. "Catholic Voting Behavior in 1988: A Critical Swing Vote." Pp. 173-87 in *The Bible and the Ballot Box: Religion and Politics in the 1988 Election*, edited by James L. Guth and John C. Green. Boulder, Colo.: Westview Press, 1991.

Kettern, B. "Social Justice: The Development of the Concept of 'iustitia' from St. Thomas Aquinas through the Social Encyclicals." Pp. 84-101 in *Principles of Catholic Social Teaching*, edited by David A. Boileau. Milwaukee, Wis.: Marquette University Press, 1998.

Kinzer, Donald L. *An Episode of Anti-Catholicism: The American Protective Association*. Seattle: University of Washington Press, 1964.

Kleppner, Paul. *The Cross of Culture: A Social Analysis of Midwestern Politics, 1850-1900*. New York: The Free Press, 1970.

―――. *The Third Electoral System, 1853-1892*. Chapel Hill, N.C.: University of North Carolina Press, 1979.

―――. *Continuity and Change in Electoral Politics, 1893-1928*. Westport, Conn.: Greenwood Press, 1987.

Knoke, David. "Religion, Stratification and Politics: America in the 1960s." *American Journal of Political Science* 18, no. 2 (May 1974): 331-45.

―――. *Change and Continuity in American Politics*. Baltimore, Md.: Johns Hopkins University Press, 1976.

Kohfeld, Carol Weitzel, and Robert R. Huckfeldt. *Race and the Decline of Class in American Politics*. Urbana, Ill.: University of Illinois Press, 1989.

Kosmin, Barry A., and Seymour P. Lachman. *One Nation under God: Religion in Contemporary American Society*. New York: Harmony Books, 1993.

Ladd, Everett, Jr., Charles Hadley, and Lauriston King. "A New Political Realignment?" *The Public Interest* 23 (Spring 1971): 46-63.

Ladd, Everett Carll, Jr., with Charles D. Hadley. *Transformations of the American Party System*. New York: W. W. Norton & Company, 1975.

Land, Philip S. *Catholic Social Teaching: As I Have Lived, Loathed, and Loved It*. Chicago: Loyola University Press, 1991.

Lannie, Vincent P. "Alienation in America: The Immigrant Catholic and Public Education in Pre-Civil War America." *Review of Politics* 32, no. 4 (Oct. 1970): 503-21.

Layman, Geoffrey. *The Great Divide: Religious and Cultural Conflict in American Party Politics*. New York: Columbia University Press, 2001.

Layman, Geoffrey C. "Religion and Political Behavior in the United States: The Impact of Beliefs, Affiliations, and Commitment from 1980-1994." *Public Opinion Quarterly* 61, no. 2 (Summer 1997): 288-316.

Layman, Geoffrey C., and Edward G. Carmines. "Cultural Conflict in American Politics: Religious Traditionalism, Postmaterialism, and U.S. Political Behavior." *Journal of Politics* 59, no. 3 (Aug. 1997): 751-77.

Lazarsfeld, Paul F., Bernard Berelson, and Hazel Gaudet. *The People's Choice: How the Voter Makes Up His Mind in a Presidential Campaign*. 2d ed. New York: Columbia University Press, 1948.

Leege, David C. "Catholics and the Civic Order: Parish Participation, Politics, and Civic Participation." *Review of Politics* 50, no. 4 (Fall 1988): 704-36.

———. "Religion and Politics in Theoretical Perspective." Pp. 3-25 in *Rediscovering the Religious Factor in American Politics*, edited by David C. Leege and Lyman A. Kellstedt. Armonk, N.Y.: M. E. Sharpe, 1993.

———. "The Catholic Vote in '96: Can It Be Found in Church?" *Commonweal* 123 (Sept. 27, 1996): 11-18.

Leege, David C., and Lyman A. Kellstedt. "Religious Worldviews and Political Philosophies: Capturing Theory in the Grand Manner through Empirical Data." Pp. 216-31 in *Rediscovering the Religious Factor in American Politics*, edited by David C. Leege and Lyman A. Kellstedt. Armonk, N.Y.: M. E. Sharpe, 1993.

———. "Preface." Pp. xi-xv in *Rediscovering the Religious Factor in American Politics*, edited by David C. Leege and Lyman A. Kellstedt. Armonk, N.Y.: M. E. Sharpe, 1993.

Leege, David C., and Michael R. Welch. "Religious Roots of Political Orientations: Variations among American Catholic Parishioners." *Journal of Politics* 51, no. 1 (Feb. 1989): 137-62.

Levine, Jeffrey, Edward G. Carmines, and Robert Huckfeldt. "The Rise of Ideology in the Post-New Deal Party System, 1972-1992." *American Politics Quarterly* 25, no. 1 (Jan. 1997): 19-34.

Lipset, Seymour Martin. *Political Man*. Anchor Books Edition. Garden City, N.Y.: Doubleday & Co., 1963.

Lipset, Seymour Martin, ed. *Party Coalitions in the 1980s*. San Francisco: Institute for Contemporary Studies, 1981.

Lopatto, Paul. *Religion and the Presidential Election*. New York: Praeger, 1985.

Macaluso, Theodore F., and John Wanat. "Voting Turnout and Religiosity." *Polity* 12, no. 1 (Fall 1979): 158-69.

Maddox, William S. "Changing Electoral Coalitions from 1952 to 1976." *Social Science Quarterly* 60, no. 2 (Sept. 1979): 309-13.

Manheim, Karl. "The Problem of Generations." Pp. 276-320 *Essays on the Sociology of Knowledge*, edited by Paul Kecskemeti. New York: Oxford University Press, 1952.

Manza, Jeff, and Clem Brooks. "The Religious Factor in U.S. Presidential Elections, 1960-1992." *American Journal of Sociology* 103, no. 1 (July 1997): 38-81.

Martinson, Oscar B., and E. A. Wilkening. "Religious Participation and Involvement in Local Politics throughout the Life Cycle." *Sociological Focus* 20, no. 4 (Oct. 1987): 309-18.

McAvoy, Thomas T. "American Catholicism and the *Aggiornamento*." *Review of Politics* 30, no. 3 (July 1968): 275-91.

———. *A History of the Catholic Church in the United States*. Notre Dame, Ind.: University of Notre Dame Press, 1969.

McBrien, Richard P. *Catholicism*. Rev. ed. San Francisco: HarperCollins Publishers, 1994.

Menendez, Albert J. *Religion at the Polls*. Philadelphia: The Westminster Press, 1977.

Miller, Arthur H., and Martin P. Wattenberg. "Politics from the Pulpit: Religiosity and the 1980 Elections." *Public Opinion Quarterly* 48, no. 1b (Spring 1984): 301-17.

Miller, Warren E. "Party Identification, Realignment, and Party Voting: Back to the Basics." *American Political Science Review* 85, no. 2 (June 1991): 557-68.

Miller, Warren E., and the National Election Studies. *American National Election Studies Cumulative Data File, 1948-1998* [computer file]. 10th ICPSR version. Ann Arbor, Mich.: University of Michigan, Center for Political Studies [producer], 1999. Ann Arbor, Mich.: Inter-University Consortium for Political and Social Research [distributor], 1999.

Moore, Joan. "The Social Fabric on the Hispanic Community since 1965." Pp. 6-49 in *Hispanic Catholic Culture in the U.S.: Issues and Concerns*, edited by Jay P. Dolan and Allan Figueroa Deck. Notre Dame, Ind.: University of Notre Dame Press, 1994.

Moore, R. Laurence. *Religious Outsiders and the Making of Americans*. New York: Oxford University Press, 1986.

Morris, Charles R. *American Catholic*. New York: Random House, 1997.

Mueller, Franz H. *The Church and the Social Question*. Washington, D.C.: American Enterprise Institute, 1984.

Mueller, G. H. "The Protestant and the Catholic Ethic." *Annual Review of the Social Sciences of Religion* 2 (1978): 143-66.

Mueller, Samuel A. "The New Triple Melting Pot: Herberg Revisited." *Review of Religious Research* 13, no. 1 (Fall 1971), 18-33.

National Conference of Catholic Bishops. *Economic Justice for All*. Washington, D.C.: United States Catholic Conference, 1986.

Neal, Marie Augusta. "Faith and Social Ministry: A Catholic Perspective." Pp. 205-26 in *Faith and Social Ministry: Ten Christian Perspectives*, edited by James D. Davidson, C. Lincoln Johnson, and Alan K. Mock. Chicago: Loyola University Press, 1990.

Nie, Norman H., Sidney Verba, and John R. Petrocik. *The Changing American Voter*. Cambridge, Mass.: Harvard University Press, 1976.

Niebuhr, H. Richard. *The Social Sources of Denominationalism*. Hamden, Conn.: The Shoe String Press, 1954.

Novak, Michael. *The Catholic Ethic and the Spirit of Capitalism*. New York: The Free Press, 1993.

O'Brien, David J. *American Catholics and Social Reform*. New York: Oxford University Press, 1968.

———. "A Century of Catholic Social Teaching: Contexts and Comments." Pp. 13-24 in *One Hundred Years of Catholic Social Thought*, edited by John A. Coleman. Maryknoll, N.Y.: Orbis Books, 1991.

O'Brien, David J., and Thomas A. Shannon, eds. *Catholic Social Thought: The Documentary Heritage*. Maryknoll, N.Y.: Orbis Books, 1992.

Page, Benjamin I., and Robert Y. Shapiro. *The Rational Public*. Chicago: University of Chicago Press, 1992.

Parenti, Michael. "Political Values and Religious Cultures: Jews, Catholics, and Protestants." *Journal for the Scientific Study of Religion* 6, no. 2 (Fall 1967): 259-69.

Parsons, Talcott. *The Social System*. New York: The Free Press, 1951.

Penning, James M. "Changing Partisanship and Issue Stands among American Catholics." *Sociological Analysis* 47, no. 1 (Spring 1986): 29-49.

———. "The Political Behavior of American Catholics: An Assessment of the Impact of Group Integration vs. Group Identification." *Western Political Quarterly* 41, no. 2 (June 1988): 289-308

Peterson, Steven A. "Church Participation and Political Participation: The Spillover Effect." *American Politics Quarterly* 20, no. 1 (Jan. 1992): 123-39.

Petrocik, John R. *Party Coalitions: Realignments and the Decline of the New Deal Party System*. Chicago: University of Chicago Press, 1981.

———. "New Party Coalitions and the Nationalization of the South." *Journal of Politics* 49, no. 2 (May 1987): 347-75.

———. "The 'Christian Democratic' Republicans." Paper presented at the annual meeting of the American Political Science Association, Boston, Mass., Sept. 1998.

Phillips, Kevin. *The Emerging Republican Majority*. New Rochelle, N.Y.: Arlington House, 1969.

Prendergast, William B. *The Catholic Voter in American Politics: The Passing of a Democratic Monolith*. Washington, D.C.: Georgetown University Press, 1999.

Reichley, A. James. *Religion in American Public Life*. Washington, D.C.: The Brookings Institution, 1985.

———. "Religion and the Future of American Politics." *Political Science Quarterly* 101, no. 1 (1986): 23-47.

Republican National Committee. *The Republican Oath*.

Rokeach, Milton. *The Nature of Human Values*. New York: The Free Press, 1973.

Rossiter, Clinton. *Parties and Politics in America*. Ithaca, N.Y.: Cornell University Press, 1960.

Rubin, Richard L. *The Democratic Coalition and the Politics of Change*. New York: Oxford University Press, 1976.

Rusher, William A. *The Making of a New Majority Party*. New York: Sheed and Ward, 1975.

Ryan, John A. "The Bishops' Program of Social Reconstruction." *American Catholic Sociological Review* 5 (March 1944): 25-33.

Sandoval, Moises. *On the Move: A History of the Hispanic Church in the United States*. Maryknoll, N.Y.: Orbis Books, 1990.

Sapiro, Virginia, Steven J. Rosenstone, and the National Election Studies. *American National Election Studies Cumulative Data File, 1948-2000* [computer file]. Ann Arbor,

Mich.: University of Michigan, Center for Political Studies [producer and distributor], 2001.

Saunders, Arthur. "The Meaning of Party Images." *Western Political Quarterly* 41, no. 3 (Sept. 1988): 583-99.

Schuck, Michael J. *That They Be One: The Social Teaching of the Papal Encyclicals, 1740-1989.* Washington, D.C.: Georgetown University Press, 1991.

Schultheis, Michael J., Edward P. DeBerri, and Peter J. Henriot. *Our Best Kept Secret: The Rich Heritage of Catholic Social Teaching.* Washington, D.C.: Center of Concern, 1987.

Shively, W. Phillips. "The Relationship between Age and Party Identification: A Cohort Analysis." *Political Methodology* 6, no. 4 (Fall 1979): 437-46.

Silbey, Joel H. "The Rise and Fall of American Political Parties, 1790-1993." Pp. 3-18 in *The Parties Respond*, 2d ed., edited by L. Sandy Maisel. Boulder, Colo.: Westview Press, 1994.

Smidt, Corwin E., ed. *Evangelical Political Involvement.* Lanham, Md.: University Press of America, 1989.

Stanley, Harold W. *Voter Mobilization and the Politics of Race: The South and Universal Suffrage.* New York: Praeger, 1987.

Stanley, Harold W., William T. Bianco, and Richard G. Niemi. "Partisanship and Group Support Over Time: A Multivariate Analysis." *American Political Science Review* 80, no. 3 (Sept. 1986): 969-76.

Stanley, Harold W., and Richard G. Niemi. "Partisanship and Group Support, 1952-1988." *American Politics Quarterly* 19, no. 2 (Apr. 1991): 189-210.

Stark, Rodney, and Charles Y. Glock. *American Piety: The Nature of Religious Commitment.* Berkeley, Calif.: University of California Press, 1968.

Stockton, Ronald R. "The Evangelical Phenomenon: A Falwell-Graham Typology." Pp. 45-74 in *Contemporary Evangelical Political Involvement*, edited by Corwin E. Smidt. Lanham, Md.: University Press of America, 1989.

Stonecash, Jeffrey M. *Class and Party in American Politics.* Boulder, Colo.: Westview Press, 2000.

Stonecash, Jeffrey M., Mark D. Brewer, Mary P. McGuire, R. Eric Petersen, and Lori Beth Way. "Class and Party: Secular Realignment and the Survival of the Democrats Outside the South." *Political Research Quarterly* 53, no. 4 (Dec. 2000): 731-52.

Strong, Josiah. *The Twentieth Century City.* 1898. Reprint, New York: Arno Press, 1970.

Sullins, D. Paul. "Catholic/Protestant Trends on Abortion: Convergence and Polarity." *Journal for the Scientific Study of Religion* 38, no. 3 (Sept. 1999): 354-69.

Sundquist, James L. "Whither the American Party System?" *Political Science Quarterly* 88, no. 4 (Dec. 1973): 559-81.

———. *Dynamics of the Party System*. Rev. ed. Washington, D.C.: The Brookings Institution, 1983.

Swierenga, Robert P. "Ethnoreligious Political Behavior in the Mid-Nineteenth Century: Voting, Values, and Cultures." Pp. 146-71 in *Religion and American Politics: From the Colonial Period to the 1980s*, edited by Mark A. Noll. New York: Oxford University Press, 1990.

Tajfel, Henri. *Human Groups and Social Categories*. New York: Cambridge University Press, 1981.

Timpone, Richard J. "Mass Mobilization or Government Intervention? The Growth of Black Registration in the South." *Journal of Politics* 57, no. 2 (May 1995): 425-42.

Tocqueville, Alexis de. *Democracy in America*, edited by Philips Bradley, 2 volumes. New York: Vintage Books, 1990.

Tracy, David. *The Analogical Imagination: Christian Theology and the Culture of Pluralism*. New York: Crossroad Publishing Company, 1981.

Trilling, Richard J. *Party Image and Electoral Behavior*. New York: John Wiley & Sons, 1976.

Tropman, John E. "The 'Catholic Ethic' vs. the 'Protestant Ethic': Catholic Social Service and the Welfare State." *Social Thought* 12, no. 1 (Winter 1985): 13-22.

———. *The Catholic Ethic in American Society: An Exploration of Values*. San Francisco: Jossey-Bass Publishers, 1995.

Turner, John C. "Towards a Cognitive Redefinition of the Social Group." Pp. 15-40 in *Social Identity and Intergroup Relations*, edited by Henri Tajfel. New York: Cambridge University Press, 1982.

———. *Social Influence*. Pacific Grove, Calif.: Brooks/Cole Publishing, 1991.

Turner, John C., with Michael A. Hogg, Penelope J. Oakes, Stephen D. Reicher, and Margaret S. Wetherell. *Rediscovering the Social Group: A Self-Categorization Theory*. New York: Basil Blackwell, 1987.

Turner, John C., and Penelope J. Oakes. "Self-Categorization Theory and Social Influence." Pp. 233-75 in *Psychology of Group Influence*, 2d ed., edited by Paul B. Paulus. Hillsdale, N.J.: Lawrence Erlbaum Associates, 1989.

Turner, John C., and Rina S. Ororato. "Social Identity, Personality, and the Self-Concept: A Self-Categorization Perspective." Pp. 11-46 in *The Psychology of the Social Self*, edited by Tom R. Tyler, Roderick M. Kramer, and Oliver P. John. Manweh, N.J.: Lawrence Erlbaum Associates, 1999.

Tyler, Tom R., Roderick M. Kramer, and Oliver P. John. "What Does Studying the Psychology of the Social Self Have to Offer to Psychologists?" Pp. 1-7 in *The Psychology of the Social Self*, edited by Tom R. Tyler, Roderick M. Kramer, and Oliver P. John. Manweh, N.J.: Lawrence Erlbaum Associates, 1999.

United States Bureau of the Census. *Statistical Abstract of the United States, 1971.* 92d ed. Washington, D.C., 1971.

———. *United States Census 2000.* Washington, D.C., 2001.

Vatican, The. "John Paul II: Encyclicals." Available at http://www.vatican.va/ holy_father/john_paul_ii/encyclicals/index.htm

Verba, Sidney, Kay Lehman Schlozman, and Henry E. Brady. *Voice and Equality*. Cambridge, Mass.: Harvard University Press, 1995.

Wald, Kenneth D. *Religion and Politics in the United States*. 3d ed. Washington, D.C.: CQ Press, 1997.

Wald, Kenneth D., Lyman A. Kellstedt, and David C. Leege. "Church Involvement and Political Behavior." Pp. 121-38 in *Rediscovering the Religious Factor in American Politics*, edited by David C. Leege and Lyman A. Kellstedt. Armonk, N.Y.: M. E. Sharpe, 1993.

Wald, Kenneth D., Dennis E. Owen, and Samuel S. Hill, Jr. "Churches as Political Communities." *American Political Science Review* 82, no. 2 (June 1988): 531-48.

———. "Political Cohesion in Churches." *Journal of Politics* 52, no. 1 (Feb. 1990): 197-215.

Wald, Kenneth D., and Corwin E. Smidt. "Measurement Strategies in the Study of Religion and Politics." Pp. 26-49 in *Rediscovering the Religious Factor in American Politics*, edited by David C. Leege and Lyman A. Kellstedt. Armonk, N.Y.: M. E. Sharpe, 1993.

Weakland, Rembert G. "Foreward." Pp. ix-xii in John E. Tropman, *The Catholic Ethic in American Society: An Exploration of Values*. San Francisco: Jossey-Bass Publishers, 1995.

Weber, Max. *The Protestant Ethic and the Spirit of Capitalism*. Translated by Talcott Parsons. London: George Allen & Unwin LTD, 1930.

Welch, Michael R., and David C. Leege. "Religious Predictors of Catholic Parishioners Sociopolitical Attitudes: Devotional Styles, Closeness to God, Imagery, and Agentic/Communal Religious Identity." *Journal for the Scientific Study of Religion* 27, no. 4 (Dec. 1988): 536-52.

Welch, Michael R., David C. Leege, Kenneth D. Wald, and Lyman A. Kellstedt. "Are the Sheep Hearing the Shepherds? Cue Perceptions, Congregational Responses, and Political Communication Processes." Pp. 235-54 in *Rediscovering the Religious Factor in American Politics*, edited by David C. Leege and Lyman A. Kellstedt. Armonk, N.Y.: M. E. Sharpe, 1993.

White, Richard H. "Toward a Theory of Religious Influence." *Pacific Sociological Review* 11, no. 1 (Spring 1968): 23-28.

Wilcox, Clyde, Ted G. Jelen, and David C. Leege. "Religious Group Identifications: Towards a Cognitive Theory of Religious Mobilization." Pp. 72-99 in *Rediscovering the Religious Factor in American Politics*, edited by David C. Leege and Lyman A. Kellstedt. Armonk, N.Y.: M. E. Sharpe, 1993.

Williams, Andrea S., and James D. Davidson. "Catholic Conceptions of Faith: A Generational Analysis." *Sociology of Religion* 57, no. 3 (Fall 1996): 273-89.

Williams, Elisha. "The Inalienable Rights of Conscience," in *Puritan Political Ideas, 1558-1794*, edited by Edmund S. Morgan, 267-304. Indianapolis, Ind.: Bobbs-Merril, 1965.

Wuthnow, Robert. *The Restructuring of American Religion: Society and Faith since World War II*. Princeton, N.J.: Princeton University Press, 1988.

Index

abortion, 24, 41, 132
Adams, John Quincy, 13
African Americans, 2, 37, 48n25, 60. *See also* blacks
Allinsmith, Wesley, and Beverly Allinsmith, 24
American Catholics: and abortion, 24; assimilation into American mainstream, 4-6, 21-22, 35, 42-43; and anti-Protestantism, 14; and civil rights, 23-24; and church attendance, 71; and the Democratic Party, *See* Catholic/Protestant Divide; as distinct from American Protestants, 2-4; and Hispanics, 58-59, 64n21-22; and immigration, 3-4, 11-15, 21-22; percentage of American population, 2, 11-12; and the New Deal, 20-21; and the "social question," 23-24, 39; and socioeconomic mobility, 21-25, 42-43
American Catholic bishops, 19, 98-99, 132
American Civil War, xv, 16
American political parties, 1; in the nineteenth century, 14-15, 26n32; and religion, *See* Catholic/Protestant divide. *See also* Democratic Party, Republican Party, Whig Party
American Protective Association, 14, 15
anti-Catholicism, 2-4, 11-14, 19-20

Baumer, Donald C., and Howard J. Gold, 103

Bendyna, Mary E., and Ted G. Jelen, 135
Benson, Peter L., and Dorothy L. Williams, 6, 136
Billington, Ray Allen, 13
Bishops' Program of Social Reconstruction, 19. *See also* Monsignor John A. Ryan.
blacks, 19, 24, 37, 40. *See also* African Americans
Blaine, James, 15
Bryan, William Jennings, 16-17, 102
Buckley, William F., 100
Burchard, Samuel, 15
Carmines, Edward G., 41
Catholic Church: and abortion, 24, 41, 132; and authority, 3, 13; and charity efforts, 17-18; in Colonial America, 2; and the common good, *See* common good; and communion, 92-93; in England, 2; and hierarchy, 14; and mediation, 92; and organized labor, 18-19, 94-97; and personal morality, 3; pre-Vatican II, 4, 57-58; and relation of adherents to God, 91-93; and sacramentality, 92; and social action, 17-19; and social justice, *See* social justice; social thought of, 93-100; Vatican II, *See* Vatican II
Catholic Ethic, 90-94, 104
Catholic/Protestant divide, and African Americans, 37-38
Catholic/Protestant divide, and age, 54-58, 122-30

157

Catholic/Protestant divide, continuation of, xvi-xvii, 5-6, 39-46, 51-62, 71-82, 121-32, 135-36
Catholic/Protestant divide, and division of Protestants, 80-82
Catholic/Protestant divide, and gender, 51-54, 122-30
Catholic/Protestant divide, and Hispanic ethnicity, 58-62, 122-31
Catholic/Protestant divide, and income level, 43-46, 122-30
Catholic/Protestant divide, and multivariate tests of, 121-32
Catholic/Protestant divide, origins of, 14-23
Catholic/Protestant divide, and religious salience, 71-79, 122-32
Catholic/Protestant divide, and southern residence, 122-30
Catholic/Protestant divide, supposed decline of, xvi, 4-5, 23-25, 33-46, 51, 135
Catholic/Protestant divide, and union membership, 122-30
Catholic worldview, xvii, 6, 87-88, 91-94, 110-12, 136-37
Census of 2000, 58
Centesimus Annus, 97
church attendance. *See* religious salience
civil rights, 23-24
Cogley, John, 2
Columbia University, 1
common good, 93-100, 102, 104-12
communal perspective. *See* Catholic Ethic and Catholic worldview
Conover, Pamela Johnston, 113n9
conservative. *See* ideology
contraception, 5, 93
Converse, Philip E., 47n16
Coolidge, Calvin, 101
Coughlin, Father Charles E., 21
crime, 23

Davidson, James D., et al., 57, 64n18
defense spending, 41, 106-7, 110
Democratic Party, and American Catholics. *See* Catholic/Protestant divide

Democratic Party: "Democratic Party Credo," 102; images of, 102-3; party convention of 1924, 19-20; platforms of, 101-2; political culture of, 100-101
Depression of 1893, 16
divorce, 5
Dolan, Jay P., 12
Dorr, Donal, 95
Durkheim, Emile, 7-8n9, 127

Economic Justice for All, 99
education, 5, 22, 24, 42-43
Eisenhower, Dwight D., 23
The Enlightenment, 2
equality. *See* Catholic Ethic and Catholic worldview
evangelical Protestants, xv-xvi, 79-83, 85n21, 86n27

Faithful Citizenship: Responsibility for a New Millennium, 99, 132
Falwell, Jerry, xv
family income. *See* income level
family planning, 5
Farley, James, 21
fertility patterns, 5
Fuchs, Lawrence, 22

Gallup, George, Jr., and Jim Castelli, 64n19, 92
Gaudium et Spes, 97-98
gender gap, 51-54, 62n5
General Social Survey, 107-8
generational effect, 54, 56-58, 62-63n6
Gerring, John, 101-2
GI Bill, 4, 22, 42
Gibbons, Cardinal James, 18-19
Ginsberg, Benjamin, 101
Gleason, Philip, 5, 56
Great Depression, 20
Greeley, Andrew M., 2, 6, 33, 36, 64n21, 87-88, 91, 137
Green, John C., 41
Greer, Scott, 24
Guth, James L., 6, 41

health care, 39, 102, 105-6
Herberg, Will, 5

Hispanics, 48n25, 58-62, 64n21-22, 65-66n32, 122, 127-31, 136
Hunt, Larry L., 61-62, 64n22
Hunter, James Davison, 78, 135

ideology, 23-24, 39-42
immigration, 3-4, 11-15, 17-18, 21-22, 58
income level, 5, 22, 24, 42-45, 122-130
"independent leaners," 34, 46n6
individualism. *See* Protestant Ethic and Protestant Worldview

Jackson, Andrew, 16
Jensen, Richard, 15-16, 24, 27n43
Johnson, Lyndon B., 48n26

Kennedy, John F., xv, 22-23, 48n26
Kleppner, Paul, 15-16, 27n43
Knights of Labor, 18-19
Know-Nothings, 14, 16
Kosmin, Barry A., and Seymour P. Lachman, 135
Ku Klux Klan, 19-20

Ladd, Everett Carll, Jr., and Charles D. Hadley, 24, 25, 26n32, 27n43, 36
laissez-faire capitalism, 20-21
Layman, Geoffrey, 36, 41
lay trustee management, 11
Leege, David C., and Michael R. Welch, 6, 136; and Lyman A. Kellstedt, 137
liberal. *See* ideology
Liege School, 18
life-cycle effect, 54
Lopatto, Paul, 48n26

Manza, Jeff, and Clem Brooks, 25, 47n16
Mater et Magistra, 97, 100
McBrien, Richard P., 92-93
McGovern, George, 23, 33
McKinley, William, 16-17
Michigan School, 1, 88
minimum wage, 19
Moral Majority, xv
Morse, Samuel F. B., 13
multivariate logit, 121-132

National Election Studies (NES), 1, 34, 46n5; and categorization of Protestant denominations, 80, 86n25; and measurement of race and ethnicity, 59-60, 65-66n32; and measurement of religious salience, 69-70, and questions about social justice and the common good, 104-7
nativism, 4, 15
New Deal Coalition, xv, 23
Nie, Norman H., et al., 25, 36
Nixon, Richard M., 33
Novak, Michael, 96

Pacem in Terris, 97
papal encyclicals, 94, 115n49-50. *See also* individual titles
Parenti, Michael, 24
Parsons, Talcott, 7-8n9
Penning, James M., 113n9
period effect, 54
the poor: Catholics as, 3, 12-13, 17-18, 24; and the Catholic Church, 94-100, 104; and the Democratic Party, 24, 102; government assistance to, 108-110
Pope Benedict IV, 94
Pope John XXIII, 96-98, 100
Pope John Paul II, 97, 98, 100
Pope Leo XIII, 21, 94-95, 100
Pope Paul VI, 92, 97, 98
Pope Pius XI, 29n82, 95-96
popery. *See* anti-Catholicism
Populorum Progressio, 97, 98
pornography, 23
Prendergast, William B., 35, 36, 64n19, 135-36
presidential campaign of 1868, 15
presidential election: of 1896, 16-17; of 1928, 20; of 1932, 20-21; of 1960, 22-23, 36, 47n16, 48n26
Protestant Ethic, 90-93, 104
Protestantism: and anti-Catholicism, *See* anti-Catholicism; and authority, 2; divisions within, 79-80; evangelical, xv-xvi, 79-83, 85n21, 86n27; and individual perspective, *See* Protestant Ethic and Protestant

worldview; mainline, 79-83, 85n21; and personal morality, 2; relation of adherents to God, 91-93
Protestant worldview, xvii, 6, 91-93, 110-12, 136-37
public education, 11

Quadragesimo Anno, 21, 29n82, 95-96, 97

race, 23-24
Reagan, Ronald, xv-xvi, 35, 64n19
The Reformation, 79
Reichley, A. James, 17
religion: definition of, 1-2, 7-8n9; and electoral behavior, xvi, 1-2, 78-79, 137, *See also* Catholic/Protestant divide; and self identity, xvi, 89-90; as worldview, xvi, 89-90, 136-137, *See also* Catholic worldview and Protestant worldview
religious salience: and church attendance, 70-75; definition of, 67; effect on electoral behavior, 71-79, 131-132; index of, 75-79, 85n16; measurement of, 68-70, 83n6
The Republican Oath, 102
Republican Party: and American Protestants, 16-17; and anti-Catholicism, 15; and gains in the electorate over the last thirty years, 36-37; images of, 102-3; platforms, 101-2; political culture of, 100-102
Rerum Novarum, 19, 21, 94-95, 97
responsibility of government to guarantee jobs and a good standard of living, 104-5, 108-12
Roe v. Wade, 24, 41
Roosevelt, Franklin Delano, xv, 20-21
Rossiter, Clinton, 101

Ryan, Monsignor John A., 19

Schuck, Michael J., 94
Sign magazine, 21
Smith, Alfred E., 19-20, 22-23
social group membership and individual identity, 88-90, 113n9
social justice, 93-100, 102, 104-12
"social question," 23-24
Society of St. Vincent de Paul, 17
socioeconomic status (SES), 4-5, 21-22, 24-25, 27n43, 42-45
Sollicitudo Rei Socialis, 97
South (American), 14-16, 20, 24, 26n32, 37, 86n27, 122-130
Stark, Rodney, and Charles Y. Glock, 91
Strong, Josiah, 13

Tajfel, Henri, 88
Tammany Hall, 19
Tocqueville, Alexis de, 6
Trilling, Richard J., 103
Tropman, John, 90-91, 104, 137
Truman, Harry S., xv, 23
Turner, John C., 88, 114n24
Vatican II, 5, 56-58, 63n10, 97-98, 100
Verba, Sidney, et al., 70
Voter Education Project, 37
Voting Rights Act of 1965, 37

Walsh, Thomas, 21
Weakland, Archbishop Rembert G., 92
Weber, Max, 90
welfare, 23, 24, 102-3
Whig Party, 15, 16
Wilcox, Clyde et al., 89
Williams, Elisha, 13
World War I, 19
World War II, 4, 21, 24, 42
Wuthnow, Robert, 6, 78, 91

About the Author

Mark D. Brewer is a Visiting Assistant Professor of Government at Colby College in Waterville, Maine. His work focuses broadly on political behavior, at both the mass and elite level. His research has been published in journals such as *Political Research Quarterly*, *Legislative Studies Quarterly*, and *Political Behavior*. His work with Jeff Stonecash and Mack Mariani, *Diverging Parties*, was recently published by Westview Press. This book examines the electoral sources of party polarization in the House of Representatives. Currently, Professor Brewer is engaged in an analysis of the substance, evolution, and electoral impact of party images in the United States. He holds a Ph.D. in political science from Syracuse University.